Advance Praise for

THE BIG FRAUD

"A Must Read for All Americans."

— Donald J. Trump

"My wife Debbie has known Troy Nehls for many years, and I met him through her. We both are super-fans of this guy. He was a terrific sheriff in Fort Bend County, Texas, and now he has brought that same practicality and bravery to Congress. This book is a candid and well-researched examination of the events surrounding the election through January 6th. Troy Nehls goes against the prevailing media narrative, which is concocted to advance the cause of the Democratic Left and makes a powerful stand here for fairness and for truth."

— Dinesh D'Souza

The BIG FRAUD

WHAT DEMOCRATS DON'T WANT YOU to KNOW about JANUARY 6, the 2020 ELECTION, and a WHOLE LOT ELSE

CONGRESSMAN TROY E. NEHLS

BOMBARDIER
BOOKS

Published by Bombardier Books
An Imprint of Post Hill Press
ISBN: 978-1-63758-721-8
ISBN (eBook): 978-1-63758-722-5

The Big Fraud:
What Democrats Don't Want You to Know about January 6, the
2020 Election, and a Whole Lot Else
© 2022 by Congressman Troy E. Nehls
All Rights Reserved

Cover photo: AP Photo/J. Scott Applewhite

Post Hill Press
New York • Nashville
posthillpress.com

Published in the United States of America
1 2 3 4 5 6 7 8 9 10

I dedicate this book to my older brother, Todd Nehls, who served our nation thirty-six years in the Wisconsin Army National Guard retiring with the rank of colonel. Todd also served his community in law enforcement for thirty-four years, with ten of those years as sheriff of Dodge County, Wisconsin. It was my brother Todd who inspired me to serve our nation twenty-two years in the Army Reserve and encouraged me to serve in law enforcement for thirty years, eight years as sheriff of Fort Bend County, Texas. Brother Todd, you are my hero!

A debt of gratitude to my mother Joyce Rasmussen, an incredible example of a loving parent. Brothers, Tim, Terry, Tyler, and twin brother Trever, sister Tammy Shaw, for always being there for me. Love You All!

TABLE OF CONTENTS

CHAPTER 1   INTRODUCTION

January 6, 2021. I was sworn in on January 3rd, so it was my third day in Congress. I went to the office knowing what I had to do. A few days before, I publicly announced my decision to object to the certification of Pennsylvania's and Arizona's electoral votes. I had no indication there was any serious threat to the Capitol, despite a staff bulletin from the House Administration Committee saying that only essential staff should come to work that day. One more COVID restriction, I thought. The main threat I was worried about was the one that endangered the integrity of our precious right to vote.

As a freshman congressman, I knew I would be facing significant criticism for questioning the validity of electoral votes, especially from the Democrats on the other side of the aisle. But I had to do what I thought was right.

Why? I was convinced "there were massive and unprecedented voter irregularities and anomalies" in Pennsylvania and Arizona, but also Wisconsin, Michigan, and Georgia. "In many cases these irregularities were caused by intentional misconduct and illegal behavior." Indeed, "on election day, there were numerous unexplained anomalies and irregularities involving hundreds of thousands of votes that have yet to be accounted for...."

What kind of irregularities? There were "electronic [voting] machines [that] transferred an unknown number of Trump votes to the Biden column." Some counties even "locked out public observers from vote counting." Election records also "show significantly more votes than voters in some precincts," and also "voters casting more than one ballot." In one county, "voter turnout was an improbable and highly suspect 98.55 percent, and after 100 percent of the precincts were reported, an additional 19,000 extra votes were recorded for Joseph Biden." There were counties that "allowed for irregular marking of ballots and failed to secure and store ballots and machinery," and "counties which prevented witnesses for candidates from observing the various aspects of the recount."

Whoever would ultimately win, I knew the "outcome cannot be certain as long as legitimate questions remain and valid ballots are being counted," and so it was "imperative that we examine any and all factors that may have led to voting irregularities and any failure of votes to be properly counted."

You're probably wondering why there are quotation marks in the paragraphs you just read. These are not my words in quotes, but come from the January 6, 2005, *Congressional Record*.[1] They are the words of the Democrat Party concerning the 2004 election of Republican George Bush over Democrat John Kerry. (Of course, I did substitute Trump and Biden for Bush and Kerry in the quotes.) Democrats back then were officially objecting to counting the electoral votes of Ohio, just as we Republicans were now (exactly sixteen years later to the day) objecting to counting the electoral votes of Pennsylvania and Arizona.

Complaints look familiar, don't they? The kinds of accusations the Democrats were making about voting irregularities back then seem almost identical to those made by Republicans in regard to the 2020 election. It was no more un-American or anti-democratic for me to object in January of 2021 than it was for Democrats

---

1   *Congressional Record*, January 6, 2005. The objections begin on p. H85, column 3. https://www.congress.gov/congressional-record/2005/01/06/house-section/article/H84-6.

in January of 2005 (and that wasn't the only election results Democrats challenged).

Those complaints make clear these kinds of things do happen, and as we'll see in a later chapter, they happened a lot in 2020. But whenever and wherever they happen, one thing is clear: we *all* need to support election integrity—both parties, every American.

But again, it seemed to me, whatever Republicans may have done in the past, the massive number of reported irregularities favoring the Democrats in the 2020 election were unprecedented.

And that's why I decided to object to the electoral votes on my third day in Congress. I could see many of my colleagues were nervous. As a freshman in the House, I certainly was. I'm not a career politician. I've spent my life in law enforcement (most recently, as the sheriff of Fort Bend County in Richmond, TX), and in the military as a member of the National Guard, and then the Army Reserve.

One way or another, we would all face some kind of political backlash, whatever we did, and as a new congressman, I thought I might get more than my share. But that wasn't going to deter me from doing what I knew was right, and I wasn't alone. There were a record number of objectors: six Republicans in the Senate and 121 Republicans in the House.

Just to put those numbers in perspective, in 2001 a handful of Democrats in the House officially objected to the election of George Bush, but no Democrat senators joined them. (And so, given the rules, if at least one senator and one representative do not formally object, the Joint Session of Senate and House then go on to certify the electoral votes.) In the 2005 objection I quoted from above, only one Democrat senator would officially object, and in the consequent voting, only thirty-one Democrats in the House voted against certification. In 2017, House Democrats objected to the electoral votes of Donald Trump, but again, no Democrat senator would join them. It was a big jump from these numbers to six senators and 121 members of the House in January 2021.

I took a seat toward the back, near the center doors leading into the House Chamber. Nancy Pelosi's COVID restrictions were in place, so we had to keep our distance, and a limited number of members from each party were allowed on the House Chamber floor. It was approximately 1:00 p.m. when we were all called to rise. Suddenly, House Sergeant at Arms Paul Irving strode down the center walkway and loudly proclaimed, "Madam Speaker, the Vice President and the United States Senate."

I stood up and applauded as staffers carrying the ballots came through the doors first, followed closely by Vice President Pence. He walked past me just feet away as I stood clapping, and I truly felt the magnitude of the moment. After Speaker Pelosi brought the House to order, Vice President Pence took the microphone at the rostrum.

"Madam Speaker, Members of Congress, pursuant to the Constitution and the laws of the United States, the Senate and House of Representatives are meeting in joint session to verify the certificates and count the votes of the electors of the several States for President and Vice President of the United States. After ascertainment has been had that the certificates are authentic and correct in form, the tellers will count and make a list of the votes cast by the electors of the several States."

We commenced the slow, official affirmation of electoral votes, state by state, beginning with Alabama. There were no objections until we hit Arizona.

"Mister Vice President, I, Paul Gosar from Arizona, rise for myself and sixty of my colleagues to object to the counting of the electoral ballots from Arizona."

"Is the objection in writing and signed by a senator?" asked Vice President Pence.

"Yes, it is," replied Rep. Gosar.

"It is," affirmed Senator Ted Cruz from Texas. A thunderous applause resounded in the Chamber.

According to the rules, the Joint Session of Congress then split for separate deliberation and debate. After the Senate retired to its Chamber, we, the members of the House, took up the task of deciding the validity of the electoral votes. Debate was not to exceed two hours, and anyone speaking only had five minutes to state his or her case.

As we were informed, we would alternate between those who objected to Arizona's electoral votes being counted and those who did not. We began with Rep. Steve Scalise, a Republican from Louisiana, making the case for the objection not just about Arizona, but "a number of States." As with me and many others, the most important objections were in regard to last-minute changes in the way elections were run, under the "cover" of emergency COVID measures, that were instituted independent of the state legislatures—and *that* was a clear violation of the Constitution's demand that the choosing of electors be done by each state "as the Legislature thereof may direct" (II.1), not judges, not governors, not special committees, or anyone else.

Following Rep. Scalise came Rep. Zoe Lofgren, a Democrat from California, then Republican Jim Jordan (OH), Democrat Adam Schiff (CA), Republican Andy Biggs (AZ), Democrat Jamie Raskin (MD), Republican Lauren Boebert (CO), Democrat Joseph Neguse (CO), Republican Mike Johnson (LA), Democrat Raúl Grijalva (AZ), then Republican Paul Gosar (AZ).

But while Rep. Gosar was speaking I noticed several uniformed personnel, as well as plainclothes personnel, rush into the chamber. Some of the plainclothes personnel swept Speaker Pelosi off the dais and escorted her out through the Speaker's Lobby, which is directly behind the House Rostrum. Not knowing what was causing the commotion, Rep. Gosar asked, "Mister Speaker, can I have order in the Chamber?"

Moments later, Speaker *Pro Tempore* (meaning temporary) Rep. Jim McGovern assumed the dais and gaveled, calling out, "Members take their seats, the House will be in order." But they continued to move about the Chamber seemingly ignoring the Speaker *Pro Tempore's* command. He let a little time pass as he scanned the room and then he gaveled again, exclaiming, "The House will be in recess." It was 2:18 p.m. That's when I noticed my colleagues starting to wander and congregate together to attempt to determine what was happening. The Speaker *Pro Tempore* called the House to order once more at 2:26 p.m., and Rep. Gosar resumed his objection, but the Speaker almost immediately recessed the Chamber again. It was now 2:29 p.m.

Minutes later, one of the Capitol Police in a suit with an earpiece raised his hands and to paraphrase exclaimed, "Ladies and gentleman, you're locked in. The Capitol has been breached. If you're near a chair, take a seat. If you're on the floor, stay on the floor. If you're sitting down, reach underneath your seat; there's a gas mask under your seat."

I noticed multiple people trying to put gas masks on. That's when the anxiety really set in. I couldn't believe what I was seeing. I wondered to myself, "Is this really happening?" Not exactly what I had in mind for my third day on the job.

There were no TVs on the House floor, so we didn't have a clue as to what was causing all the commotion. I started to get texts from my wife, Jill, and brothers asking me if I was okay. My twin brother, Trever, asked, "How are you doing pal?"

"Locked us on the House floor," I replied.

"People forcefully entering the Capitol Building?" he asked.

"Uncertain. They just locked us in," I answered.

"We are watching online. They are in the Rotunda," he replied.

"I am at the back door leading into the Chamber. I told Capitol Police I would help them," I told him.

My many years of law enforcement and military training were kicking in. I had moved to the back of the House Chamber to be with plainclothes and uniformed Capitol Police officers positioned at the center doors. Rep. Markwayne Mullin from Oklahoma was also there. (I later found out he was a mixed martial arts fighter!) He grabbed one of the wooden hand sanitizer stands and snapped off the base.

"What are you doing?" I asked.

"This is my weapon," he said.

"Great idea," I thought to myself, knowing we still had no idea what was on the other side of the doors. I saw another hand sanitizer stand not far from me and proceeded to break the stand off its base.

Moments later security asked me to leave the House floor. I responded, "No sir, I will not. I will remain here with my brothers and sisters in blue."

The doors leading to the chamber started to shake violently. People were pounding on the doors, and I could hear the protestors on the other side shouting as they beat on them. The Capitol Police were getting very worried. They were on their radios talking, and they seemed to be completely caught off guard.

I later found out that this was in fact the case (a point I'll come back to). They were brave but poorly trained, poorly equipped, and poorly coordinated. I firmly believe if things had been otherwise, what started as a peaceful protest would not have been able to be turned into a destructive riot by a small number of bad apples. More on that in a later chapter.

Back to January 6th. One of the US Capitol Police officers near me pulled out her ASP baton, a standard-issue defense weapon for law enforcement.

"Do you have another one of those?" I asked.

"No," she replied.

All the while, the doors kept shaking and rattling. Predicting whoever was trying to get in very well might, I removed my jacket and threw it aside so I would have the ability to be more mobile. If these rioters entered the chamber and tried to get violent, I wanted to be prepared to defend myself.

Jill and my brothers were seeing what was unfolding on TV and social media and were worried. She kept texting me, wondering why I wasn't responding to her texts—my phone was in my jacket.

As the doors continued to shake, other members of Congress from the Texas delegation who were nearby, including Ronny Jackson and Pat Fallon, joined the Capitol Police in barricading them with furniture. All of the sudden, as I was pushing on a piece of furniture right in front of the doors, I heard a loud "BANG," and shattered glass from the doors started flying. I ducked, as did the Capitol Police officers nearby.

One of the officers got on the radio and said, "Shots fired! Shots fired!"

I turned to my colleague from Oklahoma, Markwayne Mullin, and said, "I don't think that was shots fired"—my experience in law enforcement told me it wasn't a gun shot. As it turns out, it wasn't a gun that made the sound; it was a flagpole used to break a hole in the glass portion of the Chamber doors. If it had been a gun, I probably wouldn't be here as I was right in the line of fire.

Credit: Drew Angerer/Getty Images

As I stood back up and peered through the hole where the glass was broken, I saw a young man staring at me. I said to him, "What the hell are you doing?!"

Credit: AP Photo/J. Scott Applewhite

He saw my Texas COVID mask on my face. "You're from Texas. You should be with us!"

"No sir, I cannot be. You are interfering and disrupting this sacred chamber. This is Congress. What you're doing is un-American. It's criminal. We're in here working, and there you are breaking glass."

As a longtime law officer, I do not believe in people taking the law—as they see it—into their own hands. The First Amendment affirms "the right of the people *peaceably* to assemble, and to petition the Government for a redress of grievances." This was anything but peaceable. Making matters worse, I'm certain it undermined the possibility of any congressional investigation into election fraud. Because an unprecedented number of senators and representatives objected based upon a multitude of election irregularities, *if* the protestors had remained peaceful, *then* there might have been a congressionally mandated committee set up to scrutinize those irregularities. But the peaceful protest turned riot assured the legitimate and lawful objections brought against the electoral votes in Arizona and Pennsylvania would later be dismissed, tainted by the unlawful and violent actions of a few.

Another rioter yelled out he had lost thousands because Biden was elected. Behind him I saw someone holding a flag on a long metal pole. "That must be what broke the glass," I thought. The rioters kept surging forward. I told them, "You need to stop banging on these doors. Stop trying to breach these doors. If you don't, and you try to come in here, these gentlemen to my left and right with their guns drawn, they will kill you."

I knew this from my years in law enforcement—officers are trained not to draw their firearm unless they're in a situation where they have to use it for deadly force. Knowing bloodshed was the last thing I wanted and thinking of how I could create space between the rioters and the doors, I picked up the hand sanitizer stick I had broken off from its wooden base and began to poke it through the hole broken in the glass. "You better get back," I yelled as I continued to ram the hand sanitizer stick through the hole.

Credit: AP Photo/J. Scott Applewhite

I didn't think the situation warranted deadly force, and I certainly didn't think I would find my picture all over the news that day, even on the cover of *Time* magazine. But that was the very moment captured: Troy Nehls at the back door of the House Chamber, flanked by plainclothes officers with guns drawn on the broken window.

After repeatedly ramming the hand sanitizer stick through the hole and making it clear the rioters faced the potential of deadly force from the officers with weapons drawn, things settled down at the doors for a bit, but all the sudden things quickly deteriorated. There were loud noises all around us, sounding like flash-bangs. Then, in all the chaos, I heard something very distinct, and I knew immediately what it was, a gunshot—as I found out later, it was the gunshot in the Speaker's Lobby that killed Ashli Babbitt.

Credit: Tom Williams/CQ-Roll Call, Inc via Getty Images

Immediately after that shot rang out, a plainclothes officer ran up to me and said, "Sir, please, you must leave the chamber now!" Knowing shots had in fact been fired and the situation could deteriorate even more, I felt I didn't want to be an obstruction to Capitol Police attempting to do their job, so I complied and was escorted off the floor into another building.

After many hours, my colleagues and I returned to the House Chamber to do our constitutional duty. Speaker Nancy Pelosi called the House to order at 9:02 p.m. It was going to be a very long night. All the objections would be heard, in due and lawful order, as would all the responses to those objections. But it was clear that the violent attack on the Capitol had taken the wind out of the sails of the legitimate effort by Republicans to question the validity of the 2020 election. In the end, eight US Senators and 139 House of Representative members, including myself, voted against certifying the election. The House adjourned at 3:48 a.m., January 7th, with Joseph Biden's election now certified by Congress.

There was a lot packed into my third day at Congress—a riot at the Capitol after a year of BLM and ANTIFA "mostly peaceful" riots across America, serious and substantive allegations of election fraud, the underfunded and poorly trained Capitol Police committing the greatest law enforcement failure in the history of Congress in a year the Left pushed to defund and abolish the police, the murder of Ashli Babbitt by Capitol Police, forced government COVID mask mandates, and as I would find out later, an attempt by the liberal mainstream media to portray thousands of peaceful protestors that day as White Supremacist insurrectionists.

I've spent over a year thinking about what happened January 6th and what set the stage for it, and I'm going to spend the rest of the book unpacking that, because when we look at things more deeply than the mainstream media repeating the word "INSURRECTION" ad nauseam, we'll find there's a lot more to January 6th and the 2020 election than the media or Democrats want people to realize, much more.

It's clear Democrats will use January 6th as their main strategic weapon in the 2022 midterm election (and probably the 2024 presidential election after that). In fact, the strange events of January 6th seem suspiciously well-tailored to provide the progressive elites in both parties with an avenue to try and eliminate their greatest fear: Donald J. Trump.

Trump is the globalist, progressive elite's greatest fear because he's fighting against everything they want. They want to sell America out to China and the world, Trump wants to put America first. They want to grow the swamp, Trump wants to drain it. They want to profit from government corruption, Trump wants to root it out.

As you'll see, the evidence shows January 6th was orchestrated to give the political establishment, these progressive elites in both the Democrat and Republican parties, an opportunity to get Trump out of the way so they could get back to selling America out and pushing us ever more towards socialism and their New World Order.

That's the main reason I'm writing this book—to set the record straight about what really happened that day and warn everyone about the real insurrectionists, those who would uproot and destroy our political system once and for all, and replace it with an all-powerful globalist elite whose only aim is to implement socialism and control every aspect of our lives. That's what they were trying to accomplish in the 2020 election, but Trump and his movement are still standing. I want to provide a kind of source book for everyone who wants to ensure they don't complete their insurrection in 2022 and 2024.

CHAPTER 2

A NOT SO SHORT HISTORY OF VOTER FRAUD, SUPPRESSION, AND MANIPULATION BY THE DEMOCRATS
(THE PARTY OF SLAVERY, RACISM, AND JIM CROW)

The thousands of peaceful protestors who were in DC on January 6th were there, at heart, because of a conviction that the Democrat Party had cheated to win the 2020 election. Against this, the Democrat Party (along with the media and other like-minded people on the Left) asserted that the protest was really an insurrection of angry White Supremacists, so that January 6th was actually a kind of White race riot. For Democrats, the Capitol Hill riot was put forward as proof of what the FBI and Department of Homeland Security, under Democrats, had been (strangely) warning about for several years: that the greatest political threat facing the US was from White Supremacist groups.

But let's state the obvious. Slapping the label of White Supremacist on the tens of thousands of good folks who came to Washington that day to peacefully protest was a way for Democrats to avoid having to face widespread, legitimate concerns about the integrity of the 2020 election. This Democrat diversionary strategy needs to be stopped once and for all, and I've provided important material in this chapter to do it.

The truth is that the Democrat Party is the party of White Supremacists, the party of racists, the party that was started to protect slavery, the party of segregation and Jim Crow, *and* on top of that, the party of voter fraud, manipulation, and suppression.

The two are intimately related for Democrats. The Democrat Party not only has a long history of voter fraud, but much of it was related to the fact that it was *the* party of slavery, racism, Jim Crow, and White Supremacy. Voter fraud, manipulation, and suppression were the ways it held onto power, first to protect slavery, and then to protect the Democrat control of the South after the Civil War.

It's an ugly truth the Left and the Democrat Party conveniently ignore. That's why we're going to spend significant time in this chapter bringing to light the connection between voter fraud and racism. It's a rather complex connection, so I ask your patience in advance for the history lesson that follows. We'll begin with the surprising truth about how early voter fraud entered our elections.

EARLY FRAUD IN AMERICAN ELECTIONS

I am not making the case that there was never any voter fraud before the Democrat party formed in the first half of the 1800s. When you look back in history, you find that voter fraud and manipulation of elections is just about as old as voting, and that's true in America as well.

Even prior to 1776, American elections were rather riotous affairs, sometimes quite literally. According to historian Tracy Campbell, in colonial Philadelphia election day crowds "were often drunk and unruly," sometimes descending "into open vote fraud and bloodshed," such as the 1742 election where, so it was rumored, "illegal German immigrants were being imported to the city to swell the vote totals...."[2] It certainly didn't make things more peaceful that it was considered essential for candidates on election day to supply voters with rum, wine, brandy, and beer as a kind of "reward for travelers taking the time and expense" to vote. (Both George Washington and Thomas Jefferson did it.[3])

Outright fraud also existed, as when those seeking office got around property qualifications for voters by "giving" landless voters land for a day in exchange for their vote. Vote buying was so prevalent in the colony of Rhode Island that "Rhode Islandism" became a "pejorative term for vote-buying."[4]

A sure sign of these early problems with voter integrity was the fact that there were laws against voter fraud. As Campbell notes, "The Pennsylvania constitution of 1776 set certain punishments for bribery at the polls, and the next year the North Carolina state assembly passed a statute prohibiting bribery, ballot-box stuffing, and multiple voting. In 1784, New Hampshire made conviction of bribery at the polls a disqualification for holding office." [5]

The Constitution was ratified in the summer of 1788, but the acceptance of the Constitution as the law of the land didn't stop problems with voter integrity. According to historian Andrew Gumbel, "The first formal complaint of vote fraud" in our newly established constitutional republic "occurred as early as 1789, in the wake of a congressional race in Georgia between two generals from the Revolutionary War." General Anthony Wayne was initially declared the winner, until General James Jackson pointed

---

2   Tracy Campbell, *Deliver the Vote: A History of Election Fraud, an American Political Tradition—1742-2004* (New York: Carroll & Graf Publishers, 2005), p. 4

3   Tracy Campbell, *Deliver the Vote*, p. 5.

4   Tracy Campbell, *Deliver the Vote*, pp. 6-7.

5   Tracy Campbell, *Deliver the Vote*, p. 9.

out "that there were more votes than voters in one county, that a crooked judge had suppressed votes in another, and that the elections was marred by other 'undue and corrupt practices' such as the recording of voters who later said they had not shown up on election day at all."[6]

The lesson here is not that Americans have always been hopelessly corrupt but that Americans are sinners like everyone else in history, and *that's why election integrity must always be protected.* If you're not convinced of that now, you soon will be as we continue our history lesson in regard to the Democrat Party.

THE FIRST CASE OF PRESIDENTIAL VOTER FRAUD: SLAVE OWNER DEMOCRAT ANDREW JACKSON

The first presidential election with verified fraud was that of Andrew Jackson, the slave owning founder of the Democrat Party. Jackson felt that he was cheated out of victory in the 1824 presidential election against John Quincy Adams, and with good reason. Jackson won ninety-nine electoral votes and Adams only eighty-four (with two other candidates getting forty-one and thirty-seven votes). According to the Constitution, the winning candidate must have at least "a Majority of the whole Number of Electors…and if no Person have a Majority, then from the five highest on the List the said House [of Representatives] shall…chuse the President" (Article II, Section 1). The House chose Adams over Jackson, and that immediately put Jackson on the warpath to win the 1828 presidential election, by force or fraud.

Jackson waged a forceful campaign, organizing everything from the massive printing up of flyers, to wooing the electorate with

---

6   Andrew Gumbel, *Steal This Vote: Dirty Elections and the Rotten History of Democracy in America* (New York: Nation Books, 2005), p. 78.

barbeques and tree plantings to get out the vote, all to the tune of over a million dollars in expenditures (Jackson's wealth coming from the Hermitage, his Tennessee plantation). To make sure that he beat Adams this time, "Wagonloads of Jackson supporters, many of them from his native Tennessee, spilled over state lines to Kentucky and Ohio to cast votes in the names of citizens who had died—a technique that would become all too familiar in years to come." Fraudulently jacking up the popular vote brought Jackson a "crushing majority in the Electoral College—178 to Adam's 83...." And so, "The year 1828...marked the first presidential election with known instances of ballot fraud."[7]

Not a good beginning for the Democrat Party. We see right from the beginning that voter fraud and slavery were connected. Non-resident voter fraud, vote hauling, and the dead casting ballots—we'll see those methods again as well. At this point, they were in the service of the Democrat Party's protection of the evil institution of slavery. Jackson's election brought about the dominance of the presidency by pro-slavery Democrats up until the election of Abraham Lincoln.

The Democrats were the real racist party, not only before but after the Civil War, as the following historical account will reveal. *Every American should know this history.*

THE REAL RACIST PARTY: THE DEMOCRAT OPPOSITION TO BLACK CIVIL RIGHTS

The Founders failed to solve the slavery problem, and the Southern slave-owning states were always worried that they would be forced by the Northern states to give up their slaves—a struggle that brought the nation into the great Civil War. After the Confederates

---

7   Andrew Gumbel, *Steal This Vote*, p. 69.

lost the Civil War, the Democrat Party went from being the party of slavery to being the party of resistance to reform, the party of Jim Crow, the party of segregation, and therefore the party of voter intimidation and suppression.

During the Reconstruction period (1865–1877) Republicans tried to dismantle the remnants of slavery and uphold the newly gained civil rights of freed Black Americans—and that included their right to vote. But fierce opposition to reform came immediately from Abraham Lincoln's own vice president, Democrat Andrew Johnson, who became president after Lincoln's assassination. (Johnson had been added to Lincoln's ticket to try to draw in the vote of more moderate Democrats in the election of 1864.) President Johnson and Democrat-dominated Southern state legislatures passed a series of discriminatory laws in 1865–1866 called the Black Codes, which sought to keep newly freed Black Americans in a new kind of servitude.

When Republicans got a majority in Congress in the election of 1866, they pressed for reform against President Johnson and the Democrats. Republicans responded to the Democrats' Black Codes by passing the *first* great civil rights act, the Civil Rights Act of 1866. Going well beyond the Thirteenth Amendment, it proclaimed the following:

> *That all persons born in the United States…are hereby declared to be citizens of the United States; and such citizens, of every race and color, without regard to any previous condition of slavery or involuntary servitude…shall have the same right, in every State and Territory in the United States, to make and enforce contracts, to sue, be parties, and give evidence, to inherit, purchase, lease, sell, hold, and convey real and personal property, and to full and equal benefit of*

*all laws and proceedings for the security of person and
property, as is enjoyed by white citizens, and shall be
subject to like punishment, pains, and penalties, and
to none other, any law, statute, ordinance, regulation,
or custom, to the contrary notwithstanding.*[8]

This was the father of all American civil rights acts. It was
passed by a Republican-dominated Congress in mid-March of
1866 but then vetoed by Democrat President Johnson within two
weeks. Republicans responded by overriding Johnson's veto.

Repeated clashes with Johnson came to a head when
Republicans in the House voted to impeach him, thereby giving
the dishonor of being the first president to be impeached to a
Democrat defender of racial oppression. He missed full conviction
by one vote in the Senate.

Obviously, the Democrats didn't want the popular Ulysses
Grant to win the presidential election of 1868, and so they resorted
to both horrifying force and detestable fraud wherever they could
to push through their candidate Horatio Seymour. Keep in mind
that at this point Black Americans are devout Republicans, voting
for the party that freed them from chains.

"In the six months preceding the election, over a thousand
African-Americans were killed in Louisiana. In that same period,
Democratic vote totals more than doubled."[9] While Democrat
votes shot upwards—largely driven by the desire to reassert political control and the fear of the potential political power of freed
slaves—the Black Republican vote was suppressed. In Democrat-
controlled Georgia, there were over twenty-seven thousand Black
Republicans registered, but Grant only received 3,500 votes.
Why? If Black voters dared to come to the polls, their ballots were

---

8   Thirty-Ninth Congress, Sess. I, Ch. 31, 1866, p. 37. Text available at https://uslaw.link/
     citation/stat/14/27%E2%80%9330.
9   Tracy Campbell, *Deliver the Vote*, p. 61.

opened. If it did happen to be for the Democrat candidate Horatio Seymour—a vote likely cast out of terror—it would be accepted; but any Blacks who cast votes for Grant were immediately asked for their poll tax receipt, which, if they hadn't paid the poll tax, resulted in their votes being thrown away.[10]

During this election year, Republicans spearheaded passage of the Fourteenth Amendment (ratified, July 9, 1868) to ensure that the Civil Rights Act of 1866 could not be declared unconstitutional (as claimed by Democrat President Johnson). Republicans then pushed through the Fifteenth Amendment (ratified, February 3, 1870), which declared that "The right of citizens of the United States to vote shall not be denied or abridged by the United States or by any State on account of race, color, or previous condition of servitude."

All of this was done against the opposition of the Democrat Party. Again, Democrats did not want the recently freed Black Americans to vote and overturn the political and cultural power of White Democrats. Unfortunately, as Republicans soon found out, declaring the right to vote for Black Americans was easier said than done. The enforcement of the Fourteenth and Fifteenth Amendments was possible only through the Republican-based institutions of Reconstruction in the South (backed up by federal troops).

But Reconstruction would come to end with the contested presidential election of 1876, where a special electoral commission had to decide the victor. We need to take a very close look at this famous, and misunderstood, election.

---

10   Tracy Campbell, *Deliver the Vote*, p. 62.

THE TRUTH ABOUT THE GREAT STOLEN ELECTION OF 1876: DEMOCRAT VOTER FRAUD, VIOLENCE, INTIMIDATION, AND SUPPRESSION OF THE BLACK VOTE

Let's first remind ourselves of the historical importance of the election of 1876 for our own time. On January 6, 2021, this election came up as part of the Republican objections to widespread suspicion of voter fraud on the part of the Democrat Party. Republican Senator Ted Cruz suggested that Congress look "to history, to the precedent of the 1876 election, the Hayes-Tilden election, where this Congress appointed an electoral commission to examine claims of voter fraud," the commission consisting of "Five House Members, five Senators, five Supreme Court Justices [who] examined the evidence and rendered a judgment." Cruz continued, "What I would urge of this body is that we do the same; that we appoint an electoral commission to conduct a 10-day emergency audit, consider the evidence, and resolve the claims."[11]

Keep in mind that we had history on our side in making the case on January 6th that we needed to investigate the very serious allegations that had been brought forward since the November 2020 election.

To return to 1876, the special electoral commission was needed in the Hayes-Tilden election because of allegations of fraud in an exceedingly close vote. In regard to the contest itself, it's fair to say that neither Republican Rutherford B. Hayes nor Democrat Samuel Tilden were sparkling personalities. But it was an election that focused on principle rather than personality. At issue was the possibility that Democrats would regain national political control and roll back Republican reforms, returning Blacks to servitude. As Andrew Gumbel rightly notes, "Many genuinely feared that a

---

11   Congressional Record, Senate, January 6, 2021, S15.

Democratic Party victory [in the presidency] would lead to the reintroduction of slavery, the creation of a new wedge between North and South, and perhaps even a second Civil War."[12]

The night of the election (November 7, 1876) it certainly looked like Democrat Samuel Tilden would win. He had over a quarter of a million more in the popular vote, and 184 electoral votes out of the total of 369 at the time—just one electoral vote shy of victory. The races were very close in Florida, Louisiana, and South Carolina, but since these were Southern states, and Democrat candidate Tilden appeared to be leading the popular vote there, his victory looked assured. So Tilden himself went to bed that election night thinking he was the winner.

But while Tilden slept peacefully, a one-legged Civil War general, "Devil Dan Sickles" hatched a last-minute scheme to bend Florida, Louisiana, and South Carolina to Republican Rutherford B. Hayes. As Gumbel points out, all three states "were under Republican control" due to Reconstruction, and that included being in charge of judging the legitimacy of votes in the "returning boards." Republicans were thereby "in a position to delay, massage, or otherwise manipulate the figures to the party's advantage."[13]

The charge some historians make (and nearly all Democrats to this day) is that Devil Dan and the Republicans cheated their way to the presidential victory of Hayes, mainly by illegally throwing out enough Democrat votes to swing Florida, Louisiana, and South Carolina to the Republican side.

Democrats at the time certainly thought Republicans cheated, and so, as I said, contested the results. A special electoral commission was set up to settle the issue, and after much wrangling, the victory went to Hayes by one electoral vote—again, as Democrats to this day assert, wrongfully so. It reminds today's Democrats (bitterly)

---

12 Andrew Gumbel, *Steal This Vote*, p. 93.
13 Andrew Gumbel, *Steal This Vote*, pp. 92-93.

of the election of 2000 where Democrat Al Gore (like Tilden) won the popular vote, but was deprived of victory by Republican candidate George Bush through a combination of alleged Republican chicanery and the Supreme Court siding with Bush.

That's the standard account of the famous "stolen" election of 1876. But is that really what happened?

The problem with this assessment is that there was, in fact, widespread voter fraud and suppression *by the Democrats,* calling into question their alleged popular election victories in the South. We therefore need to look more carefully at what the Democrats did in the months leading up to election day (and it's *not* pretty).

In what follows, keep in mind how big a voting block freed slaves, now Black Republicans, actually were in the South. That's why they were such a threat if they voted. In fact, in Louisiana and South Carolina Black Republicans constituted a "majority of the registered electorate."[14]

"In all three contested states in the South," as Gumbel notes, Democrat "party supporters embarked on campaigns to intimidate, threaten, and cause physical harm to black voters."[15] Again, the demographics make clear why: freed slaves formed an enormous potential voting block whose loyalty was to the Republican party, the party that freed them.

Voter suppression and intimidation by Democrats began before the national presidential election because they also wanted to regain political power in their state governments (power that had been denied them during Reconstruction). The same tactics would also be used to ensure the vote for presidential Democrat nominee Tilden. As Michael Holt relates,

---

14   Michael F. Holt, *By One Vote (American Presidential Elections)*, University Press of Kansas, Kindle Edition, p. 215.
15   Andrew Gumbel, *Steal This Vote*, p. 95.

In these three states [Florida, Louisiana, and South Carolina], as well as elsewhere in the South, the basic Democratic message was the same: white supremacy required ousting Republicans from control of state governments or preventing them from retaking it where Democrats were already in the saddle. According to this logic, any white man who voted Republican betrayed his race and his region.[16]

There was, for example, the famous Hamburg Massacre in South Carolina in the summer of 1876. The goal by Democrats (named, locally, Red Shirts) was to intimidate the Black Republican majority in the Edgefield district by violence. "The whites came from surrounding Edgefield County and nearby Augusta, Georgia. Accounts of this fracas differ," relates historian Michael Holt, "but between five and ten blacks had been shot dead, most of them unarmed after they had already surrendered."[17]

The main guide to this shameful program of intimidation by Democrat Red Shirts was Brigadier General Martin Gary, who wrote up a plan to suppress the Black vote in South Carolina. A militant opponent of granting civil rights to newly freed Black Americans, Gary believed that the 1876 election was a "struggle for supremacy between the races and not a mere contest for honest government as has been alleged."[18] General Gray wrote up a "plan" for Democrats to ensure that the Black Republican vote would not materialize. Some of it is all too familiar, and some of it is shocking to say the least.[19] I urge everyone to read the whole thing; I'll provide a few illuminating excerpts.

---

16   Michael F. Holt, *By One Vote (American Presidential Elections)*, p. 216.

17   Michael F. Holt, *By One Vote (American Presidential Elections)*, p. 173.

18   Patrick Young, "The Plan to Suppress the Black Vote in South Carolina Revealed!: Election 1876." https://thereconstructionera.com/the-plan-to-suppress-the-black-vote-in-south-carolina-election-1876/.

19   Available on the Wayback Machine: https://web.archive.org/web/20141105180816/http://www.screconstruction.org/Reconstruction/Citations_files/GaryCampaign.pdf.

We must get the three Commissioners of Election, who are appointed by the Governor, as favorable to us as possible, and we must demand that at least one reliable Democrat is on the Commission and he must endeavor to get to be Chairman of the Commission, and the clerk that is allowed them must be a Democrat if we can possibly bring it about.

It shall be the duty of each [Democrat] club to provide transportation to old and helpless voters and assist them to the Polls, and at same time see to it that all Democrats turn out and vote.

Every Democrat must feel honor bound to control the vote of at least one negro, by intimidation, purchase, keeping him away or as each individual may determine, how he may best accomplish it.

We must attend every Radical [that is, Republican] meeting that we hear of whether they meet at night or in the day time. Democrats must go in as large numbers as they can get together, and well armed, behave at first with great courtesy and assure the ignorant negroes that you mean them no harm and so soon as their leaders or speakers begin to speak and make false statements of facts, tell them then and there to their faces, that they are liars, thieves and rascals, and are only trying to mislead the ignorant negroes and if you get a chance get upon the platform and address the negroes.

In speeches to negroes you must remember that argument has no effect upon them: They can only be influenced by their fears, superstition and cupidity. Do not attempt to flatter and persuade them. Tell them plainly of our wrongs and grievances, perpetrated upon us, by their rascally leaders. Prove to them that we can carry the election without them and if they cooperate with us, it will benefit them more than it will us. Treat them so as to show them, you are the superior race, and that their natural position is that of subordination to the white man.

Never threaten a man individually if he deserves to be threatened, the necessities of the times require that he should die. A dead Radical is very harmless—a threatened Radical or one driven off by threats from the scene of his operations is often very troublesome, sometimes dangerous, always vindictive.

In the month of September we ought to begin to organize negro clubs, or pretend that we have organized them and write letters from different parts of the County giving the facts of organization out from prudential reasons, the names of the Negroes are to be withheld. Those who join are to be taken on probation and are not to be taken into full fellowship, until they have proven their sincerity by voting our ticket.

Every [Democratic] club must be uniformed in a red shirt and they must be sure and wear it upon all public meetings and particularly on the day of election.

Secrecy should shroud all of transactions. Let not your left hand know what your right does.

In a speech in October of 1876, General Martin Gray (disgustingly) summed up his approach in one sentence: "South Carolina is a white man's State, and in spite of nigger majorities the Democrats are going to rule it."[20]

Attempts to threaten or bribe Black Americans to vote Democrat were of little avail, as Holt makes clear: "Little statistical evidence exists that a significant number of blacks actually voted Democratic in the South, although Democratic poll watchers in the three Republican states and elsewhere undoubtedly stuffed ballot boxes with fraudulent Democratic tickets purportedly cast by registered blacks who were too frightened to vote at all."[21] The main strategy was straight racist brutality. In Gumbel's words,

> *In Louisiana, where a riot by White Leaguers in New Orleans had been heavy-handedly put down by federal troops two years earlier, Democrats went on an anti-Republican rampage so brutal it 'would have disgraced Turks in Bulgaria,' according to an account in Harper's Weekly. Armed gangs burst in on Republican Party meetings and murdered a number of elected officials. In Florida, black sharecroppers were warned that anyone suspected of voting for Hayes would be subject to a 25 percent surtax by local shopkeepers, landlords, doctors, and lawyers. In one incident outside Lake City, a white gang forced a group of black men to endure a mock hanging, making them promise not to vote Republican before letting them go. Throughout the state on election day, illiterate blacks in some precincts were given Democratic ballots misleadingly decorated with Republican symbols.*[22]

---

20   Michael F. Holt, *By One Vote (American Presidential Elections)*, p. 216.
21   Michael F. Holt, *By One Vote (American Presidential Elections)*, pp. 216-217.
22   Andrew Gumbel, *Steal This Vote*, p. 95.

That's enough for us to draw the real historical lesson from the disputed Hayes-Tilden election, and it's not one that Democrats want you to learn: if there had been no such widespread voter intimidation by Democrats, and Black American freedman had been allowed to vote unhindered, the popular vote would have legitimately gone to Republican Hayes.

The election would never have been disputed if Democrats hadn't disenfranchised Black Republicans. In Holt's words, "It was clear in all three southern states [at the center of the dispute] in 1876 that thousands of black Republicans had been prevented from voting." Indeed, that's what Republican candidate Rutherford Hayes himself maintained.

> *Hayes was unquestionably right. Had blacks been allowed to vote freely, Hayes easily would have carried all three states in dispute, Mississippi, and perhaps Alabama as well. Democrats at the time and later pro-Democratic historians who cried that the election had been stolen by Republicans, that it was "the fraud of the century," conveniently ignored the clear evidence of the force, intimidation, and fraud used by Democrats to keep blacks from the polls.*[23]

But because of Democrat "force, intimidation, and fraud" the presidential election was disputed—and hotly. It soon seemed that the country might move from a contested election to war. "Democrats from around the country were threatening to use armed force to make sure Tilden was inaugurated in March," with "both northern and southern Democrats promising to raise armed vigilantes on Tilden's behalf once he gave the word."[24] Much to his

---

23   Michael F. Holt, *By One Vote (American Presidential Elections)*, p. 237.
24   Michael F. Holt, *By One Vote (American Presidential Elections)*, p. 240.

credit, Tilden counseled peaceful patience while the vote counting got sorted out.

Finally, a fatal compromise gave the election to Republican Hayes. What Democrats really wanted, above all, was the withdrawal of federal troops from the South and the end of Reconstruction. Electing Democrat Samuel Tilden was the way they first conceived of achieving that end. But (nearly) equally effective would be a compromise: agree to the election of Republican Rutherford Hayes in exchange for the withdrawal of troops and the end of Reconstruction. That would allow Democrats to reign in the South unimpeded, which of course would mean the Democrats could obstruct Blacks as they pleased. The deal struck to end the disputed election therefore meant the real beginning of Jim Crow—and that's the next essential part of our story.

Before moving on, readers should think about a rather interesting fact. Black Republicans suffered all kinds of intimidation and violence at the hands of Democrats back then; why are Black Republicans still suffering intimidation by Democrats today? What's the real reason Biden would say to Black Americans, if you voted for a Republican, "you ain't black"? Something to think about.

THE DEMOCRAT PARTY: *THE* PARTY OF JIM CROW

As a consequence of the Hayes-Tilden election, the Democrat party was *for the next eighty years* the party of Jim Crow. "We have come to call the latter half of the nineteenth century in the South as the era of 'Jim Crow,' during which the oppression of blacks throughout the region became institutionalized," notes Bruce Bartlett. "It is seldom pointed out that all of the Jim Crow laws were enacted by Democratic legislatures and signed into law by Democratic governors. It could not have been otherwise, since there were virtually no Republicans in positions of authority in state governments in the South after the end of Reconstruction in 1877."[25]

Given the length of time Democrats suppressed the Black vote—and the sheer number of Black American citizens who were unable to act upon their constitutional right to vote and have that vote counted in free and fair elections—that makes the Democrat party, *the* party of Jim Crow, the greatest source of voter suppression in the history of our nation.

I make this point so strongly, and at such great length, because today the Democrat party cries "Jim Crow!" (or "Jim Crow on steroids!" as Biden repeatedly squawked out) every time Republicans try to take any measures to strengthen voting integrity or reduce chances for voter fraud. This is not only disgustingly ironic (the Democrat party *is* the Jim Crow party), but it's the use of the injury the Democrat Party itself historically imposed on Black Americans as an instrument to advance its own radical agenda today.

That's an insult to Black Americans. To make sure there's no confusion about who is the real party of Jim Crow, let's take a closer look at Democrat Jim Crow rule in the South.

The dynamic of Democrat voter suppression is easy enough to understand. "In the South, voter suppression was driven by the fact that blacks were numerous enough to threaten white, Democratic control of government . . . if they voted."[26]

That's the "if" that worried the Democrat Party. As we noted, Democrats resorted to violence and intimidation during

---

25   Bruce Bartlett, *Wrong on Race*, St. Martin's Publishing Group, Kindle Edition, p. 24.

26   Brad Epperly, Christopher Witko, Ryan Strickler, and Paul White, "Rule by Violence, Rule by Law: Lynching, Jim Crow, and the Continuing Evolution of Voter Suppression in the U.S.," *Perspectives on Politics*, September 2020 Vol. 18/No. 3, pp. 756-769. Quote from p. 757. "To be readmitted to the Union, Southern states had to rewrite their constitutions and ensure the rights guaranteed to blacks in the U.S. Constitution and federal enforcement statues, including suffrage for black males. White Democratic Party leaders in the South wanted to reinstitute control over black citizens. But this would require substantial policy changes from the Reconstruction-era status quo, and was virtually impossible as long as many blacks voted because, even in areas lacking black majorities, blacks could be pivotal to election outcomes." Ibid, pp. 758-759.

Reconstruction in order to keep Blacks from expressing their right to vote. But once Republicans pulled back troops and bureaucratic machinery after the election of Hayes, Democrat legislatures enacted laws that allowed Democrats to shift from outright violence to "legal" suppression of the Black Republican vote.[27]

But we mustn't forget the violence was horrifyingly real. And in particular, we mustn't forget—especially in light of Democrats calling Trump a KKK White Supremacist—that the Ku Klux Klan was a Democrat organization begun after the Civil War, and lynching was a way to keep freed Blacks out of power or remove them from any political power they'd gained. Historian Tracy Campbell rightly relates, "In suppressing the black vote, the Klan became the operating arm of the Democratic party throughout the South."[28] As other historians note, "secret, targeted assassinations of black office holders or activists" by the KKK "were critical to Democrats regaining power in the South. Highly public lynchings were more akin to terrorism, creating a spectacle designed to reinforce group boundaries and strengthen white racial solidarity, *including identification with the 'white man's' Democratic Party.*"[29]

Keep in mind: that wasn't just the strategy of the KKK but the whole Democrat Party. "Though the Democrats had generally regained power in Southern governments by 1877, concerns that white [Republican] competitors and blacks could ally and threaten

---

27 "In the late 1860s some Southern states did attempt to enact laws restricting black suffrage, but these were overturned by federal legislation and enforcement of voting rights because Republicans controlling the federal government wanted to develop a national party to consolidate the political victories of the Civil War; this would require black votes in the South (Valelly 2009a). While Republicans wanted to compete in the South and stationed federal troops there to enforce voting rights, Southern states could not implement legal, institutionalized forms of suppression." Brad Epperly, Christopher Witko, Ryan Strickler, and Paul White, "Rule by Violence, Rule by Law: Lynching, Jim Crow, and the Continuing Evolution of Voter Suppression in the U.S.," pp. 756-769. Quote from p. 759.

28 Tracy Campbell, *Deliver the Vote*, p. 58.

29 Brad Epperly, Christopher Witko, Ryan Strickler, and Paul White, "Rule by Violence, Rule by Law: Lynching, Jim Crow, and the Continuing Evolution of Voter Suppression in the U.S.," pp. 756-769. Quote from p. 761.

their control remained. Thus, violence was used to suppress black voting and drive Republicans from office." The Democrat efforts were effective. "Voter turnout declined dramatically for [Republican] whites and blacks over two decades, but…black turnout declined much more dramatically than white." Yet in tribute to the courage of Black Republicans, even in the face of violence, in 1892, "fifteen years after federal troops largely left the South, the black turnout rate remained roughly 50% in some Southern states." The Democrat effort at "voter suppression was never going to be entirely effective…as long as some blacks heroically risked life and limb to continue to vote."[30]

Because continued violence wasn't enough, more ingenious and effective laws had to be devised. In the words of a delegate to the Alabama Democratic Convention of 1900, "We have disfranchised the African in the past by doubtful methods, but in the future we'll disfranchise them by law." That's the heart of Jim Crow.[31]

Jim Crow Democrats realized—and this is very important for our assessment of the massive Democrat effort to change voting requirements and gain control of election oversight leading up to the 2020 election—that "before they could effectively disenfranchise blacks, election oversight institutions also needed to be reconfigured along the lines of Democratic preferences after being controlled by Republicans during Reconstruction." Democrats were very careful in advancing, however, because of the fear of sparking federal intervention if they became too bold, too quickly.[32]

---

30 Brad Epperly, Christopher Witko, Ryan Strickler, and Paul White, "Rule by Violence, Rule by Law: Lynching, Jim Crow, and the Continuing Evolution of Voter Suppression in the U.S.," pp. 756-769. Quote from p. 759.

31 Brad Epperly, Christopher Witko, Ryan Strickler, and Paul White, "Rule by Violence, Rule by Law: Lynching, Jim Crow, and the Continuing Evolution of Voter Suppression in the U.S.," pp. 756-769. Quote from p. 759.

32 Brad Epperly, Christopher Witko, Ryan Strickler, and Paul White, "Rule by Violence, Rule by Law: Lynching, Jim Crow, and the Continuing Evolution of Voter Suppression in the U.S.," pp. 756-769. Quote from p. 760. Emphasis added to quote.

Much to the discredit of Northern Republicans, the Republican Party more or less "abandoned" attempts to enforce Black voting rights in the South, regarding it as too expensive and impractically difficult to sustain what amounted to (at least) the threat of reoccupation by federal troops. Instead, Republicans changed their focus to "the promotion of business as a way to build a national party."[33] That meant Black Republicans were at the mercy of the Democrat Party. The so-called "solid South" thus arose under the complete dominance of the Jim Crow Democrat Party.

The "legal" disenfranchisement was a step-by-step process, with Democrats testing the waters as to what might reignite Northern Republican interference again. First, those Blacks convicted of a crime were disallowed from voting—and here we need to keep in mind that Democrat lawmen would arrest Black men for just about any reason they could dream up *because* that would allow incarcerated Blacks to provide free labor in chain gangs. Then, broader laws were passed to decrease the Black vote, such as those using "poll taxes, registration requirements, multiple-box voting, secret ballots, literacy tests, property tests, understanding clauses, grandfather clauses, and the white primary."[34]

Ironically, Democrats enacting Jim Crow laws believed that legal disenfranchisement was a necessary improvement that kept the party from having to resort to outright election fraud (at least quite so frequently).[35] And Jim Crow legislation was all too effective. To take Louisiana as an example, in 1897 there were 130,344 Blacks registered to vote, and by 1900 it had been cut down to

---

33　Brad Epperly, Christopher Witko, Ryan Strickler, and Paul White, "Rule by Violence, Rule by Law: Lynching, Jim Crow, and the Continuing Evolution of Voter Suppression in the U.S.," pp. 7. Quote from p. 760.

34　Brad Epperly, Christopher Witko, Ryan Strickler, and Paul White, "Rule by Violence, Rule by Law: Lynching, Jim Crow, and the Continuing Evolution of Voter Suppression in the U.S.," pp. 756-769. Quote from pp. 761-762.

35　Tracy Campbell, *Deliver the Vote*, pp. 102-103.

5,320, a 96 percent drop. The Black Republican vote was nearly extinguished in the South.

Black Republicans did try to fight back by creating the Fusionist Party with Populists (generally poor white farmers), but Democrats fought back, literally. For example, in North Carolina in 1894 Fusionists managed to win the governor's office, a majority in the General Assembly, and a good number of local offices around the state. But in 1898, using "intimidation and blatant election fraud, the Democrats recaptured five of the state's nine Congressional seats...." In Wilmington, where Black Republicans held multiple political offices, there was an insurrection by Democrat White Supremacists, led by Alfred Waddell who instructed his followers to go to the polls on election day, "and if you find the negro out voting, tell him to leave the polls, and if he refuses, kill him." That wasn't hyperbole. Waddell led a band of four hundred followers who attacked and killed Blacks, ensuring that Democrat control would be reestablished. Democrats elected a White governor in 1900, and "amended the [state] constitution to disenfranchise African-Americans."[36]

But fraud was still alive and well in the era of Jim Crow. At the same time that Fusionists were fighting for their lives in North Carolina, Fusionists also struggled against the Democrat political machine in Louisville, Kentucky. Louisville's Democrat machine was run by burlesque theater owner John Whallen, who used every fraudulent trick to control the elections: having police intimidate Black Republican voters, stuffing ballot boxes, stealing ballot boxes in heavily Republican areas, making Republican voters wait in excruciatingly long lines with purposely slow election clerks, buying votes with great stacks of cash, padding the voting rolls with illegal voters, and throwing out Fusionist poll watchers. Whallen

---

36   Tracy Campbell, *Deliver the Vote*, p. 105.

also bribed some Blacks as thugs to scare other Blacks away from the voting booth and also as repeat voters for the Democrat Party.[37]

In the presidential election of 1920 that pitted Republican Warren Harding against Democrat James Cox, Black Republicans in Florida hoped "to transform the tradition of one-party Rule and Jim Crow." The Democrats controlling Florida had other ideas: "The KKK declared open war on black voting; with the encouragement of state authorities, an estimated 30 to 60 black Floridians were killed that [election] day, along with hundreds more wounded or chased away from the state."[38] While Republican Harding won by a landslide, Florida's electoral votes went to Democrat candidate Cox.

So, as we've seen, Democrat Jim Crow had a long rule. The civil rights movement in the mid-20th century finally overcame the resistance of the Democrat Party to giving Black Americans the right to vote. But here, too, we need to get our history right.

THE TRUTH ABOUT THE CIVIL RIGHTS MOVEMENT

As with the real history of Jim Crow, we must be clear about what actually happened in regard to passing the great 20th century civil rights legislation. The passage of the Voting Rights Act of 1965 is too often presented as a triumph of the Democrat Party over racism because it was signed into law by Democrat Lyndon Johnson.

But when we look more closely, things are a lot less rosy. The first significant civil rights act in the 20th century was the Civil Rights Act of 1957, which directly addressed the long-standing Democrat Jim Crow disenfranchisement of Black voters. It passed the House 286 to 126, *with 107 nay votes coming from Democrats.*

---

37   Tracy Campbell, *Deliver the Vote*, pp. 114-135.
38   Tracy Campbell, *Deliver the Vote*, p. 153.

It passed the Senate 72 to 18, *the 18 nay votes being all Democrats*. Republican President Dwight Eisenhower signed it into law.

The next Civil Rights Act was in 1960, once again trying to undo the ill effects of Jim Crow that had not been taken care of in the 1957 act. It passed the Senate 71 to 18, *with all 18 votes against it by Democrats*. It passed the House 288 to 95, *with 82 Democrats voting against it*. Republican President Dwight Eisenhower signed it into law.

The Civil Rights Act of 1965 did finally deal the death blow to Democrat's Jim Crow. The Senate passed it 77 to 19, *with 17 Democrats voting against it*. The House passed it 333 to 85, *with 62 Democrats voting against it*. Yes, LBJ did sign it into law, but over the protests of all too many of his own Democrat Party.

Much more could be said, but the point is clear: the Democrat Party is not only the party of slavery, but the Party of Jim Crow, and they should be ashamed, given their party's horrible history, to try to smear Republicans with the tawdry Jim Crow brush. I can only assume that Democrats think everyone is ignorant of history, and that's why I included this chapter in the book. We need to set the historical and political record straight.

At the end of the next chapter I'll answer the obvious question: "If *that* is the history of the Democrat Party, how did they become the party of Black Americans?" Before we can answer that question, we need to know other things history has to teach us about the Democrat Party that will help us understand the Democrat political machine today—especially in regard to the multitude of voting "irregularities" in the 2020 election. That's the subject of the next chapter.

CHAPTER 3

THE CORRUPT DEMOCRATIC POLITICAL MACHINES

We have seen that the Democrat Party was, historically, the party of slavery, and as a consequence, the party of Jim Crow. Democrat intimidation and violence against Black Americans and suppression of the Black vote undermined election integrity. But the Democrat Party has used other ways to undermine election integrity.

It so happens that the Democrat Party was the party of big-city political machines from the mid-1800s on and remains so to this day. Take a look at one of the maps of the 2020 election that colors the country by what *counties* (not states) went Democrat (blue) or Republican (red). Almost the whole country is red but a few densely populated blue metropolitan areas. Democrats win presidential elections by controlling big cities, and that's why we need to stand back and see how they've controlled the vote in cities historically.

This isn't merely an interesting history lesson. Adding together the last chapter with this one allows us to ask questions about the integrity of the 2020 election in the context of long-standing patterns of corruption by the Democrat Party and also allows us to see the typical patterns of cheating in elections.

If we want to understand Democrat city politics, there's no better place to begin than with Tammany Hall in New York City, which perfected every available method of voter fraud. Keep these methods in mind when we look at the 2020 election in more detail in a later chapter.

BIG CITY DEMOCRAT VOTING FRAUD: THE PARTY OF TAMMANY HALL

Tammany Hall is actually the name of a political organization, rather than (as it might sound) a place. It might be more properly called Tammany Society, or even more exactly, the Society of St. Tammany, named after the Indian Tamanend, who signed a peace treaty with William Penn. Rather than have any real connection to its namesake, it was actually a political society that began in the late 1700s and grew to be one of the greatest (and most corrupt) Democrat political machines in American history.

As you might suspect, Tammany didn't gain and maintain political power through fair and square voting, but through twisting elections in any way to win. So, for example, "In an 1843 election," historian Tracy Campbell relates, "Tammany's men imported inmates from the Blackwell's Island Penitentiary to vote in the Democratic wards. Tammany also employed paupers from the city almshouse, giving them clean clothing, money, and tickets for grog after they had cast their vote for Tammany candidates."[39]

Connecting the last chapter to this one, in the presidential election of 1844, Tammany Hall did its part to bring pro-slavery Democrat James K. Polk to victory over Whig candidate Henry Clay, with an impressive New York City voter "turnout of fifty-five thousand," even though there were "only forty-one thousand eligi-

---

39   Tracy Campbell, *Deliver the Vote*, p. 19.

ble voters,"[40] a sure sign of the Democrat Party machine "stuffing ballot boxes."[41]

That's a serious charge. Tammany literally stole the national election for pro-slavery Democrat Polk. New York State had a total of thirty-six electoral votes, enough to swing the presidential election to Clay, and New York City was the key to winning the state. Even with all the cheating, Polk won New York by only 5,106 votes.

Perhaps it was the immigrant vote that clinched it for Polk. It just so happened that "over 5,500 immigrants had been naturalized in the three months preceding the election in New York City, and twice that amount throughout the state in the same period. On election eve alone, 497 new voters had been naturalized in New York City. These votes, everyone understood, were cast for Polk."[42]

We'll come back to Tammany's "naturalization mills" below. But to finish off our discussion of the 1844 presidential election, the pro-slavery Polk won the popular vote by less than forty thousand votes, and the electoral vote (thanks to Tammany's steal) by 170 to 105. Take New York's thirty-six votes from Polk's column and put them in Clay's, and the results would have been that the Whig candidate Henry Clay would have won 141 to 134. But thanks to Tammany Hall, Democrats cheated their way to victory in the presidential election (for a second time, we remind ourselves; the first was with Andrew Jackson).

To be sure, Democrats weren't the only ones using dirty tactics. Both Democrats and the opposing party of the time, the Whigs, used "street toughs" to get out the vote, fix the vote, and suppress the other side's vote, including the use of "convicts who promised loyalty to one party or the other" who were "routinely being let

---

40   Andrew Gumbel, *Steal This Vote*, p. 78.
41   Tracy Campbell, *Deliver the Vote*, p. 20.
42   Tracy Campbell, *Deliver the Vote*, p. 24.

out of prison to enable them to cast a ballot."[43] The Whigs were no match for the Democrat's Tammany Hall, however.

Attempts at oversight to ensure election integrity had little effect. In an election of 1851, "thugs known as 'Short Boys' descended upon a district in the Eighth Ward and violently drove out the election inspectors and inserted 'ballots by the handful.'"[44] In the presidential election of 1856, when Democrat James Buchanan beat the first Republican presidential candidate, John Charles Frémont, "a conservative estimate placed the number of fraudulent votes in New York City at 10,000...."[45]

Abraham Lincoln (who was actually the second Republican presidential candidate) won the state of New York in the election of 1860, but because of the usual Democrat tactics of force and fraud, Lincoln didn't win in Tammany-controlled New York City. "In the Twelfth Ward of New York City alone, 500 of the 3,500 registered names were fictitious. Tammany Hall, in firm opposition to Lincoln and the Republicans, registered nearly a thousand false names in the Ninth Ward. Not surprisingly, Lincoln lost New York City by nearly 30,000 votes."[46]

In the election of 1864, Republicans discovered "countless false names in an investigation of the New York City registry roles, and the absentee soldier vote was a vulnerable point of corruption. Thousands of forged registration papers had been filed for soldiers, officers' certificates had been forged, and numerous sick, disabled, and dead soldiers had been illegally registered." Lincoln sent six thousand troops to watch over the election, which certainly quieted things down, but significant fraud still occurred.[47]

---

43   Andrew Gumbel, *Steal This Vote*, p. 79.
44   Tracy Campbell, *Deliver the Vote*, p. 20.
45   Tracy Campbell, *Deliver the Vote*, p. 21.
46   Tracy Campbell, *Deliver the Vote*, p. 50.
47   Tracy Campbell, *Deliver the Vote*, p. 56.

The Democrats declared themselves the champions of the Defunding the Police Movement in the 2020 election. Ironically, what really allowed "Tammany's clout" in the 1800s was "its control of the city's police force," which looked the other way "while Tammany men brought axes and pistols to the polling places to destroy ballots boxes and threaten voters," and even used the police force itself "as an active agent to steal votes or intimidate voters...."[48]

Police protection and intimidation kept the machine running smoothly. When elections came around—local, state, and national—police stood cheerfully by as "armed gangs poured out of saloons, flophouses, and gambling dens and flocked to the polls to do their worst on behalf of the Tammany Hall political machine." The gangs were divided by task. "Some were under instruction to stuff ballot boxes with fraudulent votes, or to oversee the count so the result would correspond to a predetermined outcome. Others were simply wreckers out to vandalize polling places favored by the Republican opposition and beat up the other side's election officials." But the greatest number were the "repeaters," those who "had been given five dollars, as much liquor as they could hold, and a list of the recently deceased whose names they were to use to cast as many ballots as possible."[49] Small wonder that Democrats didn't want to clean up voter rolls.

Democrat repeat voting was a real art in New York City in the 1800s. "The repeaters carried changes of clothing, including several sets of coats and hats, so they could plausibly come forward a second or third or fourth time in the guise of an entirely new person."[50] One of the most amusing tricks to allow repeat voting was cheerfully explained by Tammany's Big Tim Sullivan.

---

48 Tracy Campbell, *Deliver the Vote*, p. 21.
49 Andrew Gumbel, *Steal This Vote*, p. 74.
50 Andrew Gumbel, *Steal This Vote*, p. 74.

"When you've voted 'em with their whiskers on, you take 'em to a barber and scrape off the chin fringe. Then you vote 'em again with the side lilacs and a mustache. Then to a barber again, off comes the sides and you vote 'em a third time with the mustache. If that ain't enough and the box can stand a few more ballots, clean off the mustache and vote 'em plain face. That makes every one of 'em good for four votes."

Big Tim was under the corrupt leadership of "Boss" Tweed, the most famous of the Democrat machine bosses who controlled New York City and New York State politics from just before the Civil War up until his downfall in 1871.

I include Big Tim's amusing instructions on the art of multiple voting not only because it reflects the ingenuity and depth of voter fraud in the Democrat's Tammany Hall, but also because it was quoted by Justice John Paul Stevens in the Supreme Court's *Crawford v. Marion County Election Board* (2008). It's worth taking a bit of a detour to look at the *Crawford* case.

In that 2008 case, the Democrats tried to argue (in regard to an Indiana law) that having to provide photographic identification to vote unfairly disenfranchised poor voters (who mostly voted Democrat). The Democrat argument was that voter fraud was not a significant issue, so that photo IDs were entirely unnecessary. The majority opinion disagreed: voter fraud was and is a real danger to democracy. "It remains true," wrote liberal-leaning Justice Stevens, "that flagrant examples of such fraud in other parts of the country have been documented throughout this Nation's history by respected historians and journalists, that occasional examples have surfaced in recent years, and that Indiana's own experience with fraudulent voting in the 2003 Democratic primary for East Chicago Mayor—though perpetrated using absentee ballots and not in-person fraud—demonstrate that not only is the risk of voter fraud real but that it could affect the outcome of a close election."[51]

Justice Stevens offered Big Tim Sullivan's cheeky advice in a footnote as an illustration of how long voter fraud and lack of proper voter ID have been problems. Steven's words are also important because they make us aware of the fact that absentee ballot manipulation isn't something new for the Democrat party.

But let's return to Tammany Hall because there are other lessons to be learned about how Democrats controlled the vote. As I've mentioned, one especially rich source of vote-stacking was immigration, and Democrats had been doing it for some time (and not just in New York).

In Kentucky in 1840 Whigs called for having an official registry of voters because, they claimed, "Democrats resorted to importing voters in a large number of elections," something that couldn't occur if there were well-maintained, official voter rolls. Republicans later joined Whigs in this demand in several states for the same reason, but efforts "to enact registry laws…failed in Iowa, Indiana, and New York, where Democrats opposed Whig and Republican attempts to enact a registry law because it would shut off the naturalization 'mills' in which so many immigrants were added to the rolls in the days leading up to an election."[52]

That leads us to an important insight. Have you wondered why our southern borders opened up under Democrat leadership after the 2020 election? The strategy goes back to Tammany Hall. As Campbell notes, "The source of Tammany's power, and later of that of its legendary leader William M. 'Boss' Tweed, was located in its ability to corral armies of immigrants into quick naturalization mills and then into voting booths."[53]

---

51   *Crawford v. Marion County Election Board* (2008), Majority opinion written by Justice Stevens, Part II, pp 11-12.
52   Tracy Campbell, *Deliver the Vote*, pp. 14-15.
53   Tracy Campbell, *Deliver the Vote*, p. 18.

Gumbel likewise notes that Tammany Hall excelled at "the fraudulent naturalization of tens of thousands of Irish immigrants who could be counted on to vote for the Democratic Party ticket." During the 1860s, about nine thousand immigrants became citizens every year. But Tammany Hall needed more votes than that, so it "put in a request for an initial forty thousand application forms as it opened a dedicated naturalization office in a saloon," which soon enough "sent almost sixty thousand names to the New York Superior Court" to be approved for citizenship and hence voting.[54] Since Boss Tweed owned the courts, approval was exceedingly quick and indiscriminate.

So it was that "Tweed…perfected a way to fast-track the naturalization process to generate tens of thousands of new immigrant votes, an idea he originally filched from his archrival, Fernando Wood," a fellow Democrat but rival to Tammany Hall.[55] How fast? It wasn't unusual for a judge to process eight hundred in a day.[56]

In the presidential election of 1868, Boss Tweed did his part to try to keep Republican Ulysses Grant from being elected: "Tammany Hall's well-known naturalization mills worked feverishly before the 1868 election," resulting in "over 65,000 people… naturalized" in the month before the election.[57] The Democrat candidate Horatio Seymour carried New York state, thanks to Tweed, but Grant won the presidential election.

But Tammany Hall succeeded in helping Democrats steal the election of 1884 that pitted Democrat Grover Cleveland of New York against Republican James Blaine. Cleveland beat Blaine by less than fifty-eight thousand popular votes, resulting in an electoral college win of 219 to 182. Cleveland inched out a win in his home state of New York by a mere 1,149 votes, no doubt made pos-

---

54   Andrew Gumbel, *Steal This Vote*, p. 75.
55   Andrew Gumbel, *Steal This Vote*, p. 14.
56   Tracy Campbell, *Deliver the Vote*, p. 19.
57   Tracy Campbell, *Deliver the Vote*, p. 62.

sible by the voter fraud in New York City, and that gave Cleveland the presidency. (New York had thirty-six electoral votes, so if there were no typical Tammany cheating, Blaine would have had 216 to Cleveland's 183.)[58]

If that weren't enough to taint the election of 1884, Jim Crow was at work providing votes for Cleveland from the Democrat South. For example, ballots were accepted through a slit in the wall in one Mississippi county where "the official casually counted all Democrat votes and discounted as many Republicans as he desired." Florida Democrats threatened Blacks away from the polls and stole ballot boxes. In a tribute to the effectiveness of Jim Crow, in Mississippi, Georgia, and South Carolina there were a total of ninety-eight counties that had Black majorities, but all were carried by the Democrats. I agree with Campbell's assessment when he asks rhetorically, "With one portion of the country so thoroughly intimidated that Republicans could never expect a fair return, could *any* presidential race in this era be excluded from the list of elections where fraud was rampant and influential?"[59]

How many presidential elections have Democrats actually stolen, taking into account the intimidation of Black Republican voters in the South and the corruption by Democrat political machines in the North?

But to return to Tammany again, Cleveland carried New York, and hence the presidency, because of Tammany Hall. Keep this lesson firmly in mind: flooding the ballot box with the immigrant vote through "fast-track naturalizations" was one of the most important ways that New York City's Democrat political machine built and retained power—in New York City itself, New York State, and because of the number of electoral votes in the state,

---

58   Tracy Campbell, *Deliver the Vote*, p. 91. Campbell erroneously states that Cleveland won New York state by less than a thousand votes.

59   Tracy Campbell, *Deliver the Vote*, p. 92.

the nation. Again, something to keep in mind in regard to illegals flooding over our southern border today.

It's important to understand that political machines like Tammany Hall did provide real services for its constituents in the cities, especially the vulnerable immigrants, just like the Democrats of today provide welfare handouts. Like mob bosses, they often got things done for those on their side. But the help they gave in exchange for votes came at a significant price, as Boss Tweed illustrates. "Before he took over, the standard kickback on city contracts was 10 percent. Once he asserted control"—between 1863 and 1871—"the rate shot up to 35 percent, with Tweed taking 25 percent for himself." Thus, millions and millions of dollars were looted out "of the public purse" for the Democrat politicians of New York City.[60] Democrat government largesse benefits the givers far more than those whose votes it buys.

SOME REPUBLICAN MACHINE CORRUPTION

We don't want to be unfair to Democrats, however. While the Democrat Boss Tweed may be the most famous of the crooked city machine bosses, there were some less famous but equally corrupt Republican city machines, such as in Philadelphia under James McManes and the "Gas Ring," and even more under Matthew Quay.

Philadelphia's bosses also ruled by voter manipulation and fraud, going all the way back to the founder of Philly's political machine, Simon Cameron, who was Abraham Lincoln's first secretary of war. One oft-repeated story gets to the heart of Cameron's lack of character. Aware of the rumors about Cameron, Lincoln asked abolitionist congressman Thaddeus Stevens about Cameron's dishonesty. Stevens replied, "I do not believe he would steal a red

---

60   Andrew Gumbel, *Steal This Vote*, p. 85.

hot stove." Cameron, upon later hearing the remark, demanded that Stevens retract his statement in the presence of the president. Stevens then reportedly said to Lincoln, "I believe I told you he would not steal a red hot stove. I will now take that back."[61] An equally famous statement by Matthew Quay gives us a glimpse of his less than noble character. He defined politics as "the art of taking money from the few and votes from the many under the pretext of protecting the one from the other."

THE DEMOCRATS' CHICAGO FRAUD MACHINE

But historically, the Democrat Party has really been the big city political machine party, and nowhere is that more clear than in Chicago, especially under Mayor Richard Daley (mayor from 1955–1976).

In didn't start with Daley. Corruption in Chicago had a very long history, and that included massive voter fraud of multiple kinds. In the 1884 Chicago mayoral race, Democrat candidate Carter Harrison won with 57 percent, no doubt helped by the interesting fact "that George Washington, Thomas Jefferson, John Hancock, and similar notables had registered and voted." Corruption was rife in nearly every precinct. "In the end, only seven of 171 precincts did not evince irregularities."[62] Cheating also marked the national aspect of the 1884 presidential election race between Democrat Grover Cleveland and Republican James Blaine: secretary of the Illinois state Democrat committee, Joseph "Chesterfield" Mackin,

---

61 The story is repeated many times, with slight variations. See "Matthew Quay: The Political Boss Who Made Two Presidents!" August 11, 2019. https://fascinatingpolitics.com/2019/08/11/matthew-quay-the-political-boss-who-made-two-presidents/.

62 James L. Merriner, *Grafters and Goo Goos: Corruption and Reform in Chicago* (Southern Illinois University Press, 2004), p. 44.

was caught in a great ballot box stuffing scheme that earned him both national notoriety and a trip to the penitentiary.[63]

Mackin wasn't the only one famous for dishonesty in Chicago. There was Democrat Chicago alderman Michael "Hinky Dink" Kenna, a notoriously corrupt lord of Chicago's 1st Ward from the end of the 1890s up until the 1940s. "Kenna perfected methods of vote fraud, such as rounding up vagrants and shuttling them from precinct to precinct to cast multiple ballots at fifty cents a vote. Beyond the half-dollar, tramps were given lodging, food, and beer for days before an election."[64]

Multiple techniques of voter fraud were perfected in Chicago's Democrat machine over the years, including "chain voting," where a corrupt poll worker would obtain a blank ballot, and the local boss would fill it out and hand it to a bribed voter, who would then go in to vote, get another blank ballot, drop his pre-filled ballot in the box, and sneak out the blank ballot, which would be given to the boss to fill out, and so on. There was also the "four-legged voter," which was a "vote-fraud practice in which an election judge (a machine worker at the polling place) accompanied a voter into the polling booth, allegedly for assistance, but actually to ensure that the correct [political] machine votes are cast." Let's not forget the "short pencil" technique, in which a "pencil secretly [was] used by election judges to deface and thus invalidate nonmachine ballots [i.e., of the opposition party]. Adepts employed a piece of pencil lead secured under the thumbnail with sealing wax. Others palmed a pencil stub."[65]

The history leading up to Daley was bad enough, but the Daley machine wins the prize for voter fraud, as had been wonderfully

---

63   See *New York Times*, "Ballot Box Stuffers in Jail," March 13, 1885. https://www.nytimes. com/1885/03/13/archives/ballot-box-stuffers-in-jail-mackin-and-gallagher-of-chicago-to-go.html.

64   James L. Merriner, *Grafters and Goo Goos*, p. 68.

65   James L. Merriner, *Grafters and Goo Goos*, Chicago Political Glossary, pp. 283-285.

detailed by the city's own great newspaper, *The Chicago Tribune*. As James Merriner notes, "The Tribune won a Pulitzer Prize in 1973 for its own vote-fraud series after the primary and general elections of 1972. The newspaper covertly sent twenty reporters and the BGA [Better Government Association] ten staffers to serve as election judges and poll watchers in fourteen notorious precincts on the West and South sides in the March primary. The planted election workers noted firsthand the techniques, developed by Hinky Dink [Kenna] and even those before him," still being used over thirty years later. Forty people were indicted in September of 1972 for vote fraud in the primary. "As with the conviction of 'Chesterfield Joe' Mackin and others in 1884, the techniques were so crude that even a routinely competent Chicago board of election commissioners should have detected them."[66]

Writing in 2004 about continuing corruption in Democrat-dominated Chicago, Merriner asserted that "the favored techniques of fraud now occur not in the polling place but in manipulations of absentee voting."[67] As we'll see, Democrats were to make absentee voting the key to winning the 2020 election.

MAYOR DALEY "FINDS" THE VOTES TO ELECT PRESIDENT KENNEDY: ANOTHER QUESTIONABLE PRESIDENTIAL WIN BY THE DEMOCRAT PARTY

But it was actually before the humiliating exposure of Daley corruption that his machine scored its biggest and most famous win when it "secured" the victory of Democrat John Kennedy over Republican Richard Nixon in the 1960 election.

---

66   James L. Merriner. *Grafters and Goo Goos*, pp. 200-201.
67   James L. Merriner. *Grafters and Goo Goos*, p. 201.

Kennedy won the national popular vote by a razor slim margin of less than 120,000 votes out of sixty-nine million votes cast, and Illinois (or more exactly Chicago) was the hinge of Kennedy's inching out Nixon. At the time, Illinois had twenty-seven electoral votes. That meant a Daley-orchestrated vote manipulation of a relatively small number of votes could hand the twenty-seven electoral votes to Kennedy. How small? Kennedy won Illinois by a mere 8,858 votes.

That's an important point to keep in mind when we look at questions of voter fraud. To rig an election doesn't require cheaters to win everywhere; they only need to win a small number of votes where it's close *and* where there are a lot of electoral votes awarded by that state. (Almost all our states abide by this winner-take-all method of awarding all of their electoral votes to the candidate who wins the majority, so winning a state's major city vote often means winning all the electoral votes of the entire state.)

Other states in the 1960 election also teetered on the balance and barely tipped to the Democrats. Kennedy won Hawaii's three electoral votes by a mere 115 popular votes, Nevada's three electoral votes by 2,493 popular votes, and New Mexico's four electoral votes by 2,294 popular votes. But given the much greater population of Illinois, and the well-known fact of the Daley machine's corruption, Republicans had every reason to suspect that something fishy had occurred in Chicago.

And they were right. In the month before the election, the Chicago *Daily News* reported that there were "thousands of illegal names on the poll list" ripe for vote stealing. It also brought attention to the fact that "the Board of Elections Commissioners" who would oversee the election "was little more than an extension of Daley's machine, considering that 176 of 180 positions on the Board were held by Daley Democrats."[68]

---

68   Tracy Campbell, *Deliver the Vote*, pp. 245-246.

And so, to no one's surprise, Daley indeed delivered the vote to Kennedy. As Robert Dudley and Eric Shiraev note, Kennedy's "victory in Illinois came from the city of Chicago. Mayor Richard J. Daley held back much of Chicago's vote *until the late morning hours* of November 9. The efforts of Daley and the powerful Chicago Democratic organization gave Kennedy an extraordinary Cook County victory margin of 450,000 votes, thus overcoming the heavy Republican vote downstate."[69]

A sudden appearance of votes in the wee hours of the morning. Sounds familiar. What's the strategy?

As Tracy Campbell notes, the Democrats' refusal "to release the [election] returns from over two hundred Chicago precincts until they learned of returns from other parts of the state," is "*one of the oldest election tricks in the book.*"[70] Experienced election fraudsters realize that if you want to steal an election, you have to be careful to act in accordance with what we might call the Goldilocks Principle of Election Stealing: not too few votes, not too many votes, but just the right number to comfortably win without it being obvious the votes were manufactured out of thin air (or, more exactly, by stuffing ballot boxes, filling in absentee ballots, double-voting, and so on).

That's why fraudsters win elections in the wee hours of the morning, after they hear how many votes they need to magically produce to win. Daley did just that and delivered the crucial votes to Kennedy. Sudden victories in the early morning hours is a tactic that also appeared in 2020.

While scholars still debate whether the fraud committed in Chicago was sufficient to bring about Kennedy's victory, it's clear that there was so much corruption under Daley, both in the years

---

69   Robert Dudley and Eric Shiraev, *Counting Every Vote: The Most Contentious Elections in American History*, Vol. 1st ed (Potomac Books, 2008), p. 93.

70   Tracy Campbell, *Deliver the Vote*, p. 247.

before and the years after the 1960 presidential election, that the charge remains highly credible.

But it wasn't just Chicago that made Nixon and the Republicans suspicious about the integrity of the election. Nixon believed that he had been cheated in Texas as well (which he lost by 46,242 popular votes, thereby giving twenty-four electoral votes to Kennedy). He had good reason: in all too many places in Texas, "the votes for president exceeded the number registered," a sure sign of fraud. On top of that, the Texas ballot was exceedingly confusing, causing "spoiled ballots," ballots incorrectly filled in that would then have to be judged as acceptable or declared void. In some counties in Texas, the rate of spoiled ballots approached 30 percent. Much to the anger of Republicans, "Democratic county judges were quick to count those 'spoiled ballots' for the Democrats, while denying the same to Republicans."[71]

LBJ CHEATING HIS WAY TO THE TOP

Even aside from the suspicious goings-on in Texas, it certainly helped the Democrat ticket in the Lone Star State that Kennedy had chosen Texan Lyndon Baines Johnson as his running mate. Johnson had run against Kennedy in the Democratic primary and accused Kennedy of winning the state of West Virginia by a combination of vote buying and bribery of county bosses—most likely an accurate charge, but one that he conveniently forgot when Kennedy chose him as his VP.

That LBJ should accuse anyone else of political shadiness was certainly ironic. When Johnson was first climbing the political ladder in the early 1940s, running in a Senate race against the equally corrupt Democrat Pappy O'Daniel, vote buying in Texas was com-

---

71   Tracy Campbell, *Deliver the Vote*, p. 250.

monplace, especially along the southern border. "Illiterate Mexican Americans would be escorted to the polls by pistoleros, who would pay off their poll taxes and offer them a shot of tequila in exchange for their vote." Often ballots were marked in advance, or sometimes illegal and illiterate voters would be handed strings with knots that helped them identify which candidate they were supposed to vote for. This was not a one-time problem. "Illegal voters from Mexico proper would routinely come across the border to swell the numbers for favored candidates."[72]

As it turned out, LBJ couldn't out-cheat Pappy O'Daniel in that election, although he came close. But he was determined not to lose in his next bid for the Senate in 1948 against Democrat Coke Stevenson, who likewise sought to run as one of the Democrat senators. Johnson was amply bankrolled, so he engaged in a fervent negative campaign against Stevenson on the radio, had himself flown around in a helicopter to campaign events, and handed out "fat rolls of dollar bills to cover poll worker 'expenses,'...."[73]

But most importantly, LBJ enlisted the support of the powerful corrupt local boss of the important Texas border county of Duval, George Parr. Parr delivered for the future Democrat president: "Turnout in Duval County was an utterly implausible 99.6 percent, and Johnson won there with a similarly preposterous 99 percent of the vote,"[74] a sure sign of election fraud.

There was another sure sign of corruption, a convenient overnight discovery of just the right number of votes for Johnson to win. The following episode from Johnson's Senate race might seem familiar to those skeptical of Joe Biden's miraculous overnight gains in the 2020 presidential election. "On election night, Stevenson was ahead by 854. The following night, Johnson made up almost all the difference, thanks to late-breaking returns from Houston

---

72 Andrew Gumbel, *Steal This Vote*, pp. 19-20.
73 Andrew Gumbel, *Steal This Vote*, p. 21.
74 Andrew Gumbel, *Steal This Vote*, p. 22.

and one precinct from Duval County," the county LBJ had Parr fix. Yet, despite these efforts, Stevenson pulled ahead again, and it looked like—after six days of wrangling and recounting—Stevenson would win by 113 votes. "Johnson needed a miracle, and he got one, courtesy of an enforcer by the name of Luis Salas in Jim Wells County, one county over from Duval." Salas "found" a box of yet-uncounted 202 votes—all for Johnson![75]

LBJ went on to win his seat in the United States Senate, soon became the leader of the Senate Democrats, ran for the Democrat nomination for the 1960 presidential election, but came in below John Kennedy. As already noted, the defeat was sweetened by becoming Kennedy's running mate. Such was the moral caliber of LBJ, soon to become president after Kennedy's assassination.

Given the history of voter fraud in Texas evident in LBJ's political climb, it's hard to think that there wasn't significant fraud in the 1960 presidential election that, combined with Mayor Daley's late-night contribution of votes, brought victory to Democrats Kennedy and Johnson. I think it's fair to say that this is one more presidential election stolen by the Democrat Party.

CONTINUING CORRUPTION IN CHICAGO: AN ALL TOO FAMILIAR STORY

To return to Chicago, Mayor Richard J. Daley died in 1976, but corruption continued to blossom in the city of Chicago and the state of Illinois—an important point because of the importance of both as centrally defining the Democrat Party.

All kinds of corruption was uncovered in the Chicago and Illinois general election of 1982. Witnesses brought forward to testify reported "forging signatures, impersonating voters, registering

75   Andrew Gumbel, *Steal This Vote*, p. 22.

ineligible voters, 'assisting' older or disabled voters, bribing voters, illegally dispensing and voting absentee ballots, and using weapons and force to persuade voters and campaign workers. One official was accused of running a ballot through the tabulator two hundred times in order to increase his candidate's margin of victory."[76]

Anything sound familiar?

There's more. Republican US attorney, Dan Webb, who, as having federal jurisdiction, was brought in to investigate the alleged fraud, used a computer "to determine how many dead people were registered to vote or registered in more than one location throughout the city's 2,910 precincts. Overall, 10 percent of Chicago's one million votes for governor, major, city council, and other public officials were alleged to be fraudulent."[77]

Vote-buying is not always expensive. In Chicago's 27th Ward, 17th Precinct, "votes were bought and sold for a cup of cocoa, two dollars, a glass of wine, or a cigarette. Other kinds of voter fraud had been used since the 1800s. The ringleader was Democratic precinct captain Raymond Hicks, who coordinated ballot box stuffing with the assistance of precinct election judges." Votes were mined at nursing homes. Hicks counseled precinct officials to gather votes at residential care homes where they should ensure that the elderly and disabled (whom Hicks considered "crazy") "punch 10" on the absentee ballots, thereby voting straight Democrat. In his investigation of this fraud, Dan Webb "discovered one resident whose full name appeared signed on his application, even though he had 'no fingers or thumbs and can write only an "X" by holding a pen between the stumps of his hands.'"[78]

---

76 Mary Frances Berry, *Five Dollars and a Pork Chop Sandwich: Vote Buying and the Corruption of Democracy* (Boston: Beacon Press, 2016), pp. 95-96.
77 Mary Frances Berry, *Five Dollars and a Pork Chop Sandwich: Vote Buying and the Corruption of Democracy*, p. 96.
78 Mary Frances Berry, *Five Dollars and a Pork Chop Sandwich: Vote Buying and the Corruption of Democracy*, p. 97.

In Hicks's plea bargain testimony, he reported "visiting every hotel and flophouse in the West Side ward to pay for votes and obtain lists of people who had died or moved and would not be voting," so he could cast votes in their names. That was, he remarked, "standard operating procedure." Absentee ballots made this old-fashioned method even more effective in rigging the election.[79] Edward Howard and Thomas Cusack were indicted by Webb because they "helped cast absentee ballots for fictional, non-existent, or deceased ward residents."[80]

Again, we emphasize the importance of absentee ballots for fraudsters. As Mary Frances Berry makes clear in her *Five Dollars and a Pork Chop Sandwich: Vote Buying and the Corruption of Democracy*, "Absentee ballots have proven particularly susceptible to vote buying because campaign workers collaborate with county clerks and voting registrars to accept ballots signed and submitted in bulk."[81] Berry also notes the problem that continues to exist on our southern border. "In Texas, the widespread use of the buying, hauling, and abuse of absentee ballots in rural areas among Latino *politiqueras* has become entrenched,"[82] another point to keep in mind in regard to the Democrats' open-border policy as a means to turn Texas blue.

But to return, once again, to Chicago, it's important to understand that the Windy City is not an island of corruption in an otherwise stellar state; it's part of the epic corruption of Illinois itself. Essential reading in this regard is a 2012 Southern Illinois

79   Mary Frances Berry, *Five Dollars and a Pork Chop Sandwich: Vote Buying and the Corruption of Democracy*, p. 97.

80   Mary Frances Berry, *Five Dollars and a Pork Chop Sandwich: Vote Buying and the Corruption of Democracy*, p. 98.

81   Mary Frances Berry, *Five Dollars and a Pork Chop Sandwich: Vote Buying and the Corruption of Democracy*, p. 13.

82   Mary Frances Berry, *Five Dollars and a Pork Chop Sandwich: Vote Buying and the Corruption of Democracy*, p. 4.

University Anti-Corruption Report, "Chicago and Illinois, Leading the Pack in Corruption."[83] That's 2012—not very long ago at all.

The report begins, "New public corruption conviction data from the U.S. Department of Justice shows the Chicago metropolitan region has been the most corrupt area in the country since 1976. In addition, the data reveal that Illinois is the third most corrupt state in the nation."[84] It continues, "Since 1970, four Illinois governors have been convicted of corruption. Yet only seven men have held this office in this time, meaning more than half of the state's governors have been convicted in the past forty-two years."[85] Three of the four were Democrats.

In Chicago itself, "Since 1973, 31…aldermen have been convicted of corruption. Approximately 100 aldermen have served since then, which is a conviction rate of about one-third."[86] In fact, "Recent conviction data shows that the [sic] Chicago is the most corrupt city in the United States, and the State of Illinois is the third most corrupt state. Since 1976, a total of 1,828 elected officials, appointees, government employees and a few private individuals have been convicted of public corruption in Illinois—an average of 51 per year. Illinois is surpassed only by California with 2,345 convictions (65 per year) and New York with 2,522 convictions (70 per year)."[87]

Interesting, all Democrat-dominated states.

While New York and California may have more convictions, since Illinois has fewer residents, its per capita corruption rate is actually higher (at 1.42 convictions per 10,000 residents). It doesn't hold first place in the nation, however. "Coming in first is

---

83 Dick Simpson, et al, "Chicago and Illinois, Leading the Pack in Corruption," Anti-Corruption Report Number 5, February 15, 2012 (Updated April 18, 2012). https://studylib.net/doc/8274458/chicago-and-illinois--leading-the-pack-in-corruption.

84 Dick Simpson, et al, "Chicago and Illinois, Leading the Pack in Corruption," p. 1.

85 Dick Simpson, et al, "Chicago and Illinois, Leading the Pack in Corruption," p. 2.

86 Dick Simpson, et al, "Chicago and Illinois, Leading the Pack in Corruption," p. 3

87 Dick Simpson, et al, "Chicago and Illinois, Leading the Pack in Corruption," p. 5.

the District of Columbia, which with only 602,000 residents has a per capita conviction rate of 16.02 per 10,000 residents."[88]

That's over eleven times the corruption rate of famously corrupt Illinois! Need I mention that DC is dominated politically by the Democrat Party?

FROM THE CHICAGO MACHINE TO THE NATIONAL DEMOCRAT PARTY MACHINE

The 2012 report came out right in the middle of President Obama's two terms, and it's not altogether beside the point to recall that Obama came from Chicago and helped (along with the Clintons) to define the Democrat Party as it moved into the 21st century.

In 1992, Democrat Bill Clinton beat the elder George Bush by almost six million popular votes, and in 1996 Clinton beat Bob Dole by over eight million. Clinton's lackluster vice president, Al Gore, allegedly won the popular vote in 2000 against the younger George Bush by over a half a million but lost the electoral vote, setting off an enormous effort by Democrats at recounting in Florida, an effort that (as we noted) ultimately ended up with the Supreme Court deciding for Bush.

As I noted in the first chapter, Democrats declared that both the 2000 and the 2004 victories by the younger Bush were stolen elections and sought to overturn the electoral votes in Congress, but without success.

Barack Obama gave us some relief from contested elections, beating John McCain in 2008 by almost ten million popular votes and Mitt Romney in 2012 by nearly five million votes.

Given Barack Obama's victories, Hillary Clinton was supremely confident she could carry the 2016 election, especially since the

---

88   Dick Simpson, et al, "Chicago and Illinois, Leading the Pack in Corruption," pp. 5-6.

opposition candidate, Donald Trump, was a complete outsider to the entrenched political class in Washington and a man who rubbed a great percentage of the establishment, globalist Republicans the wrong way. She was so confident she assumed the blue-collar Democrat base was (as usual) in the bag for Democrats and foolishly thought not campaigning in blue-collar states wouldn't affect her. Trump saw his opportunity and won the blue-collar vote, which helped guide him to a resoundingly huge electoral college victory even though he allegedly lost the popular vote by almost three million, many votes that President Trump and I believe were fraudulent.

The disputed vote deficit of nearly three million was one big reason Democrats allegedly never accepted the election of Donald Trump as legitimate. That's why the Democrat Party's political machine vowed not to take any chances in the 2020 election and decided *by any and every means* to ensure that Trump would not serve a second term.

I emphasize *by any and every means* because, as we have seen in our overview of voter fraud and suppression by the Democrat Party, the Democrats have had a long history of experience in voter manipulation from which various devious methods could be chosen. That's why the charge of multiple violations of voting integrity in the 2020 election have significant clout: such violations would be in full continuity with the Democrat Party's past. They would fit a long-standing pattern we've already seen of not allowing voting rolls to be purged of voters who've moved or died so ballots could be filled out in their names, of non-resident voting, of hauling prepaid voters to the polls, of racking up more votes than eligible voters, of using felons to vote, of ballot box stuffing, of using bulk absentee voting as a means of illegally jacking up the vote, of mining nursing homes for votes, of fraudulently naturalizing immigrants for voting purposes, of discovering piles of uncounted ballots in the middle of the night, and of intimidating Republican voters.

We also know that there have been multiple presidential elections where Democrat fraud and voter suppression or intimidation were demonstrable and significant, oftentimes leading to victory as with Andrew Jackson (1828), James Polk (1844), Grover Cleveland (1884), and John Kennedy (1960). We also know of elections where it was demonstrable and significant, even though it didn't lead to Democrat victory, as with the two elections of Lincoln and in the famous Hayes-Tilden disputed election of 1876. And finally, given the amount of voter suppression by Jim Crow Democrats in the South, the number of presidential elections stolen by Democrats has yet to be fully counted.

Does that mean that we know for certain that there was significant voter fraud by the Democrat Party in the 2020 election?

While we obviously have reasonable suspicions, there's more evidence that we need to examine before looking at the integrity (or lack of it) in the 2020 election itself. But remember, we are not just looking at the election but also want to understand the Capitol Riot on January 6th and how the two are related. So, in the next chapter we'll be examining the year of riots leading up to the election as offering us yet another set of clues as to what really happened in both. Before we do that, I've got some unfinished business.

HOW THE DEMOCRATS GOT THE BLACK VOTE

As I said at the end of the last chapter, there's an obvious question: After all the horrible history of Democrat mistreatment of Black Americans, how did the Democrats move from being the party of slavery, and then the party of Jim Crow, segregation, and Black voter suppression, to being the political party that counts on Black Americans as an essential part of its voter base? You'll see why I waited until the end of this chapter to give an answer.

Recall how the northern Democrat big city political machines of Boss Tweed and Mayor Daley worked. While southern Democrats lorded over their unchallenged political domain through Jim Crow, northern Democrats were (as we've noted in this chapter) the big city machine party whose power was based in the immigrant vote, and since immigrants picked up the lower-class, blue-collar jobs, the blue-collar vote as well.

In exchange for their vote, the Democrat machines provided real help to struggling immigrants (what we might now call "social programs") thereby getting their political loyalty. It also protected blue-collar workers against wealthy industrialists (who tended to be Republican), especially in Democrat support of the unions. But this wasn't all merely charity. It was a way to secure political power and become very rich as politicians. Democrat political power was a way to control tax dollars and patronage jobs dealt out by the political bosses like Tweed and Daley, who always took a healthy cut for themselves.

How, then, did the Democrat Party become the party of Black Americans? Ironically, because of the racial sins of the Democrat Party!

Prior to 1900, almost 90 percent of Black Americans lived in the South. The injustices and horrors of Democrat-imposed Jim Crow and segregation kept them poor and powerless. During World War I and II, the slowing of immigration from Europe and the surge of manpower sent overseas to fight left huge labor shortages in northern cities. That triggered a series of Great Migrations of Black Americans northward—some six million plus—who flocked to the big cities of New York City, Chicago, Detroit, Philadelphia, Pittsburgh, Cleveland, Baltimore, and Washington, DC, (as well as

Los Angeles) looking for higher wages and real economic and political opportunity. Black Americans escaping from Democrats in the South thereby became *yet another immigrant class* in the northern cities that supported the power of the northern Democrat big city political machines.

This shift is more than ironic, but it makes clear how the Democrat Party, with its deplorable history of slavery, oppression, voter intimidation, Jim Crow, and segregation, rather suddenly became the party claiming to protect the civil rights of Black Americans. It also makes clear why the northern Democrats cut ties with the southern Democrats (the so-called Dixiecrats) at about the mid-20th century. The northern Democrats counted on the Black vote in the cities. The northern Democrats won out, making the most significant transformation during the presidency of Lyndon Johnson, whose Great Society programs were, in a very real sense, the nationalization of big city machine politics, dispensing social welfare programs in exchange for votes and the power of political patronage.

There's an interesting and important twist to this story. It wasn't long after LBJ that Democrats also decided to become the party of the sexual revolution as well. That set up for a real tension in the Democrat base between the White elite of the sexual revolution, and the much more conservative blue-collar, Hispanic, and Black base. If that weren't enough to alienate its base, in line with the takeover of the universities by the Left, the Democrat party became the party of Hollywood pseudo-intellectuals and the Left intelligentsia.

The election of Barack Obama in 2008 and 2012 reinvigorated the Black voter base of the Democrat party, and it seemed to Hillary Clinton that the Clinton political machine would sweep her to victory in 2016 against the political nobody, Donald Trump.

Hillary was too confident. She believed that she could ignore and insult White blue-collar workers as deplorables unworthy of the Leftist intelligentsia's attention and depend on their vote. Meanwhile, Trump was expertly campaigning for their vote, putting forth issues the blue-collar base really cared about. Trump also made significant headway among Hispanics, who are much more economically and culturally diverse than Black Americans, and among Blacks themselves. Hillary lost in 2016 because the Democrat base was slipping away, and Trump introduced the country to a new brand of politics, one where the globalist elites would not run the show, one where the power was returned to we the people. In the aftermath of their devastating defeat, Democrats were desperate, in preparing for 2020, to ensure Trump could never win again.

That desperation will, in part, explain why 2020 was a year of riots, the subject of the next chapter.

CHAPTER 4 THE LEFT'S INSURRECTION: THE 2020 RIOTS, ANTIFA, AND THE DEMOCRATS

Given the material we've covered, I think you can now see how hypocritical the Democrat claim to be *the* party of Black Americans really is. You can also see the reason why the Democrat Party was so intensely supportive of the "race riots" of 2020 and Black Lives Matter (BLM), no matter how much damage came from the rioting. In fact, there are several reasons.

First, the support from the Democrat Black base was slipping, and to say the least, Hillary was no Obama. Democrat support of the race riots and the BLM movement were ways to reinvigorate Black support of the Democrat Party.

Second, and related, that support was also a way for Democrats to divert attention from their own horrible history of slavery, racism, voter suppression, and Jim Crow, and pin all their own sins on the "racist" Republicans.

Third, the riots were useful for voter intimidation. The months of rioting were a kind of warning: if Trump wins the 2020 election, expect even more riots to break out all over America.

To add to the second point, as the radical Left was destroying multiple cities with Democrat approval, there was a very strange effort to paint Trump and his supporters as dangerous insurrections in the months leading up to the election (most famously by the Transition Integrity Project). This effort was entwined with the intelligence community's narrative that the number one threat to the US was White Supremacist organizations (which allegedly all supported Trump).

The White Supremacist narrative fit with the reasons for all the rioting by the Left. According to that narrative, the police, the judicial system, and America itself were hopelessly racist and needed to be torn down. And so, the riots were justified, as was violent opposition to the reelection of Donald Trump, White-Supremacist-in-Chief.

This all cleverly fit together to advance the political agenda of the Democrat Party, creating a lose-lose situation for Trump and the Republican Party. If Trump won again in 2020, as he had in 2016, America would burn, and it would deserve to burn because it was essentially defined by racism. If Trump lost, and there was *any* effort to call into account the integrity of the election (as had been done by the Democrats in regard to the 2000, 2004, and 2016 elections), then it would be a sign of an expected political insurrection by White Supremacists that must be suppressed.

All very nicely laid out. And note this: *if* a peaceful protest by Trump supporters on January 6th could be turned into a riot, *then* it would divert attention from the serious charges of voter fraud and also justify a harsh response to the protestors as the anticipated White Supremacist insurrectionists.

We won't be going into all this complex web of connections in this chapter. Our main focus now is on understanding more deeply what was actually going on in the months of rioting leading up to the 2020 presidential election. When we do so, we'll see who the *real* insurrectionists are.

WHY ARE THEY RIOTING?

Let's begin with the obvious: the year leading up to the 2020 presidential election was a year of rioting, especially the summer. I recall sitting in my backyard, day after day, among family and friends, our eyes constantly focused on the awful destruction taking place across many large cities from coast to coast—Minneapolis, St. Paul, Columbus, Washington, DC, Los Angeles, Portland, Richmond, Seattle, Phoenix, Denver, Atlanta, Chicago, Detroit, Dallas, Milwaukee, New York, Louisville, Pittsburgh, Philadelphia, Charleston, Birmingham, and on and on.

Storefront windows were smashed and stores looted and set aflame. Police stations were attacked, state and federal government buildings vandalized or burned. Churches were desecrated and torched. The night we watched St. John's Episcopal Church burn (May 31), my eight-year-old daughter Tori burst into tears. She ran over to me and said, "Daddy, why would anyone burn a church?"

That was a question I simply couldn't answer at that point, one of many.

Why did tens of thousands of Americans take to the streets, causing over $2 billion in destruction of stores, homes, businesses, churches, and state and federal buildings? Why did some of these same people violently attack and beat innocent people, killing some, with many of those victims complete strangers? Why did the Democrat Party and the Left-leaning media ignore the evident destruction caused by the riots and even herald the rioters as heroes, especially members of Black Lives Matter and Antifa? Weren't they engaged in a kind of political insurrection? Why did they express such contempt, even hatred for police? Why were those who opposed the rioters called Nazis, Fascists, and White Supremacists?

I now think I have the answers. When you add everything up—and it will take a bit to lay out the important details, so bear with me—it turns out that it's the *Left*, aided and abetted by the Democrat Party, who are the real insurrectionists (not the Trump supporters at the Capitol on January 6th). Let's begin by getting an overview of the riots of 2020.

THE DEATH OF GEORGE FLOYD: AN UNJUSTIFIED USE OF FORCE

The 2020 riots began with the reaction to the death of George Floyd, the first protests erupting the day after on May 26th in Minneapolis, MN. Along with everyone else in America, I watched the video of Officer Chauvin resting his knee on Floyd's neck for several minutes.

The video was very disturbing to watch, as a human being and as a police officer trained in the proper use of force. My law enforcement experience immediately told me there was a problem. According to the police standard five-level Use of Force Continuum, when subjects do not respond to the mere presence of police (Level One) or to verbal commands of officers (Level Two), then officers should move to Level Three and employ what's called "Empty Hand Control," using *only* the physical force necessary for control. If that doesn't work, officers may use Less-than-Lethal instruments such as pepper spray, a baton, or taser (Level Four). Only as a last resort do officers have recourse to Lethal Force (Level Five).

Officer Chauvin used Empty Hand Control (Level Three) in a way that escalated to Level Five, Lethal Force. To say the least, Officer Chauvin's knee on Floyd's neck for several minutes would be extremely difficult to justify because Floyd was unable to move and no longer a threat to Chauvin or others. Again, in Level Three, police are trained to use *only* the physical force necessary for control. Officer Chauvin came across more like a cowboy who'd wrestled a calf to the ground rather than a policeman dealing with a human being. To me, it appeared as if he wanted the world to see that he'd defeated Floyd; his face showed a total lack of respect and disregard for Floyd's life. That total lack of respect and disregard for life ended with Floyd's death, something that never should have happened.

A SURPRISE CALL: ENSURING GEORGE FLOYD'S PEACEFUL FUNERAL

Much to my surprise, I soon found I was to help make George Floyd's funeral peaceful. Serving as sheriff of Fort Bend County in 2020, I was notified that George Floyd's body would be arriving in Houston for a funeral ceremony scheduled on June 9, 2020. The Houston Police Department stated that Floyd would be transported to a funeral home just outside Fort Bend County in Pearland, Texas, the night prior to the funeral. We were told to expect large crowds and that demonstrations would take place.

My job was to make sure that things would remain peaceful. I immediately assembled my command staff and devised a plan. Our detailed plan called for deploying several uniformed sheriff's deputies around the funeral home as a show of force. It also included a Quick Reaction Force (QRF) stationed a few miles away from the funeral home, which could immediately respond to any disturbance or civil unrest. Finally, we had a large bus capable of holding several prisoners should any arrests happen.

The orders I issued to my deputies called for the arrest of any person who violated Texas state laws. My job as sheriff was to ensure that demonstrators would be protected as long as they were peaceful. It was also incumbent upon me to ensure that traffic along State Highway 6, where the funeral home was located, would remain open.

My deputies were given clear and direct instructions relating to Use of Force measures—that's the way it should always be. We felt most protestors would travel to the funeral home to pay respect to George Floyd, but we anticipated that some might want to create chaos and lawlessness. Our intent was to immediately identify agitators and remove them quickly from the area. Fortunately, we did not experience the anticipated crowds. No arrests were made. Fort Bend County and Brazoria County remained peaceful that day, as they have for years.

But that peace was not to be shared by the rest of America. A great number of America's cities were already being torn up by riots, and that would continue for some time.

THE MAJOR CITIES CHIEFS ASSOCIATION REPORT ON THE 2020 SUMMER OF RIOTS

A good place to begin to understand the year of riots is the Major Cities Chiefs Association (MCCA) "Report on the 2020 Protests and Civil Unrest." It came out in October of 2020 and sets out as well as anything the nature of the rioting leading up to January 2021.[89]

The MCCA is comprised of "Chiefs and Sheriffs of the sixty-nine largest law enforcement agencies in the United States and nine largest in Canada." These aren't the people who report on the riots, or academics and media types who pontificate about the riots, but the actual people who dealt with the 2020 riots on the front line. As a long-time sheriff, I can tell you I respect their take on things.

As noted, the riots began after the death of George Floyd. Media outlets rolled this video countless times a day, with activist groups taking notice. One couldn't turn on a television for days without seeing a reference to Floyd. You could see this story beginning to build with more and more people discussing it on social media platforms. As a consequence, the riots spread like wildfire. According to the MCCA analysis,

> *there were 8,700 protests that took place in most major cities between May 25th and July 31st, 2020. While the vast majority of these protests were peaceful, a large portion did include non-violent acts of civil disobedience such as the takeover of a roadway or dis-*

---

89   According to their document, "The Major Cities Chiefs Association (MCCA) is a professional organization of police executives representing the largest cities in the United States and Canada.... MCCA membership is comprised of Chiefs and Sheriffs of the sixty-nine largest law enforcement agencies in the United States and nine largest in Canada. They serve 79.9 million people (65.7 US and 14.2 Canada) with a workforce of 251,082 (222,973 US and 28,110 Canada) officers and non-sworn personnel." https://majorcitieschiefs.com/resources/.

ruption of commerce. Additionally, there were 574 protests that involved acts of violence, some of which were severe. This violence was limited to only 7% of all protests and in most cases, the acts were perpetrated by individuals or small groups that infiltrated the larger protests.

That gives us a clearer picture of what actually happened during those two months. But it also gives an essential insight to January 6th. As with the racial riots taking place all over America, so also in Washington, DC, at the Capitol: *the violence was limited to only a small percentage, and in most cases, the acts were perpetrated by individuals or small groups that infiltrated the larger protest.*

Peaceful citizens were concerned about the death of George Floyd in May, just as peaceful citizens were concerned about allegations of wide-scale voter fraud in November. The First Amendment was set forth to protect both, declaring "the right of the people *peaceably* to assemble, and to petition the Government for a redress of grievances."

But even though many were peaceful, we cannot downplay the violence. It was real and worrisome. When we take a closer look at the data in the report, it's clear the number of violent protests wasn't evenly spread over cities but clustered in a smaller percentage of the major cities.

Three cities had by far the greatest percentage of protests involving violence: Denver, CO (68 percent), Columbus, OH (63.8 percent), and Portland, OR (62.5 percent). Then there is a big gap to the next level: Miami Dade, FL (26.1 percent), Milwaukee, WI (25.4 percent), Tulsa, OK (21.4 percent), Minneapolis, MN (20 percent), and Oakland, CA (20 percent).

According to the report, "In cities where violence did occur, assaults on police officers, looting, and arson were the most common criminal activities. Approximately, 72% of major city law enforcement agencies had officers harmed during the protests." The total number of police officers injured was 2,037. There were 2,385 incidents of looting, 624 acts of arson, and ninety-seven police cars burned. Protestors threw flaming Molotov cocktails, rocks, bricks, frozen water bottles, hammers, fire extinguishers, cinder blocks, and fireworks. They swung baseball bats and metal poles. They used spray paint and lasers to blind officers.

And there were firearms. A bit over 50 percent of the law enforcement agencies "were also confronted with firearms, most of which were legally carried based on open carry laws. In these instances, protesters often carried semi-automatic assault weapons such as AR-15s, shotguns, and handguns."

Violent protestors seemed unconcerned about the safety of peaceful protestors. As officers on the front line reported, a "common tactic was to use peaceful protesters as human shields while violent individuals attacked officers and attempted to incite violence by throwing objects from deep within the crowds."

Moreover, almost all the agencies reported a significant number of out-of-state protestors, and nearly a third were paid protestors. Unsurprisingly, "violence seemed to spike on days where out-of-state protesters were present." Since the violence was directed at police officers, we know the concerted efforts at bringing violent disorder came from the Left. But we should note that while "more than three quarters of agencies (78%) discovered persons that seemed to self-identify with violent far-left ideologies,…more than half (51%) discovered persons that seemed to self-identify with violent far-right ideologies," such as the Boogaloo Bois, who (along with Antifa) hate the police and hope to tear down the government they defend.

That isn't the whole picture of the 2020 protests. Again, there was good news. Of the 8,700 protests, "approximately 4,434

(51%) were both peaceful and lawful." That's the way it should be: no violence, no destruction of property, no takeover of buildings, no blocking of roads, no harassing outdoor diners. Peaceful, lawful assembly, as guaranteed by the First Amendment.

But the number of peaceful but *unlawful* assemblies where such things did happen was 3,692, about 42 percent of the 8,700 protests. Unlawful and peaceful protests are, of course, better than unlawful and violent protests, but something is deeply wrong when our cities have almost nine thousand protests in a two-month period, and protestors establish a habit of unlawful or violent behavior half of the time. Why were violent protests clustered disproportionately in a few cities? Is there something to this pattern?

DEMOCRAT MAYORS AND RIOTING CITIES: A PATTERN OF DISORDER

Yes, Democratic leadership. As the report notes, some cities experienced unlawful activity in 100 percent of the protests. Denver, Columbus, and Portland, of course, but also Detroit, Memphis, Sacramento, San Diego, and Tucson as well. One thing that Denver, Columbus, and Portland have in common is Democrat mayors leading up to and during 2020. Michael Hancock has been the Mayor of Denver since 2011, Andrew Ginther has been the mayor of Columbus since 2016, and Ted Wheeler has been the Mayor of Portland since 2017. In fact, all the cities on the 100 percent list I've just mentioned have Democrat mayors.

To widen our perspective, we might also ask, which cities had the highest murder rates in 2019, the year leading up to 2020? The top five were St. Louis, then Baltimore, Birmingham, Detroit, Dayton, and finally Baton Rouge, and all five had Democrat mayors. The top five cities that saw the greatest increase in murder rates between 2019 to 2020 were (in order) Seattle, New Orleans, Atlanta, Chicago, and Boston.[90] You guessed it. All had Democrat mayors at the helm. Keep that in mind.

If there's going to be law and order, then those who resort to violence must be arrested. According to the MCCA report, there were a total number of 16,241 arrests made for 8,700 protests in the 2020 riots, an average of about two arrests per protest. It's rather interesting, by comparison, that there were over 725 arrests in the single riot on Capitol Hill on January 6th.[91] Curious difference.

Even if we just count the protests in 2020 that were violent (3,692), the average number of arrests per violent protest would be about 4.4. That means, comparing apples to apples, that the arrest rate was over 160 times higher for the January 6th riot than it was for the 2020 race riots. Not only that, but the 2020 riot arrests seldom led to convictions. For the most part, it was catch and release, where many would simply return to the protest. There were even bail funds for rioters championed by the Left, even Vice President Kamala Harris, such as the Minnesota Freedom Fund; whereas, those arrested in the Capitol riots are still languishing in jail, sometimes without bail, and often in solitary confinement. Interesting. For Democrats, all rioters aren't equal.

A TENTATIVE ASSESSMENT

That's a general overview of the year leading up to the January 6, 2021, Capitol riot. What I faced that day in the House Chamber as a brand-new congressman was part of a year-long pattern of

---

90   Niall McCarthy, "Major U.S. Cities Saw Unprecedented Murder Spike In 2020 [Infographic]," *Forbes*, January 12, 2021. https://www.forbes.com/sites/niallmccarthy/2021/01/12/major-us-cities-saw-unprecedented-murder-spike-in-2020-infographic/.

91   Nik Popli and Julia Zorthian, "What Happened to Jan. 6 Insurrectionists Arrested in the Year Since the Capitol Riot," *Time*, January 6, 2022. https://time.com/6133336/jan-6-capitol-riot-arrests-sentences/.

protests that were spoiled by unlawful activity and violence. I don't approve of the destruction and violence of either side. Yet, it's clear that the rioters of the Left were treated much more leniently than those in the Capitol Hill riot.

But we need to go beyond this general overview in order to understand the real roots of all this disorder. Why did protests turn into riots? I want to set aside the Capitol Hill riot until a later chapter and look now at the others in 2020 leading up to it.

I'm going to give you a very simple answer. The majority of protestors were marching for what they believed to be racial injustice and police reform. I believe there needs to be some police reform, too, especially in Democrat-controlled cities. That's why, as sheriff of Fort Bend County Texas, I made sure the deputies under me were connected to the community in a positive way, creating a climate of deep trust and mutual respect.

Fort Bend County, TX, is the most diverse county in Texas and the fifth most diverse county in America. Our racial breakdown makes that clear: White (29.6 percent), Hispanic (24.1 percent), Asian (22.1 percent), and Black (20.5 percent).[92] Despite Fort Bend County's diverse population, I never witnessed or experienced civil unrest during my tenure as sheriff. Regardless of the racial tensions that were inflamed across our country in 2020, not once were we disturbed by a riot or civil chaos. There was no ill will towards law enforcement, and I credit that to our proactive community outreach and engagement.

Community policing is all about creating good relationships and trust with the community you serve. When those relationships

---

92   Kaia Hubbard, 'The 15 Most Diverse Counties in America," U.S. News & World Report, August 24, 2021, https://www.usnews.com/news/health-news/slideshows/the-15-most-diverse-counties-in-the-us?slide=12. In 2010, Fort Bend was reported as being the most diverse county in the US. See also Carol Christian, "Fort Bend County is nation's most ethnically diverse, leading Houston region's 'most diverse' status," *Houston Chronicle*, April 2, 2013, https://www.chron.com/news/houston-texas/houston/article/Fort-Bend-County-is-nation-s-most-ethnically-4403675.php.

don't exist, law enforcement has a tough time getting information from the community and adequately protecting that community. A lack of communication and coordination leads to distrust of law enforcement. I've always found it important for law enforcement to humanize the badge. Get officers out into their communities and interact with those they serve. Know your community; serve your community.

But many Antifa and Far Left radicals in the race riots of 2020 did *not* want to reform the police. They wanted to *abolish* the police. In fact, these groups want to abolish the United States, its entire way of life, and its economic, political, and judicial structure. They cause disorder because they have as their stated goal the overthrow of the entire social, political, economic, judicial, and we should add, moral order.

They want to abolish the police because they want to abolish America. They are the real domestic terrorists, the real insurrectionists, and we know this *because they say it, loudly and clearly*. They were the ones, primarily, bent on turning peaceful protests into riots.

ANTIFA: THE REAL INSURRECTIONISTS

So who are the real insurrections? Antifa, and to a lesser extent, Black Lives Matter, along with an assortment of additional anarchist-communist groups allied with them in the same tactics and goals. I'll be focusing, for the most part, on Antifa in this chapter (and Black Lives Matter in the chapter dealing in more detail with crime and the Defund the Police movement).

First, be clear about this: Antifa and the Far Left do not represent the Black community. The great majority of Black Americans outraged by the treatment of George Floyd want to *reform* the police, *not abolish* the police. They want safe streets, they want the crime and violence in their neighborhoods to stop, they want Black on Black murders to stop. They want what the eight hundred thousand citizens of Fort Bend got under my leadership: burglaries down 60 percent, aggravated assaults down 27 percent, robberies down 31 percent.

But Antifa and radical Left liberals don't care about any of that. They want to destroy America, and they're very happy to *use* the plight of the Black community as a means to that end. While the mainstream media would have us believe that our greatest danger is extreme-Right, White Supremacist groups, the real danger comes from the Leftist extremist groups, principally Antifa.

Antifa activists don't want to protect the right to peacefully assemble as set forth in the First Amendment. They want to destroy the Constitution and the Bill of Rights, and the entire structure of our government. That's why I can rightly call them the real *insurrectionists.*[93]

I use that term purposely. According to Article 1, Section 8 of the Constitution, Congress has the power (the duty, really) to "suppress Insurrections." An insurrection isn't a mere riot; it's an attempt to rebel against and overthrow the American government. Congress has the duty to suppress Antifa.

The peaceful protestors on January 6th were not insurrectionists. But you can see why Congressional Democrats and the mainstream media were bent on calling the Capitol riot an "insurrection." That allowed them to tag all Trump supporters as violent revolutionaries, so they could invoke the powers of Congress to call "forth the Militia" against political opponents. That's why they incarcerated those arrested at Capitol Hill without due process,

---

93   According to 18 U.S. Code 2383, "Whoever incites, sets on foot, assists, or engages in any rebellion or insurrection against the authority of the United States or the laws thereof, or gives aid or comfort thereto, shall be fined under this title or imprisoned not more than ten years, or both; and shall be incapable of holding any office under the United States."

keeping them without bail in solitary confinement (while Antifa and Black Lives Matter protestors, no matter what destruction they caused, were continually released soon after being arrested, if arrested at all).

In making this charge, I am taking Antifa at its word. Antifa proudly boasts that its main goal is insurrection—and the destruction of *all* police is part of that goal. But don't take *my* word for it. Let's go to the history of Antifa itself, where we'll see that (contrary to Joe Biden's statement that Antifa is "an idea, not an organization") Antifa is a worldwide insurrectionist organization that's been around for almost a century.

Please bear with me through some of the details in what follows because it will help make a whole lot more sense of what happened in all of 2020 as well as on January 6th, and will make evident the real reason why the Democrat Party stood by and watched the riots—it's part of the insurrection.

A (FAIRLY) SHORT HISTORY OF THE WORLDWIDE ANTIFA MOVEMENT

Antifa didn't just pop up in 2020 in response to the death of George Floyd. It's been around since the early 1930s. And since Antifa was formed as a paramilitary organization of the German Communist Party, it really goes all the way back to communism's founder in the mid-1800s, Karl Marx, the sworn enemy of capitalism and liberal democracy. The name "Antifa" is short for Antifascist Action (in German, *Antifaschistische Aktion*).

You may have wondered why so many on the Left, but especially Antifa, are so obsessed with calling everyone a "fascist"—everyone who supports the US government and the Constitution, everyone who wants peaceful reform rather than violent insurrection, all the military and police, anyone who supports private property, anyone who believes in God, in fact, anyone who disagrees with them on anything. And above all, Donald Trump.

That's a rather complex—and important—story that will help us understand far more deeply what happened in the riots of 2020, as well as what's happening with the Left and the Democrat Party today.

To understand, we must situate Antifa in the turmoil of the 20th century. The fight against fascism obviously began in Italy as a response to Benito Mussolini's National Fascist Party, founded in 1921. Since fascism aimed at a kind of totalitarian *nationalism*, it conflicted with communists who wanted a *worldwide* workers' revolution that would destroy all nation states. Fascism also conflicted with the anarchist movement, which (like communists) wanted to destroy all nation-state authority. Italian anarchists and communists both understood themselves as *anti-fascists*, and both opposed Mussolini.

Keep that in mind: Antifa is anarcho-communist in origin.

Now we move to Germany, in particular, the weak and unstable Weimar Republic in the 1920s. The German Communist Party, true to its doctrine, wanted to overthrow Weimar's democratic government and institute a workers' dictatorship that was to be part of the worldwide communist revolution. While they failed, Adolf Hitler succeeded as the head of the *National Socialist* German Workers' Party (that is, the Nazi Party).

Like Italian fascism, Nazism aimed at racially based totalitarian *nationalism*, glorifying the Aryan race as the master race that must dominate or destroy all other races in the Darwinian struggle for survival (the Jews being the favored target for Nazi destruction). German communists opposed this form of fascism (just as Italian communists had opposed Italian fascism) because it conflicted with the communist goal of the revolutionary destruction of all nations that would herald in the worldwide communist utopia. They also rightly condemned Nazi racism. Consequently, in parallel to what happened in Italy, the German communist opposition to the Nazis came to be defined as anti-fascist and anti-racist. But the German communists also called socialists and social democracy "fascist" because in their minds both supported the capitalist order (at least indirectly), rather than embrace full-blown communism.

And so see that the original Antifa in Germany (*Antifaschistische Aktion*) was in fact defined against the Nazis' form of fascism, but since it was a communist-defined organization, members of Antifa labeled "fascist" *anyone who was not a communist.*

In agreement with communism's founder Karl Marx and the communist revolutionaries of the Soviet Union, Antifascist Action in Germany believed that any non-communist state was really an evil capitalist state that must be entirely destroyed—everything about it—as part of the worldwide, violent communist revolution. Anyone who opposed that revolution in any way was labeled a "fascist." (That's where today's Antifa gets the habit of calling anyone who opposes it a fascist and/or a Nazi, a habit taken on by the Left in general.)

After the war, Germany was divided—torn apart, really—into West and East Germany. The West (Federal Republic of Germany) was defined by liberal democratic principles, and the East (the German Democratic Republic) was defined by communism.

The Berlin Wall was built in 1961 by East Germany. Hard as it is for us to believe, the Berlin Wall was referred to by the East German communists as the Anti-Fascist Protection Wall (*Antifaschistischer Schutzwall*)—as if West Germans were continually trying to escape into the gray "paradise" of the harsh, totalitarian East Germany!

We need to dwell on this irony because it shows us a fatal blind spot of Antifa today (and the Left in general), a blind spot that's important to our assessment of the violence of the race riots of 2020.

There was no Antifa in East Germany because it allegedly embodied Antifa's desire for the great communist revolution, one that actually produced a horrible totalitarian state (as was the case everywhere else communism gained political control). Antifa activists can't see the horrors of communism, even when it's right in front of their eyes. They are certainly blind to its real destruction in world history. We now know that 20th century communism was responsible for well over one hundred million deaths and more likely over 150 million. Since the fall of the Soviet Union and East Germany, we also know very clearly how wretched and miserable life really was under communism. Finally, we also know how ruthless, invasive, and oppressive the KGB and the Stasi were (the police forces of the Soviet Union and East Germany).

Yet Antifa both then and now remains entirely silent about the horrors of actual communism, and even worse, Antifa activists are still animated by the desire to bring about a communist revolution.

That's why they riot. That's why they were rioting during 2020 in America. They think they can create that wonderful communist utopia promised by Marx. That's why they continually agitate for revolution.

If I might quote Mark Bray, an academic Antifa activist and historian, "Anti-fascists are, simply, revolutionaries…their revolutionary socialist [i.e., communist] ideology advocates the global expropriation of the capitalist ruling class and the destruction (or capture) of all existing states by means of an international popular uprising that most believe will necessitate violent confrontation with state forces."[94]

That's as clear a statement of Antifa's goals as you can get. Pure Karl Marx.

In some sense, Antifa sees some evil for what it is. Antifa rightly opposes, then and now, Nazism and fascism for all the misery and

---

94   Mark Bray, *Antifa: The Anti-Fascist Handbook* (Brooklyn and London: Melville House, 2017), p. 159.

deaths they caused and the totalitarian states they produced. But like the Left in general, they seem entirely unaware of the equally great, if not far greater, misery and death caused by the various communist revolutions. In fact, they seem to believe that capitalism (the ultimate evil for communist revolutionaries) is supported by Nazism and fascism wherever and whenever it occurs! Therefore, if you now support the freedom to engage in legitimate and profitable business activities and you affirm the right to private property, according to Antifa you are a Nazi and a fascist!

We'll come back to these important points later, but some more historical details will help us get a clearer picture of Antifa as it's been transplanted in America.

From Germany, let's follow the spread of Antifa into England. We're doing it not to fill pages in a book, but to make clear that Antifa has long been an *international* revolutionary movement, one that (true to its communist roots and aims) has always aimed at insurrection in every nation. In 1930s England, as well as after World War II, its most immediate aim was combatting the spread of actual fascism.

During this period, Oswald Mosley had formed the British Union of Fascists (BUF), which, because of the anti-Semitism it took from the Nazis, was successfully opposed by a number of anti-fascist Jewish groups. The BUF was banned in 1940, but British fascism arose again after the war, with its advocates blaming the Jews for both World War II and the deprivation that followed. In response, Jews again formed their own militant anti-fascist, direct-action organizations, most notably the *43 Group*, which would disrupt fascist meetings and beat up self-declared fascists.

By about 1950, the success of these tactics had brought about the momentary fading of the British anti-fascist movement, but the increase of Afro-Caribbean immigration in England set off a British anti-immigration movement, resulting in the ascendance of such organizations as the White Defense League (founded in

1957) and the reinvigoration of Oswald Mosley's Union Movement (founded in 1948).

So-called Teddy Boys, white working-class toughs defined by the new rock 'n' roll music, attacked immigrant communities. The anti-fascist movement reignited to combat White violence against immigrants, and, more generally, any anti-immigrant, White Supremacist organizations or sentiments. This kind of battle continued with the wave of Asian immigrants to Britain in the 1970s. The Teddy Boys were replaced by neo-Nazi skinhead punk rockers, and the BUF was replaced by the political organization, the National Front. British anti-fascism revived in response.

That's an overview of the roots of Antifa in Europe. We can see it's a worldwide, long-standing movement, not just something that popped up in our 2020 riots.

Whatever we think of anti-fascist tactics, we can rightly affirm that stopping the spread of *actual* self-proclaimed fascists, Nazis, and racist White Supremacists is a good and noble thing. But the problem with Antifa, as it developed, is that *it came to see all opposition to communism as rooted in fascism, Nazism, and (now we may add) White Supremacy.* If you disagree with them on anything, you must be a fascist or a Nazi.

That's why Antifa members today are blind to the thoroughly documented evils of communism and literally cannot see why anyone would suggest that communism has been just as destructive, if not more so, than actual fascism and Nazism.

That's why Antifa views any conservative criticism of communism and socialism as yet another manifestation of fascism and/or Nazism, and any questioning of open-border immigration as a form of White Supremacy.

As pro-Antifa historian Bray recounts, anti-fascist groups spread all over Europe—to France, Norway, Sweden, Ireland, Denmark, Spain, Canada, Austria, Switzerland, the Netherlands, Greece, and, of course, to America.

ANTIFA COMES TO AMERICA

We can see from our short history of Antifa in Europe why members of Antifa in America see themselves as part of an ongoing, worldwide, violent anarcho-communist revolution against every form of government, and in particular, against capitalism and liberal democracy. That's why they regularly turn peaceful protests into violent riots, and in America, use the First Amendment to destroy it, as well as the Constitution and the whole government it defines.

In addition to Bray's book, another important document for understanding Antifa's rise and spread in America is Rory McGowan's "Claim No Easy Victories: An Analysis of Anti-Racist Action and Its Contributions to the Building of a Radical Anti-Racist Movement."[95] This is a pamphlet regularly given out to Antifa recruits in America to help them understand the history of the movement and how they need to fit in.

As McGowan explains, Anti-Racist Action (ARA) it one of the most significant pre-Antifa groups that helped define the movement in the US. It began in Minneapolis in the 1980s as anti-racist, anti-Nazi skinheads in the punk rock/skinhead scene. It spread out from there (both geographically and ideologically), and finally in 2013 morphed into its expanded form, the Torch Antifa Network, the largest Antifa network in America.[96]

According to McGowan, from the beginning the ARA (known at first as the "Baldies") expounded "righteous violence" against their enemies—originally, as in Europe, against far-Right, Nazi-friendly skinheads. The ARA understood its fight against Nazi

---

95 Rory McGowan, "Claim No Easy Victories: An Analysis of Anti-Racist Action and Its Contributions to the Building of a Radical Anti-Racist Movement," published in *The Northeastern Anarchist*, Issue 7, Summer 2003. https://theanarchistlibrary.org/library/rory-mcgowan-claim-no-easy-victories.

96 Atlanta Antifa, "William 'Bill' Fisher: Arizona White Supremacist and Grassroots Republican Activist," Torch Network, March 27, 2022. https://torchantifa.org/.

skinheads to be part of a war against racism itself. In this respect, one can have some sympathy with the Baldies, in the same way that we can understand why Antifa in the early 1930s in Germany would organize against fascism. They called themselves Anti-Racist Action because (unlike Europe) there were no actual fascist parties to oppose, and "racism" was a more compelling focus, given the history of slavery in the American South.

That's an extremely important point. It helps illuminate why the Left in general and Antifa in particular continually use the race card. The charge of fascism by anti-fascists in Italy and Germany (and even England) hits painful, historical soft spots. But there was never really any actual fascism in America. For America, the soft spot is racism because of slavery, and so anyone who opposes or criticizes or mildly disagrees with American Antifa or its goals must be a racist.

Back to our historical narrative. The ARA soon expanded. Entirely without irony, McGowan declares that by the 1990s ARA "was an overwhelmingly anti-authoritarian organization. A sizable segment of the membership identified as anarchist and were now in a position to argue for anarchist models of organizing."

What an organization founded on not being organized might look like is anyone's guess, but for the ARA anyone who believed that human beings need governmental structures at all (and a police force to guard its laws) was a fascist and a racist. This prepared the ARA to accept more deeply the European communist notion that once the structures of capitalism have all been destroyed, the state and all its structures will "melt away," leaving a state-less, peaceful communist utopia with no need of a military or a police force.

That's why Antifa today sees no harm in defunding the police. It's a needed revolutionary step to creating a peaceful, earthly paradise.

Yet, McGowan confides, during this time, the ARA struggled with internal problems. Under pressure from women joining the ARA, it added feminism to its base of fundamental beliefs (and therefore abortion rights to its platform, again, in parallel to European anti-fascists). However, frequent sexist mistreatment of women persisted precisely because ARA's model of anarchist organizing avoided governing structures that could deal with disputes and difficulties!

Adding all this together, Antifa soon became entirely identified with the Left. As just noted, in parallel to what happened in Europe, America's ARA absorbed the Marxist, anti-capitalist position of the Left, as well as embracing the Left's globalism (against nationalism), radical feminism, and the LGBTQ movement. Also in agreement with European anti-fascism, the ARA attacked racism, "Islamophobia," Colonialism, White Supremacy, and any restrictions on immigration, and adopted a kind of Critical Race Theory abhorrence of the White race.

Thus, by the year 2000, the American anti-fascist ARA understood its crusade to be part of a worldwide, revolutionary movement defined by the full suite of issues championed by the radical Left, and this prepared the way for its final transformation into Antifa in 2013.

Antifa groups spread all over the US: Rose City Antifa (Portland, OR), Milwaukee Antifa, Antifa Sacramento, Western North Carolina Antifa (Asheville, NC), Rocky Mountain Antifa (Denver, CO), Atlanta Antifa, Pacific Northwest Antifa, Antifa Seven Hills (Richmond, VA), Central Texas Antifa (Austin), Northern California Antifa, South Side Chicago Antifa, Philly Antifa (Philadelphia), Hoosier Anti-Racist Movement (Indiana), Anti-Racist Action (Los Angeles), Bay Area Antifa (Oakland, CA), Michigan Antifa, Smash Racism (Washington, DC)—and the list goes on and on. It looks strikingly close to the list of cities in which there were violent riots in 2020.

One thing is clear, however. Contrary to Joe Biden's assertion that Antifa is an idea not an organization, we can see that it was an international revolutionary communist organization that had a network of cells in a host of American cities—long before the 2020 year of riots in which they participated.

That's why you can match the Antifa organizations to the above-noted cities that experienced the worst riot damage in 2020. The network was ready for rioting, and that's why riots sprang up so quickly, almost instantaneously, during those two months in the summer of 2020. Using social media, Antifa organizations across America were able to turn protests into riots everywhere at once and did so according to what we might call their "rules of riot."

ANTIFA'S RULES OF RIOT

Antifa groups aren't mere random rioters. They are very strategic in causing maximum disorder and destruction to achieve their goals. That's why they were so ever-present in the riots and were so effective in inciting destruction. In another pamphlet handed out by Antifa called "Blockade, Occupy, Strike Back: A Collection of Tactical Knowledge for Students and Others"[97] we find a clue to the reason peaceful protests turned violent in 2020.

As the revolutionary pamphlet makes clear, there's no working peacefully within the political system for Antifa. Relying on some government bureaucracy to effect the desired changes is fruitless, we are told. Revolutionaries must resort to "self-organizing" into

---

97   "Blockade, Occupy, Strike Back," 2012, https://archive.org/details/BlockadeOccupyStrikeBack/mode/2up. This pamphlet is typical of the kinds of material handed out at Antifa events and among adherents. It was originally directed to those rebelling against universities, but its advice is applicable for any Antifa event.

"crews," i.e., small groups of fellow revolutionaries "who organize without hierarchy." The major reason revolutionaries should organize into these small crews is that the "decentralization of action planning renders repression of social movements more difficult." That's why Antifa splits itself into crews guided by Antifa cells rather than having a single centralized organization (and why they are so hard to hit with something like RICO, the Racketeer Influenced and Corrupt Organizations Act).

For Antifa, the enemies are those in power, "our rulers and keepers—politicians, bosses, police, judges…." Direct action crews are the "counterforce." They should not be interested in marching in peaceful protests, which are merely "ritualized processions from point A to point B." Instead, crews should "organize to disrupt the functioning of the economy…through blockades, sabotage, occupations, and other forms of action." They must ensure that "police stations, banks, gentrifying apartments or restaurants are never safe." They must "steal from big businesses, such as expropriating groceries to pass out for free in their neighborhoods." They should "approach the police when they are hassling someone on the street," "attack the immigration machine that deports and imprisons," "stop the landlord trying to evict their neighbors," "de-arrest someone at a demonstration," and "smash banks and other spaces which exist to reproduce capitalism."

Smashing, burning, and looting—not out of anger at a particular incident but as a means to bring about a communist destruction of capitalism by revolution.

Look at some footage of the riots where Antifa presence is obvious. Peaceful protest is clearly not their aim; they are disrupters. "Protests are boring, poorly attended, and ineffective. Peaceful marches or rallies reduce us to passive observers of what is supposed to be our own activity. We are told [by those who wish us to peacefully demonstrate] to express our anger and frustration by shouting or chanting, but otherwise, we are asked to exercise restraint."

There can be no restraint for Antifa. Peaceful protests must be turned into violent protests, and that involves a maximum of property destruction. Journalist Andy Ngo has been covering Antifa for some time. As he reports, the way that a small number of Antifa members routinely turns peaceful protests into violent protests is by smashing windows, breaking into stores, and setting fires. Such acts set off a kind of psychological "chain reaction" in the larger crowd. "Antifa know the effect that smashed windows, breached businesses, and fires have on crowd mentality." Such acts "can turn protesters into rioters. That's why antifa teaches this in their literature that is widely disseminated and in real life" instruction of its recruits.[98]

Actual insurrection is necessary because all those in charge are entirely bent on ensuring that "nothing actually changes." "Nothing short of full-scale *insurrection*" can achieve the desired changes, because "they've never responded to petitions or requests, only force." The whole democratic process is corrupt, we are told. "We have been criticized for…ignoring the democratic process. We have seen the results of that process too many times."

Democracy doesn't work. Everything needs to be torn down so that the utopia envisioned by such Antifa anarcho-communists can be realized. "We will take whatever measures are necessary both to destroy this world as quickly as possible and to create, here and now, the world we want: WITHOUT WAGES, WITHOUT BOSSES, WITHOUT PRISONS, WITHOUT POLICE, WITHOUT BORDERS, WITHOUT STATES."

Sound a little like the Far-Left side of the Democrat Party? Karl Marx's *Communist Manifesto*?

---

98   Andy Ngo, *Unmasked: Inside Antifa's Radical Plan to Destroy Democracy* (New York: Center Street, 2021), p. 16.

It's quite clear, in reading these instructions on how to engage in "direct action," that America's Antifa organizations understand their turning of peaceful protests into destructive riots as part of a worldwide plan to replace the American governmental and economic structure with the communist utopia they envision. They are really insurrectionists bent on revolution.

But as we've seen, the original anti-fascist, anti-Nazi starting point of Antifa has been broadened so that it is now fighting for the entire array of issues embraced by the Far Left. That's why we saw Antifa in the race riots of the summer of 2020, but also, since then, as disrupters in anti-abortion and anti-lockdown demonstrations. And why they support LGBTQA, pro-abortion, and even pro-COVID vaccine events.

Antifa has simply become the paramilitary organization of the Far-Left-defined Democrat Party, just as the original *Antifaschistische Aktion* was the paramilitary of the German communist party. And that brings us, finally, to Antifa and Donald Trump.

ANTIFA AGAINST DONALD TRUMP

One thing that pro-Antifa historian Mark Bray makes very clear is how the election of Donald Trump revitalized the American Antifa movement. Antifa experienced "a relative lull" from about 2005 up until the election of Donald Trump.[99] As an organization that thought it could use the charge of racism against American institutions in order to bring about a communist revolution, there simply wasn't much to do in a country that had duly elected Barack Obama, our first Black president. But Trump was a White Republican who challenged the open-border immigration policy of the Left, and so he became a kind of poster boy at which Antifa (and the entire Left

---

99   Mark Bray, *Antifa: The Anti-Fascist Handbook*, p. 106.

and Democrat Party) could direct all its hatred. He could now be proclaimed the fascist in chief, a White Supremacist and Nazi *who must be de-elected by any means.*

Given the above history of Antifa we noted above, we can see how well Trump fit the needs of Antifa for an enemy of its revolution. This is important, so let's take it point by point.

Donald Trump's turn from globalism to American nationalism to protect American interests and its economy (especially against China) became a sure sign that he was equivalent to Mussolini's fascist nationalist glorification of Italy and Hitler's Nazi racial purity politics in Germany.

Trump's goal to stem the tide of illegal immigration that was benefitting American corporations who wanted cheap immigrant labor (which should horrify even communists), was taken to be the racist equivalent to the Britain's fascist White Defense League's antagonism to Caribbean immigrants in England or the Nazi hatred of Jews.

Since Antifa absorbed the Left's radical feminism, Trump's promise to champion the pro-life cause also branded him as a fascist (since, again, "fascist" now meant anyone who disagrees with all the positions of the Left).

As far as Antifa was concerned, everything Trump did or said was a sure sign that he was a member of the so-called "alt right," which clearly meant that Trump was an irredeemable White Supremacist, Nazi, and fascist (although, for Antifa, everything to the right of Far Left is "alt right").

Antifa did everything it could to derail Trump's campaign (as did the mainstream media and the Democrat Party), for example, "infiltrating Trump speeches to disrupt the proceedings," as Antifa-apologist Bray boasts. Then, when that didn't work, and Trump was elected, Antifa protestors disrupted his inauguration in January of 2017, smashing windows of businesses and cars, pelting the police with rocks, and doing everything they could to inter-fere with peaceful Trump supporters who had come to the nation's capital, including shouting to drown out Trump's swearing-in cer-emony. Not coincidentally, riots against Trump's election victory also broke out in other cities where Antifa resides—New York, Seattle, Dallas, Chicago, and Portland.

But they weren't treated like the protestors who showed up on Trump's behalf on January 6, 2021. Why? Because, as I said, Antifa is the paramilitary arm of the Democrat Party and the Left, and protected by the mainstream media as well.

For the next four years, Trump and Trump supporters were deemed racist Nazis and fascists by Antifa, the Left, the mainstream media, and even many Democrats. But Trump remained extremely popular among his base, which Antifa advocates like Bray can only attribute to "frustrated racist white people"[100] trying to hold onto "white privilege." Mark Bray is, by the way, White (as are most members of Antifa).

Since Trump represents all that Antifa seeks to overturn, there is no debating—there is only revolution. In the "era of Donald Trump…militant antifascism refuses to engage in terms of debate that developed out of the precepts of classical liberalism that under-gird both 'liberal' and 'conservative' positions in the United States. Instead of privileging allegedly 'neutral' universal rights, anti-fas-cists prioritize the political project of destroying fascism…."[101] "For revolutionary socialist [i.e., communist] antifa, the prime question is the political struggle against fascism; from their perspective, the rights promoted by capitalist parliamentary government are not inherently worthy of respect."[102] That's why Trump supporters have no rights.

---

100   Mark Bray, *Antifa: The Anti-Fascist Handbook*, pp. 109-110.
101   Mark Bray, *Antifa: The Anti-Fascist Handbook*, p. 144.
102   Mark Bray, *Antifa: The Anti-Fascist Handbook*, p. 150.

Since everything about America is irredeemable, there is only insurrection for Antifa, and that's why they do not respect the First Amendment. They don't care about "freedom of speech" or "the right of the people peaceably to assemble." They don't believe in dialogue. They reject the Constitution, the United States government, our economic system, the laws which stem from them, *and the police who defend these laws.*

Joe Biden probably doesn't understand anything about Antifa, and that's perhaps why he claimed that Antifa was "an idea, not an organization" during the presidential debates. Hours after Biden was sworn in, Antifa activists rioted in Portland, Denver, Sacramento, and Seattle, burned American flags, and in Portland smashed the windows of the Democratic Party of Oregon's headquarters and the nation's first Starbucks in Seattle. Along with a lot of expletives directed at the new Democratic president, one of Antifa's banners read, "We don't want Biden. We want revenge."

Just an idea, Joe?

AN ASSESSMENT OF ANTIFA INSURRECTIONISTS

Let's stand back and assess. This overview of Antifa's historical origins and ideology, its tactics, and its spread across the globe and across America explain a lot about the riots of 2020.

First, we can see exactly why the Left-leaning mainstream media and the Democrat Party did not condemn Antifa or the obviously destructive riots that took place in supremely liberal cities like Portland. Antifa and its fellow anarcho-communist organizations are the militant branch of the entire Woke Revolution embraced by the Left and the Democrat Party. They are engaged in the same revolution, even if they go about it in different ways.

Second, it explains why liberal cities with liberal Democrat mayors experienced so much destructive rioting. They *agreed* with Antifa on every fundamental issue. As the militant branch of the Woke movement, Antifa brought the half-century long Leftist revolution that came to dominate the universities, the media, government bureaucracies, and municipal governments into the streets. That's why Democrat mayors let the riots happen and told police to stand down. That's why the mainstream media refused to cover the actual carnage and instead called it "mostly peaceful." That's why local, state, and national Democrats cheerfully pushed for defunding the police. They all agreed with Antifa's revolutionary vision.

Third, as already noted, it explains why Antifa and fellow activists call everyone who disagrees with them Nazis, racists, and fascists, and why the Left and the Democrat Party do so as well. While the original Antifa actually did arise in Italy and Germany in a fight against fascism and Nazism, Antifa expanded its list of enemies to all those who disagree with the sexual and political revolution of the Left, so that all opponents of the Left's agenda are now fascists. That makes everyone who disagrees with the radical political agenda of the Democrat Party a fascist, and that's someone you don't need to debate with but destroy by any means.

And so, if you believe that a nation must have a border and protect it, you're a fascist. If you oppose abortion, you're a fascist. If you have any issue with gay marriage, you're a fascist. If you don't want transgenders twerking in front of your children at the local library, you're a fascist. If you voted for any Republican, especially Donald Trump (the greatest racist fascist of all), then you are a fascist. If you think the Constitution was well-framed and should be the document that defines the powers and limits of government (even against attempts by Leftist Progressives to push their agenda), then you are a fascist.

The union of the Democrat Party, Leftist Wokeism, and Antifa became so complete that Antifa began attacking (literally) anyone questioning mask mandates and forced vaccinations as fascist. Of course, questioning the integrity of the 2020 election makes one a fascist.

Fourth, it explains the wanton destruction of property and the vehement attacks on police during the 2020 riots (and, again, the complicity of Woke Democrats). Private property is the fundamental evil the communist revolution claims that it will cure, and its destruction will bring about the communist utopia. Since police protect private property according to "capitalist" laws, they must be attacked, defunded, and ultimately destroyed. Furthermore, looting is merely the beginning of the communist reappropriation and distribution of capitalist goods to the people. The destruction of businesses strikes at the heart of the evil capitalist empire, and the destruction of the police allows it to happen.

All of this destruction is, for Antifa and the Left, not only excusable but heroic because on the other side of the destruction is a perfectly wonderful anarcho-communist utopia.

So we are told.

If you want to get a glimpse of what that looks like, study what actually happened in East Germany, the Soviet Union, or communist China—or the six-block Capitol Hill Autonomous Zone (CHAZ) in Seattle, surrounded by its own Anti-Fascist Protection Wall and overseen by its own thuggish Antifa Stasi.

And that brings us to a fifth point, one that allows me to answer my little girl's question about why anyone would burn a church. (Actually, multiple churches were vandalized or torched in the riots.) Antifa's Marxist origins explain it all too clearly. For Marx, religion was one more tool of the ruling class that helped it oppress the working class. As happened in all communist countries, churches had to be destroyed as well.

Sixth, beyond a shadow of any doubt, Antifa and like-minded anarcho-communists are self-declared *insurrectionists*. They purposely and strategically turn protests into riots, and those riots are not merely letting off a little steam, nor are they focused on reform. Antifa means to turn them into revolutionary riots. *For this reason, the full force of our government's intelligence community and federal law enforcement capabilities need to be brought to bear on rooting out Antifa.*

This will be hard to do, since Antifa now accepts the entire set of issues defining Woke Culture embraced by the pulled-ever-Leftward Democrat Party. But that means that the Democrats—*not the Republicans*—are guilty of aiding and abetting insurrection.

If the single Capitol Hill riot was an assault on democracy, then so were several thousand of the riots that took place during the summer of 2020.

Here's the difference, however. The Capitol Hill rioters were not trying to destroy the Constitution and the US government along with it; they were actually trying to preserve the integrity of the vote, the very foundation of the democratic system. They were going about it the wrong way, but I stand with those who peacefully and lawfully demanded voter integrity and fair elections. That is what I had intended to do on January 6th.

Finally, a seventh point, drawing much of this together. Now that we understand the connection between the violent insurrectionist of Antifa and the Woke Revolution that so deeply defines the Democrat Party, we can see how Antifa's reaction to Donald Trump fit so well with the Democrat Party's.

That reinforces the charge that Democrats were using the 2020 riots as a way to intimidate Trump voters, letting them know what they'd face if the American people dared to vote him in for a second term. The connection between the aims of the radical Democrats and Antifa also explains why both would misleadingly characterize Trump's win as a manifestation of White Supremacy and racism.

One wonders whether Antifa members know that the Democrat Party is historically the party of slavery, racism, and White Supremacy?

CHAPTER 5

BLACK LIVES MATTER, DEFUNDING THE POLICE, THE RIOT OF CRIME, AND REAL CRIMINAL REFORM

Readers may have noticed that in the last chapter on rioting I focused almost exclusively on Antifa as the Far-Left organization that turned peaceful demonstrations into riots in 2020. What about Black Lives Matter? Weren't they an even more visible participant in those riots?

Of course, we are examining things for the sake of understanding the 2020 election, the Democrat Party and its agenda, and the Capitol Hill riot of January 6th. As we've just seen in the last chapter, the year of riots caused immense destruction, allegedly on behalf of calling attention to racial injustice. Hence the importance of BLM.

But it was also used by the Democrat Party to reinvigorate waning political support from Black Americans, as well as to serve as a kind of warning of what would happen if Donald Trump were reelected. The hidden assumption was that the Democrat Party's agenda was really working for the good of Black Americans and that only Democrats passionately affirm that Black Lives Matter (not Republicans).

I think that's false, so I'm going to take a different tack than most treatments of Black Lives Matter. I'm not going to herald the organization as wonderful, nor spend much time recounting its defects. Instead, I'm going to spend the bulk of this chapter on the issues at the heart of the movement (crime in the Black community and its relationship to the police), and then relate that to the issues at the heart of this book (the destructive agenda of the Democrat Party).

If you think Black Lives Matter—*really matter*—then you should read this chapter very carefully.

BLACK LIVES MATTER, THE DEFUND THE POLICE MOVEMENT, AND WHAT BLACK AMERICANS REALLY THINK

As I made clear already, Antifa members hate the police. They don't want to reform them but to defund and then destroy them. To them, the police protect the political and social order that they want to tear down. You may have seen ACAB on Antifa propaganda like flags, shirts, or even COVID masks. It stands for All Cops Are Bastards. There are no good cops for Antifa.

Black Lives Matter is another group that wants to defund the police, and they often appear with members of Antifa in the protests of 2020 and after that as well. Some in the conservative media assume that Black Lives Matter is, like Antifa, just another communist revolutionary organization—and not without cause. One of the founders, Patrisse Cullors, stated in a 2015 interview, "The first thing, I think, is that we actually do have an ideological frame. Myself and Alicia in particular are trained organizers…We are trained Marxists. We are super-versed on, sort of, ideological theories. And I think that what we really tried to do is build a movement that could be utilized by many, many black folk."[103]

Cullors, Alicia Garza, and Opal Tometi founded Black Lives Matter in July of 2013 in response to the acquittal of George Zimmerman in the shooting death of Trayvon Martin. BLM became nationally known for its activism after the deaths of two other black men, Michael Brown and Eric Garner. With the George Floyd incident, BLM led the way, with the help of Antifa, in nationwide protests. As with Antifa, BLM also quickly aligned itself with every issue dear to the Left, from climate change to LGBTQ rights. In a now-deleted section on its website, "What We Believe," BLM stated:

> We disrupt the Western-prescribed nuclear family structure requirement by supporting each other as extended families and "villages" that collectively care for one another, especially our children, to the degree that mothers, parents, and children are comfortable.
>
> We foster a queer-affirming network. When we gather, we do so with the intention of freeing ourselves from the tight grip of heteronormative thinking, or rather, the belief that all in the world are heterosexual (unless s/he or they disclose otherwise).[104]

Once the BLM hierarchy made this affirmation, they were alienated from the actual conservative social and moral beliefs of most Black Americans. In other words, they sided with the Far Left in the Democrat Party hierarchy, thereby creating a significant tension with actual Black Americans.

---

103 Yaron Steinbuch, "Black Lives Matter co-founder describes herself as 'trained Marxist,'" *New York Post*, June 25, 2020. https://nypost.com/2020/06/25/blm-co-founder-describes-herself-as-trained-marxist/.

104 The deleted webpage is available on the WayBack Machine: https://web.archive.org/web/20200408020723/https://blacklivesmatter.com/what-we-believe/.

One is therefore not surprised to find BLM leadership supporting, along with Antifa, the Defund the Police movement as well. But it's extremely important to note that, in this instance as well, Black Americans do *not* agree. They do not think that defunding the police is a good idea. Even in the middle of the summer of race riots in 2020 a Gallup poll found the following about what Black Americans actually think (as opposed to BLM leadership).[105]

A total of 81 percent of Black Americans want police to spend the same amount of time or more time in their neighborhoods. In fact, the number of Black Americans who want the police to spend more time (20 percent) exceeds the number of White Americans (17 percent). Just as interesting, the number of Hispanic Americans wanting a greater police presence is even more than Black Americans, 24 percent.

BLM's and Antifa's goal to defund the police is therefore in direct contradiction to the communities they claim to represent. Obviously, the same can be said for the Defund-the-Police Democrats like avowed socialist, Rep. Alexandria Ocasio-Cortez, Rep. Ilhan Omar, Rep. Ayanna Pressley, Rep. Rashida Tlaib, Rep. Jamaal Bowman, Rep. Mondaire Jones, Rep. Cori Bush, and others.[106] They represent the radical Left.

I repeat: reforming the police where reform is needed—that's a position I agree with wholeheartedly. Police need the proper training and proper oversight. That's why I made very clear to those under my charge in Texas that they follow the proper protocol in regard to Use of Force. But just as important, they need to be connected more deeply to the communities they serve and be involved in rehabilitative programs for prisoners—and I'll come to that kind of reform at the end of this chapter. But, if police departments are

105 Lydia Said, "Black Americans Want Police to Retain Local Presence," Gallup, August 5, 2020. https://news.gallup.com/poll/316571/black-americans-police-retain-local-presence.aspx.

106 Republican Study Committee, "Looking Back: Democrats Push to Defund the Police," https://rsc-banks.house.gov/democrats-push-defund-police.

defunded, no amount of reform will help because they won't be able to do the job they're sworn to do: protect the community.

We need to understand why the Defund the Police movement is harmful rather than helpful, especially for Black Americans, and so why its adoption by Democrats was so harmful. We're going to begin by taking a much larger look at the history of violent crime itself. That will allow us to put the situation in America today in a much clearer context so that we can understand especially how harmful Democrat policies are.

CRIME, THE BIG HISTORICAL PICTURE

Harvard psychologist Steven Pinker wrote a book, *The Better Angels of Our Nature*, that gives us an interesting perspective on crime.[107] In it, he presents the *big* historical picture of the actual rates of violence in societies (our main interest being in homicide rates). Sociologists and historians use homicide rates to give them a picture of how orderly or disorderly any society is, because it's a good indicator of the presence of all kinds of crime and social disorder.

So, what do we find when we look at the big historical picture? Where and when you live (or lived) makes a big difference, but in general, violent crime has *gone down* over the last seven hundred years in the West.

If you lived in Italy at about 1400, you'd be living in a pretty violent place and time with a homicide rate of about 100 per 100,000 people. In less hot-headed England, the homicide rate at the same time was about a third of Italy's. But over the centuries, Western Europe's homicide rate came steadily downward, reaching

---

107 Steven Pinker, *The Better Angels of Our Nature: Why Violence Has Declined* (New York, NY: Penguin, 2011).

a low just prior to the 1960s of a little over 1 homicide per 100,000 people. And then, in the 1960s, it started to rise again.[108]

Keep those numbers in mind for reference: 100 homicides per 100,000 people as the high, and 1 homicide per 100,000 as the low. Where a society finds itself within that range will tell you how safe or unsafe it is.

Those were numbers from Western Europe. In its more compressed history, America also underwent a decline in violence, although there is also significant variation in time and place. In 17th century New England, homicide rates hit the 100 per 100,000 mark, but as things got more civilized, it dropped to about 1 per 100,000 by the 18th century and stayed there through the 19th century. However, in the cities of Boston and New York, the 19th century rate was closer to 10 per 100,000.[109]

But there's a big exception, the 19th century American Wild West. In the Wild West "annual homicide rates were fifty to several hundred times higher than those of eastern cities and midwestern farming regions: 50 per 100,000 in Abilene, Kansas, 100 in Dodge City, 229 in Fort Griffin, Texas, and 1,500 in Ellsworth, Kansas…87 per 100,000 in Aurora, Nevada; 105 in Leadville, Colorado; 116 in Bodie, California; and a whopping 24,000 (almost one in four) in Benton, Wyoming."[110]

Even the Wild West got less wild. By the year 1900, American homicide rates had come down to about 7 per 100,000, rose to over 9 in the 1930s, fell to under 5 per 100,000 at about 1950, and then between 1960 and the mid-1990s doubled to about 10 per 100,00. After peaking in the mid-1990s, it then came back down to about 5 per 100,000.[111]

So, we see the general pattern: high rates in early America that gradually fell by the beginning of the 20th century, rose again

---

108 Steven Pinker, *The Better Angels of Our Nature*, graphs on pp. 63-64.
109 Steven Pinker, *The Better Angels of Our Nature*, graph on p. 96.
110 Steven Pinker, *The Better Angels of Our Nature*, p. 103.
111 Steven Pinker, *The Better Angels of Our Nature*, graphs on pp. 92, 117.

during the Great Depression, dropped in the 1940s and 50s, then in 1960 went significantly upward, coming down again by the mid-1990s.

Again, the Wild West in the 19th century sticks out like a very sore thumb.

As one would expect, homicide rates in cities are, for the most part, higher than the national average. In 1870 in Chicago, for example, the rate was only 2.6 per 100,000. By 1930, it had almost doubled to 4.6 but fell again; then it rose a bit, bobbing from about 7–10 per 100,000 from 1940–1960. But after 1960, things really jump upward: 24 in 1970, 28.7 in 1980, and whopping 32.9 per 100,000 in 1990 (reaching up to all-time highs of about 35 between 1991-1995). By 2000, the homicide rate in Chicago had come down from that all-time high to 22.1 per 100,000.[112]

A bit strange, isn't it. Homicide rates were often lower in Chicago than the national average up until 1960, and then leaped upward two to over three times the national average from about 1960 to the mid-1990s, then came back down (even though it's still high) to over four times the national rate. Chicago is a very dangerous place.

The same thing happened in New York City, although for some reason, it was able to reduce its homicide rate far more significantly than did Chicago. To focus on the important "leap" years, in 1965 NYC's homicide rate was 4.6 per 100,000, about the national rate. By 1990, it had risen to 14.5 per 100,000, but in 1995 it started to decline, from 8.5 to a low of 2.8 in 2017.[113]

Whatever New York was doing, it was doing it better than Chicago, rising less than half the rate of Chicago during the Great

---

112 "Chicago Homicide Rates per 100,000 Residents, 1870-2000," http://www.encyclopedia. chicagohistory.org/pages/2156.html; Kyle Bentle, Jonathon Berlin, Ryan Marx, and Kori Rumore, "40,000 Homicides: Retracing 63 Years of Murder in Chicago," *Chicago Tribune*, April 27, 2021, https://www.chicagotribune.com/news/breaking/ct-history-of-chicago-homi-cides-htmlstory.html.

113 "New York Crime Rates 1960-2019," https://www.disastercenter.com/crime/nycrime.htm.

Crime Wave from 1960 to the mid-1990s and then falling to *lower* than the overall US rate.[114]

The pattern of dramatically rising homicide rates beginning in the 1960s, climbing especially high in the 1980s, and even higher in the early 1990s, followed by a welcome decline can be seen in Los Angeles, Philadelphia, and Houston as well, with the homicide rates of New York dropping the most significantly, especially as compared to the still very high rates of Chicago and Philadelphia.[115]

So, looking at the really big historical picture, that thirty-five-year crime spike from 1960 to 1995 is significant. In fact, it was quite alarming because it certainly seemed that for whatever reason a centuries-long downward trend in homicide rates (and crime in general) was suddenly being reversed. Yet, there did appear to be good news. The thirty-five-year crime spike did finally come down.

Then, in 2020, the homicide rates jet upward again and have been rising ever since (along with other crime).

THE CURRENT RISE IN CRIME

The upward spike in 2020 coincides with the year of rioting and the year of the "Defund the Police Movement" that plagued so many US cities. It was also the year that Far-Left criminal justice reform policies pushed by radical George Soros-funded district attorneys really began to take effect. Given Biden's election, these Far-Left policies embraced by the Democrat Party were given full sway in 2021. While all the rioting suddenly declined (except in Portland, where Antifa continues to agitate), crime skyrocketed.

The FBI released its 2020 crime statistics at the end of September 2021, and the news was not good. "The United States

---

114 "New York Murder/Homicide Rate 1979-2018," https://www.macrotrends.net/states/new-york/murder-homicide-rate-statistics.

115 "Factsheet: 2020 Shootings & Murders," https://criminaljustice.cityofnewyork.us/wp-content/uploads/2021/01/2020-Shootings-and-Murder-factsheet_January-2021.pdf.

in 2020 experienced the biggest rise in murder since the start of national record-keeping in 1960," the *New York Times* reported[116] (a significant admission by the leading newspaper representing the Left).

Unsurprisingly, given the way police were being treated during 2020, there were "large increases in retirements between April 2020 and April 2021." While there was about a 45 percent increase in retirements in 2020 as compared to 2019, there was also a reported 18 percent increase in resignations.[117] That's what happens when police are demonized and disrespected.

. When we delve into the details of the FBI's Uniform Crime Report for 2020, we find that the overall homicide rate rose to 6.5 per 100,000, the highest rate since 2001. Put in terms of lives lost, there were 4,901 more murder victims than in 2019, an astounding increase of 29.4 percent in just one year. The violent crime rate rose 5.2 percent to its highest level since 2012. Aggravated assault rose by 12.1 percent.[118] Those are enormous leaps for one year, and the first half of 2021 saw an additional 16 percent rise in homicides and a 9 percent rise in aggravated assaults.

Let's focus on particular cities. The Council of Criminal Justice reports that from the first half of 2020 to the first half of 2021 Austin, Texas, experienced over a 110 percent increase in homicides, Pittsburgh a 100 percent increase, Louisville about an 80 percent increase, and Nashville around a 60 percent increase.[119] In 2021, Philadelphia had a record 559 homicides, the highest it's

---

116 Jeff Asher, "Murder Rose by Almost 30% in 2020. It's Rising at a Slower Rate in 2021," *New York Times*, September 22, 2021. https://www.nytimes.com/2021/09/22/upshot/murder-rise-2020.html.

117 Police Executive Research Forum, Survey on Police Workforce Trends, June 11, 2021. https://www.policeforum.org/workforcesurveyjune2021.

118 Crime in the United States, 2020, Offenses Known to Law Enforcement, Table 1, Volume and Rate per 100,000 Inhabitants, 2001-2020. https://crime-data-explorer.app.cloud.gov/pages/downloads.

119 Council on Criminal Justice, Richard Rosenfeld et al, "Pandemic, Social Unrest, and Crime in U.S. Cities, June 2021 Update," p. 6. https://counciloncj.org/impact-report-1/.

been since 1960 when the Great Crime Wave began, and already in 2022 the murder rate is even higher.[120] In Atlanta, GA, homicides are already up 43 percent over 2021, and if that continues, homicides will top last year's record 158 murders, a thirty-year high.[121] Chicago had a record 797 homicides in 2021, the most it's had in twenty-five years, which was a twenty-five-homicide increase over 2020.[122] Minneapolis had more homicides in 2021 than any year since 1995, the peak of the Great Crime Wave.[123] Baltimore has one of the highest homicide rates of any city in America, and its 2022 homicide rate is already outpacing the 2021 rate.[124] In 2021, Los Angeles experienced an 11.8 percent increase in homicides over 2020, the highest rate since 2007.[125] New York City's 2021 murder rate likewise surpassed its 2020 rate.[126]

In addition to a rise in homicides, liberal policies in big cities have resulted in an epidemic of "smash-and-grab" robberies in broad daylight and increasing random acts of violence by those with long criminal records who have been let out on the streets in accordance with liberal policies. Liberal district attorneys ensured criminals

120 Tom MacDonald, "Philly DA: City's 2022 murder rate already outpacing record-deadly 2021," WHYY, January 25, 2022. https://whyy.org/articles/philly-da-citys-2022-murder-rate-already-outpacing-record-deadly-2021/.

121 Nicole Wells, "Atlanta 2022 Crime Stats: Rapes Up 236 Percent, Homicides Up 43 Percent," Newsmax, February 21, 2022. https://www.newsmax.com/newsfront/crime-atlanta-spike-statistics/2022/02/21/id/1057818/.

122 Stephanie Pagones, "US murder rate highest it's been in 25 years as big cities shatter records," Fox News, January 18, 2022. https://www.foxnews.com/us/us-murder-rate-violence-big-cities-records.

123 Andy Mannix and Jeff Hargarten, "Minneapolis closes in on homicide milestone at end of violent year," Star Tribune, December 30, 2021. https://www.startribune.com/a-most-violent-year-in-minneapolis/600131444/.

124 Annie Rose Ramos, "Harrison Calls For More Witness Cooperation To Combat Baltimore's Crime Problem," CBS Baltimore, February 15, 2022. https://baltimore.cbslocal.com/2022/02/15/baltimore-violent-crime-commissioner-harrison-challenges-residents/.

125 Richard Winton, "Homicides and shootings in L.A. are down so far this year, but robberies are up, LAPD chief says," Los Angeles Times, January 25, 2022. https://www.latimes.com/california/story/2022-01-25/homicides-and-shootings-in-la-down-this-year-robberies-up.

126 Craig McCarthy, "Grim Apple: NYC murders in 2021 to near 500 for first time in a decade," New York Post, December 30, 2021. https://nypost.com/2021/12/30/nyc-murders-in-2021-to-near-500-for-first-time-in-a-decade/.

would have free reign by either not arresting criminal offenders or releasing them almost immediately because of "bail reform."

It was quite obvious all the rioting, the Defund the Police movement, bail reform, and the decriminalization of stealing embraced by Democrats has not been very helpful; rather, it looks like it is leading us back into the Great Crime Wave of 1960 to 1995.

But this doesn't yet directly address the main focus of this chapter: the relationship of crime to Black Americans in particular, how that is related to the police, and whether Democratic policies actually affirm that Black Lives Matter. In order to sort that out, we need to look more carefully at who was killing whom during the period of the Great Crime Wave onward.

WHO IS KILLING WHOM: FROM THE 1960 CRIME WAVE ONWARD

Remember the historical homicide rate range: 100 per 100,000 is high, and 1 per 100,000 is low. That range helps us understand whether things are improving or getting worse.

The first thing we learn when we look at the statistics is that *males* are the vast majority of offenders and victims. If we look at a Department of Justice report for 1980–2008, we find that "males represented 77% of homicide victims and nearly 90% of offenders. The victimization rate for males (11.6 per 100,000) was 3 times higher than the rate for females (3.4 per 100,000). The offending rate for males (15.1 per 100,000) was almost 9 times higher than the rate for females (1.7 per 100,000)."[127] Males do almost all the killing and are over three-quarters of those killed.

---

127   U.S. Department of Justice, Alexia Cooper and Erica L. Smith, "Homicide Trends in the United States, 1980-2008," November 2011, p. 3. https://bjs.ojp.gov/library/publications/homicide-trends-united-states-1980-2008.

And not just any males but young males: "Approximately a third (34%) of murder victims and almost half (49%) of the offenders were under age 25. For both victims and offenders, the rate per 100,000 peaked in the 18 to 24 year-old age group at 17.1 victims per 100,000 and 29.3 offenders per 100,000."[128] Importantly, in this peak age group, 70.9 percent of the homicides were drug related, and 68.8 percent were gang related.[129]

Here, we need to stop and ask a really obvious question, one that concerns how intelligent police work should proceed. Would it be any wonder if police believed that *young males* (of whatever race) were more prone to criminal activity, both as offenders and victims? Wouldn't they be foolish to be keeping a special eye on forty-five-year-old women rather than young men?

Let's look even more closely. What about if we change our focus from gender and age to race and age? Let's look at the data from 1990–2010. When we do, we find that Black homicide rates in the age range of 10–24 years were astoundingly out of whack with other races, especially during the peak crime years of the 1990s, with the Black rate reaching up to about 65 per 100,000, the Hispanic being about 27, and the White about 16 per 100,000.[130] *Those are the individuals being murdered.* Black youth are being murdered at almost 2.5 times the rate of Hispanic youth and over 4 times the rate of Whites. Shouldn't police be that much more worried about the lives of young Black men and women? Shouldn't they be especially concerned to patrol in the neighborhoods where they live?

128 U.S. Department of Justice, Alexia Cooper and Erica L. Smith, "Homicide Trends in the United States, 1980-2008," November, 2011, p. 3. https://bjs.ojp.gov/library/publications/homicide-trends-united-states-1980-2008.

129 U.S. Department of Justice, Alexia Cooper and Erica L. Smith, "Homicide Trends in the United States, 1980-2008," November, 2011, Table 2, Homicide type, by age, 1980-2008, p. 5. https://bjs.ojp.gov/library/publications/homicide-trends-united-states-1980-2008.

130 Center for Disease Control and Prevention, "Homicide Rates Among Persons Aged 10–24 Years — United States, 1981–2010, FIGURE 3. Homicide rates among persons aged 10–24 years, by race/ethnicity — United States, 1990–2010." https://www.cdc.gov/mmwr/preview/mmwrhtml/mm6227a1.htm#fig1.

What if we add gender back into our analysis and focus only on males between 20 and 24 years old? Shifting a bit to the time period 1974–2010, we find that the homicide rate for White males in the 20–24 age group was 16.1 per 100,000, but the rate for Black males was 129.9 per 100,000. The homicide rates for Black males in the surrounding age groups are almost as astounding: ages 15–19 (118.5), ages 25–34 (110.2), ages 35–44 (121.3).[131] That's the alarming rate at which Black men, especially young Black men, are being killed.

How alarming?

These are the kinds of homicide rates, among young Black American males today, that compare with the absurdly high homicide rates of the Wild West in the 19th century.

That's more than tragic; it's an epidemic.

Just looking at these startling statistics about who is most likely to be murdered, we can ask the obvious question: *Who needs the most protection from police?* The answer would seem to be young, Black men, particularly those between 20–24 years old (and we may add, especially those in areas where drug trafficking and gangs are prevalent).

As sad as it is to note, these trends go back long *before* the crime spike of 1960. As far back as the 1920s the homicide victimization rates of Blacks were far higher than Whites. Historian of crime Barry Latzer reports that "in the 1920s…black [homicide] rates were approximately seven times those of whites, and in the 1930s…there was a roughly eightfold difference."[132]

The decades thereafter offered no improvement. In 1940 the White homicide rate was 4.9 per 100,000, and the Black rate was 54.4, over eleven times higher. In 1950, when crime was at a low

---

131 Randolph Roth, "Criminologists and Historians of Crime: A Partnership Well Worth Pursuing," *Crime, History, and Societies* 21, no. 2 (2017), pp. 389-401. Data conveniently available at https://journals.openedition.org/chs/2064.

132 Barry Latzer, *The Rise and Fall of Violent Crime in America* (New York: Encounter, 2016), p. 29.

point, the White rate was 3.8, and the Black rate had dropped to 47. But even though lower, the Black homicide rate was still over twelve times as high as the White rate. In 1960, the White rate inched up to 3.9 per 100,000, while the Black rate dropped to 42.3—good news, but still the Black rate was almost eleven times higher than the White rate. When the crime boom really kicked in by 1970, the Black rate was again almost eleven times the White homicide rate: the White rate rose to 7.2, almost twice what it was in 1960, but the Black homicide victimization rates leaped up to 78.2 per 100,000, nearing the Wild West levels of violence.[133]

We can see in this historical overview that the Black homicide rate followed the general contours of the rise in crime, but at much, much higher levels, and has done so for at least a century. That is a horrible long-term trend of Black Americans being murdered, and there should have been more police protection—if Black lives truly matter. And they do, as do all lives.

If we zero in on victimization rates of young males (ages 25–34) in the 1940s, we find (as Latzer shows) that the up-and-down flow of homicide victimization rates of Black and White males is almost identical, *but* the young White male rate flows up and down between about 5.5 and 8 per 100,000, and the young Black male rate flows up and down between about 85 and 125 homicides per 100,000. [134]

So, long before the Great Crime Wave of the 1960s, young Black men were being murdered at the levels experienced in the Wild West.

And again, the most important question is *who is doing the killing?*

Let's focus first on the time period from 1960 onward. As the Department of Justice makes clear, "Blacks were disproportion-

---

133 Barry Latzer, *The Rise and Fall of Violent Crime in America*, p. 29.
134 Barry Latzer, *The Rise and Fall of Violent Crime in America*, p. 30.

ately represented [in 1980–2008] as both homicide victims and offenders. The victimization rate for blacks (27.8 per 100,000) was 6 times higher than the rate for whites (4.5 per 100,000). The offending rate for blacks (34.4 per 100,000) was almost 8 times higher than the rate for whites (4.5 per 100,000)."[135]

But *which race* is killing which? In the same time period, according to a National Institute of Justice report, we find that "The vast majority of homicides are intra-racial, with 84 percent of white victims killed by whites and 93 percent of black victims killed by blacks." The number of Black on White homicides is a bit more than 5 percent of all homicides, and the number of White on Black homicides is about half of that low number.[136]

If Black lives matter—and I repeat they do, as do all lives—then police need to be actively engaged among those who need the most protection from those who are most likely to do them harm. The mainstream media and BLM tend to focus on police actions in regard to Black male perpetrators, but they unjustly forget the victims. Who are the victims? From the same report, "Black males between the ages of 18 and 24 are dramatically overrepresented in homicide. Homicides of young black males in this age category peaked at 195.9 victimizations per 100,000 in 1993 and subsequently declined to 91.1 victimizations per 100,000 in 2008."[137]

To repeat, *these are the kind of homicide rates among young Black males that are associated with the most violent episodes of the 19th*

---

135 U.S. Department of Justice, Alexia Cooper and Erica L. Smith, "Homicide Trends in the United States, 1980-2008," November 2011, p. 3. https://bjs.ojp.gov/library/publications/homicide-trends-united-states-1980-2008.

136 National Institute of Justice, Anthony A. Braga and Rod K. Brunson, "Police and Public Discourse on 'Black-on-Black' Violence," May 2015, p. 6, Figure 3. Homicides, by Race of Offender and Victim, 1980-2008, https://www.ojp.gov/ncjrs/virtual-library/abstracts/police-and-public-discourse-black-black-violence.

137 National Institute of Justice, Anthony A. Braga and Rod K. Brunson, "Police and Public Discourse on 'Black-on-Black' Violence," May 2015, p. 6. https://www.ojp.gov/ncjrs/virtual-library/abstracts/police-and-public-discourse-black-black-violence.

century Wild West.[138] And the overwhelming number of the killers are Black—over 90 percent.

And let's not forget the context in which this violence occurs. "Research has consistently documented that violence driven by conflicts within and among gangs, drug-selling crews and other criminally active groups generate the bulk of urban homicide problems."[139] I repeat: if we want to save lives, we need to provide law and order where and for whom it is most needed.

These statistics are both shocking and sad. Did things change in 2020, the year of the race riots? The year of Black Lives Matter? The year of Defund the Police?

No. Blacks were almost 56 percent of the murder victims (9,913 out of 17,754),[140] although they were only 14.2 percent of the population.

Who did the killing in 2020 and beyond? No change. Almost 39 percent of the killers were Black males (which is undoubtedly significantly under the real number, since the FBI reports that the race of 31.4 percent was unknown).[141] Whites were 46 percent of those arrested for murder, and Blacks were just under 51 percent.[142]

Who killed whom by race in 2020? As before, intra-racial killing is the norm. According to the available data, over 85 percent of Blacks were murdered by other Blacks (with Whites killing Whites

---

138 To cite a few more examples from the Wild West for comparison: 129 per 100,000 in Dodge City, Kansas (1876-1885); 198 in Los Angeles (1850-1865); 119 in mining towns (1862-1872); 65 per 100,000 for nine counties in California (1850-1865); and, statewide, 137 per 100,000 in Colorado, and 167 in Wyoming, and 212 in Montana (1865-1868). Randolph Roth, Michael Maltz, and Douglas Eckberg, "Homicide Rates in the Old West," *Western Historical Quarterly*, Summer 2011, pp. 173-195; numbers from pp 177, 183, 188, 190, 192.

139 National Institute of Justice, Anthony A. Braga and Rod K. Brunson, "The Police and Public Discourse on 'Black-on-Black' Violence," May 2015, p. 8. https://www.ojp.gov/ncjrs/virtual-library/abstracts/police-and-public-discourse-black-black-violence.

140 Expanded Homicide Data Table 1, Murder Victims by Race, Ethnicity, and Sex, 2020. https://crime-data-explorer.app.cloud.gov/pages/downloads.

141 Expanded Homicide Data Table 3, Murder Offenders by Race, Ethnicity, and Sex, 2020. https://crime-data-explorer.app.cloud.gov/pages/downloads.

142 FBI, Crime in the United States, Persons Arrested, 2020, Table 43a, Arrests by Race and Ethnicity, 2020. https://crime-data-explorer.app.cloud.gov/pages/downloads.

a bit over 78 percent of the time). What about interracial killing? Blacks killed Whites almost exactly twice as often as Whites killed Blacks.[143]

The numbers make clear a very unpleasant but predictable truth: the year of riots, 2020, witnessed a significant increase in murders and violent crime, and Black Americans were the main victims and offenders. Black on Black violence is a long-term trend that we are failing to address, one that removing or defunding the police can only make worse.

How long-term a trend? Again, from what historians can gather, it precedes even the 1960s crime wave. In late 1930s and mid-1940s, the deep-South city of Birmingham, Alabama, was about 40 percent Black. As Latzer reports, "An examination of coroner's files uncovered 500 homicide victims in the city between 1937 and 1944. An astonishing 427 of those killed (85.4 percent) were black. What is more, 418 of the killers (84.9 percent) were African American."[144] Blacks comprised less than 18 percent of Saint Louis's population in 1949, but they were "81 percent of the city's homicide victims. Ninety-five percent of the perpetrators in these black victim cases were African Americans." Cleveland, Ohio, was about 16 percent Black around 1950, but Blacks were victims in over 70 percent of the homicide cases and were the accused in these crimes over 98 percent of the time.[145]

Black on Black violence is not something that rose with the Great Crime Wave that started in the 1960s, but something that existed in shocking numbers long beforehand, and only became worse during the Great Crime Wave.

That's the data. What caused this horrible disproportion of violence that has plagued Black Americans for so long? I think the

---

143 Expanded Homicide Data Table 6, Murder: Race, Sex, and Ethnicity of Victim by Race, Sex, and Ethnicity of Offender, 2020. https://crime-data-explorer.app.cloud.gov/pages/downloads.
144 Barry Latzer, *The Rise and Fall of Violent Crime in America*, p. 30.
145 Barry Latzer, *The Rise and Fall of Violent Crime in America*, p. 31.

Democrats would say—predictably—racism. And they would be right—except it was *their racism*. There's nothing about being Black that makes someone a criminal. But being subjected for so long to the terrible institution of slavery, and then the economic, social, and political degradation of Jim Crow for about a century after the Civil War—all that would seem to go a long way in explaining the cultural, social, and political causes of these sad statistics. Even after Black Americans escaped the Democrat-controlled South in the Great Migration to northern cities, the Democrat machines seem to have been more interested in keeping Black Americans as a dependent voting block rather than improving their lot.

But I leave further investigations in this area to others far more expert than I am. Whatever the ultimate causes of these disproportions, the *effects* are clear: the single greatest danger to the lives of young Black men is other young Black men, and it's been that way for a very long time. That's not unjust racial profiling, any more than it's unjust gender or age profiling. That's the cold, hard truth.

And that means, in regard to policing, that in order to save young Black men, police officers are going to be involved in far more incidents having to use force with young Black men who are offenders.

THE ARREST RECORD FROM 1995 TO 2019: JUSTICE FOR THE VICTIMS

In all the media noise, we seldom hear the side of law enforcement, the ones charged with the difficult task of protecting citizens from lawless behavior. As a law enforcement officer for almost thirty years, allow me to provide some perspective from the side of those charged with providing law and order, and hence those who must do the arrests. And here again the numbers don't lie, and they make full sense in regard to the homicide statistics we've just spent so much time reviewing.

In 1995, which was near the peak year for homicides in the 1960–1995 crime spike, the total number of criminal arrests for all crimes, according to the FBI, was 11,386,627, of which 7,607,522 were White and 2,523,409 were Black. Doing the math, that means 66.8 percent were White and 30.9 percent were Black.[146] The percentage of the population by race in 1995 was 73.5 percent White and 12.7 percent Black.[147] Whites were arrested at under their total population percentage; Blacks were arrested at about 2.5 times their population percentage.

As I said above, generally speaking, homicide rates are a good indication of overall crime rates. Does that mean that Blacks are being arrested at an unfair rate? Or does it mean that Blacks are committing disproportionately more crimes and therefore have significantly more interactions with police?

Before you answer that question, *remember who the victims are*, at least in regard to homicide. As we've already seen in detail in regard to homicide rates, young Black men commit a dispropor-tionate amount of homicides *and* account for a disproportionate number of victims. In 1995, Black murder arrests were 54.4 per-cent of the total 16,691 (over four times their percentage of the population).[148] But that seemingly disproportionate percentage of arrests reflects the disproportionate number of Black perpetrators *and* victims.

Here's the truth. *If young Black men were not being arrested for homicide at a higher rate, that would indeed be unjust—unjust to the victims who, over 90 percent of the time, are Black.*

---

146 FBI, Uniform Crime Report, Crime in the United States 1995, Section IV, Table 43.—Total Arrests, Distribution by Race, 1995, p. 226. https://ucr.fbi.gov/crime-in-the-u.s/1995.

147 FBI, Uniform Crime Report, Crime in the United States 1995, Section IV, Table 43.—Total Arrests, Distribution by Race, 1995.. https://ucr.fbi.gov/crime-in-the-u.s/1995.

148 FBI, Uniform Crime Report, Crime in the United States 1995, Section IV, Table 43.—Total Arrests, Distribution by Race, 1995, p. 226. https://ucr.fbi.gov/crime-in-the-u.s/1995.

Would it be better if police arrested 2.5 times fewer young Black perpetrators of homicide? What would Black victims' families think of that kind of "equity"?

But homicide isn't the only kind of crime police must deal with. If we look at other kinds of crime in 1995, when the crime rate was just starting to come down from the highs in the early 1990s, we find even greater disproportions by race. Blacks accounted for 42.4 percent of forcible rape arrests, 59.5 percent of robberies, and 38.4 percent of aggravated assaults.[149]

There is good news, however. By the year 2000, and using the same FBI data, we find the total number of arrests had gone down somewhat to under ten million. The Black percentage of arrests had also dropped to 27.9 percent (from 30.9 percent). They accounted for 48.8 percent of the homicide arrests, 34.1 percent of forcible rape, 53.9 percent of robberies, and 34.0 percent of aggravated assaults. In five years since 1995, all the numbers were down.[150]

Even better, the number of victims went down as well in the years following, setting a long-term trend. In 2005, the rate of violent victimization (per 1,000, not 100,000) for Whites was 27.1, for Blacks 32.7, and for Hispanics 25.9. By 2019, all had dropped, but Black victimization most of all: Whites were down to 21.0, Blacks to 18.7, and Hispanics to 21.3.[151] The rate of Black victimization of violent crime dropped by 43 percent. Just as interesting, the Black arrest rate itself had also fallen from 30.9 percent to 26.6 percent. But then, as we've seen, the year of rioting, the year Biden was elected, the year that liberal policies in our big cities really began to kick in, crime shot back up again.

---

149 FBI, Uniform Crime Report, Crime in the United States 1995, Section IV, Table 43.—Total Arrests, Distribution by Race, 1995, p. 226. https://ucr.fbi.gov/crime-in-the-u.s/1995.

150 FBI, Uniform Crime Report, Crime in the United States 2000, Table 43 Arrests by Race, 2000, p. 234. https://ucr.fbi.gov/crime-in-the-u.s/2000.

151 Department of Justice, Bureau of Justice Statistics, "Violent Victimization by Race or Ethnicity, 2005-2019," Table 1 Rate of violent victimizations, by victim race or ethnicity, 2005-2019, p. 1. https://bjs.ojp.gov/library/publications/violent-victimization-race-or-ethnicity-2005-2019.

Now we must ask the really hard question: What can be done to save Black Americans from being crime victims, especially murder victims?

MAKING THE NEW WILD WEST LESS WILD

I've mentioned several times the connection between the current homicide rates among Black Americans, especially young, Black, male Americans, and the homicide rates of the Wild West. As a former sheriff, I think that connection is more than merely accidental.

Everybody knows the shoot-'em-up lawlessness of the Wild West towns, where men took the law into their own hands because there was no sheriff in town. At the slightest provocation or insult, or if there was a conflict over land, whiskey, horses, or cattle, the guns came out, and the undertaker had even more business.

This isn't mere Hollywood fantasy; it actually represents what real life (and death) was like in the Wild West towns I listed that had such high homicide rates. One of the main reasons that men took the law into their own hands, or embraced frontier lawlessness for their own profit and pleasure, was (as Steven Pinker notes) that "the criminal justice system," if it existed, "was underfunded, inept, and often corrupt."[152]

What brought the homicide rates down? The first thing was the arrival of an effective and honest sheriff and a judge who had the power, and the backing of the town, to settle disputes according to the law and to punish offenders.[153] Defunding the sheriff and undermining the criminal justice system were exactly what people didn't need; they needed law and order. And our cities need law

---

152 Steven Pinker, *The Better Angels of Our Nature*, p. 103.
153 Steven Pinker, *The Better Angels of Our Nature*, p. 105.

and order now, especially for the sake of the victims, most of whom are Black.

How do we know that can work now? Recall how many times I've noted above that the crime wave that began in 1960 was finally brought down again in the mid-1990s. What happened to bring it down?

Remember that I noted above that New York City's crime rate fell to levels even lower than the national rate. The reason was a combination of increasing and reforming police forces, and a smarter approach to policing.

As to the first, Americans became sick of ever-increasing crime, and beginning in the 1980s and into the '90s, police forces were enlarged, a trend greatly helped by *Democrat* President Bill Clinton's promise to put one hundred thousand more police on America's streets. The legislative result was the Violent Crime Control and Law Enforcement Act of 1994. It was sponsored by then-Senator Joe Biden, supported by the Congressional Black Caucus, and affirmed by Black religious leaders (who stated, "We believe in putting 100,000 well-trained police officers on the streets of our most violence-plagued communities and urban areas"[154]).

But merely adding police is insufficient if there isn't a smarter approach to policing, and that was brought about by a rather famous *Republican* Mayor of New York, Rudy Giuliani, and his police commissioner, William Bratton. They introduced a sophisticated computer program (CompStat) to track crimes by precinct (holding precinct commanders responsible for crime increases in their jurisdictions), added zero-tolerance policing that removed the seeds of crime before they took root (thereby cleaning up areas plagued by vagrants and drug addicts), assigned special patrols for crime hotspots, and paid particular attention to public drug deal-

---

154 "Statement by African-American Religious Leaders," August 16, 1994. https://clinton-whitehouse6.archives.gov/1994/08/1994-08-16-african-american-religious-leaders-support-crime-bill.html.

ers. In addition to the greater arrest rate, tougher sentencing was meted out to those convicted.[155]

All of this resulted in finally bringing down the crime wave, way down. To state the obvious, it also brought up the numbers of those imprisoned, and that meant a disproportionate number of Black males in prison in relationship to the Black population. As Latzer states, "This outcome was predictable, if unsettling." It's predictable because, as we've seen in great detail, the Black offender rate, especially in regard to homicides, is so much higher. But again, we must remember who were the main victims of these offenders. Latzer continues:

> [I]t must also be noted that crime reductions gained in part by incarcerations positively affected African Americans and their communities much more than they did white communities. Black victimization, overwhelmingly at the hands of black offenders, was extraordinarily high. For homicide, for instance, blacks were 47 percent of all victims between 1976 and 2005, and 94% of those black victims were killed by other African Americans. So the crime drop unquestionably saved countless black lives and spared thousands of African Americans from nonlethal victimizations.[156]

We don't have to defend everything about the police and criminal reforms that brought the Great Crime Wave down. We can sort through and keep what worked and reject what didn't. But one thing that surely will bring the crime wave back—in fact, did bring it back—is the notion that we should defund the police, especially in our cities, and add to that a host of other liberal "reform" policies.

---

155 Barry Latzer, *The Rise and Fall of Violent Crime in America*, pp. 221-227.
156 Barry Latzer, *The Rise and Fall of Violent Crime in America*, p. 233.

If we continue to engage in such foolishness, then the crime spikes in 2020 and 2021 are going to create another Great Crime Wave.

These are Democrat policies. Democrats embraced the 2020 riots, the Defund the Police movement, and the liberal "criminal justice reform" movement. According to a report by the House Judiciary Committee, we have the following list of which cities championed defunding the police, with the amount cut.[157] To make the point, I'll add the political party in charge of the city in 2020.

Austin, TX ($150 million cut), Democrat mayor
Baltimore, MD ($22 million cut), Democrat mayor
Boston, MA ($12 million cut), Democrat mayor
Burlington, VT ($1 million cut), Democrat mayor
Columbus, OH ($23 million cut), Democrat mayor
Denver, CO ($55 million cut), Democrat mayor
Hartford, CT ($2 million cut), Democrat mayor
Los Angeles, CA ($175 million cut), Democrat mayor
Madison, WI ($2 million cut), Democrat mayor
Minneapolis, MN ($8 million cut), Democrat mayor
New York, NY ($1 billion cut), Democrat mayor
Oakland, CA ($14.6 million cut), Democrat mayor
Oklahoma City, OK ($5.5 million cut), Republican mayor
Philadelphia, PA ($33 million cut), Democrat mayor
Portland, OR ($15 million cut), Democrat mayor
Salt Lake City, UT ($5.3 million cut), Democrat mayor
San Francisco, CA ($120 million cut), Democrat mayor
Seattle, WA ($69 million cut), Democrat mayor
Washington, DC ($15 million cut), Democrat mayor

Additionally, the cities currently contemplating defunding the police (Chicago, Ithaca, Kansas City, and New Orleans) all have Democrat mayors.

---

157 House of Representatives, Judiciary Committee, Cities That Have Defunded the Police.

The pattern is obvious: except for one outlier (Oklahoma City), those at the helm of cities defunding the police are all Democrats. If Black lives really did matter, Democrats should be investing more in creating law and order, rather than undermining the safety of their citizens, especially their Black citizens.

How well did defunding the police work for these cities? Here's a sampling of the increases in murders from 2019 to 2020: Austin (over 55 percent increase), Minneapolis (over 72 percent), St. Louis (over 34 percent), Washington (over 19 percent), Boston (over 54 percent), Oakland (over 37 percent), Philadelphia (over 35 percent), New York (over 39 percent), Los Angeles (over 30 percent), Portland (over 51 percent), Seattle (over 74 percent), San Francisco (over 32 percent), Denver (over 38 percent), Madison (400 percent), and let's add Chicago (over 55 percent) and New Orleans (over 61 percent).[158]

The most important areas where more, not less, police are needed are related to gangs and drugs. Recall, as noted above, "that violence driven by conflicts within and among gangs, drug-selling crews and other criminally active groups generate the bulk of urban homicide problems." Most homicides occur among young Black men who are connected to gangs and illegal drugs—the equivalent of Wild West gangs who engaged in illegal activities and absorbed a lot of whiskey in the process.

We know that gangs and drugs cause skyrocketing homicide rates from more than this inference from the Wild West and the data cited above. In 2020, the most dangerous cities in the world (as measured by homicide rates) were almost all in Mexico, Central America, and South America where gangs and drugs cause so much chaos. Not coincidentally, the homicide rates of the top four cities were nearly identical to the young Black male homicide rates in the

---

158 Cheryl Corley, "Massive 1-Year Rise In Homicide Rates Collided With The Pandemic In 2020," NPR, January 6, 2021. https://www.npr.org/2021/01/06/953254623/massive-1-year-rise-in-homicide-rates-collided-with-the-pandemic-in-2020.

US: Los Cabos, Mexico (111.3 per 100,000), Caracas, Venezuela (111.2), Acapulco, Mexico (107), and Natal, Brazil (102.6).

Sadly, the first city outside of this region in the list of most dangerous cities in the world is St. Louis, Missouri, with a 2020 homicide rate of 65.8. Also making the top fifty were Baltimore (55.5), New Orleans (40.1), and Detroit (39.7).[159] The mayors of St. Louis have all been Democrat since 1949. The mayors of Baltimore have all been Democrat since 1967. The mayors of New Orleans have all been Democrat since 1872. The mayors of Detroit have all been Democrat since 1962. That should be an indication of what policies *don't* work.

Needless to say, since the running of drugs by gangs is illegal, the young men can't look to the police and the justice system to settle disputes and avenge insults and attacks. So, they are put into a position of the lawless Wild West, where they have to act as their own "sheriffs," with guns settling the score. Since they resort to their own "frontier" justice so often, they have proportionately far more run-ins with the actual police. Just like the Wild West, what is needed is more police protection, not less, to bring law and order to those who need it the most.

The second thing that brought the homicide rates down in the Wild West was marriage. In these wild towns there were very few women and a whole lot of men. The taming of the Wild West occurred with the arrival of enough women so that the men were turned from whiskey, fighting, and visiting prostitutes, to marriage and taking care of a wife and children. In Pinker's terms, "cads"

---

159 Statista, "Ranking of the most dangerous cities in the world in 2020, by murder rate per 100,000 inhabitants." https://www.statista.com/statistics/243797/ranking-of-the-most-dangerous-cities-in-the-world-by-murder-rate-per-capita/. Other sites using slightly different data yield somewhat different results in the details, but agree with the fact of the most dangerous cities being in Mexico, Central America, and South America, and including St. Louis, Baltimore, and Detroit in the top fifty. See, for example, World Atlas, "The Most Dangerous Cities in the World." https://www.worldatlas.com/articles/the-most-dangerous-cities-in-the-world.html.

were thereby turned into "dads." The civilizing effect of marriage was transformative. To quote Pinker at length,

> *The West was eventually tamed not just by flinty-eyed marshals and hanging judges but by an influx of women.... As the women arrived, they used their bargaining position to transform the West into an environment better suited to their interests. They insisted that the men abandon their brawling and boozing for marriage and family life, encouraged the building of schools and churches, and shut down saloons, brothels, gambling dens, and other rivals for the men's attention. Churches, with their coed membership, Sunday morning discipline, and glorification of norms of temperance, added institutional muscle to the women's civilizing offensive.*[160]

And the homicide rates went down. "The idea that young men are civilized by women and marriage may seem as corny as Kansas in August, but it has become a commonplace of modern criminology."[161]

But young Black men are not getting married. As if the bad effects by Democrats of slavery and Jim Crow were not enough, they also gave us the sexual revolution that brought "under attack... marriage and family life, which had done so much to domesticate male violence in the preceding centuries."[162] The result, in Pinker's words, was the "de-civilization in the 1960s" that tore apart the social fabric built up by strong marriages and ushered in the Great Crime Wave.[163]

---

160   Steven Pinker, *The Better Angels of Our Nature*, p. 105.
161   Steven Pinker, *The Better Angels of Our Nature*, p. 106.
162   Steven Pinker, *The Better Angels of Our Nature*, p. 111.
163   Steven Pinker, *The Better Angels of Our Nature*, pp. 106-116.

The decline of marriage since the Left's sexual revolution of the 1960s is something that afflicts all races but Blacks in particular. According to a Hoover Institute study,

> *In the 1950s, after at least seventy years of rough parity, African American marriage rates began to fall behind white rates. In 1950, the percentages of white and African American women (aged fifteen and over) who were currently married were roughly the same, 67 percent and 64 percent, respectively. By 1998, the percentage of currently married white women had dropped by 13 percent to 58 percent. But the drop among African American women was 44 percent to 36 percent—more than three times larger. The declines for males were parallel, 12 percent for white men, 36 percent for African American men.*[164]

As Pinker notes, "The 1940s and 1950s, when crime hugged the floor, were the great age of marriage."[165] The drastic drop in marriage rates from sometime in the 1950s to 1990s, especially among Black Americans, corresponds with the drastic rise in crime rates that we've just set out above. That's not a coincidence; it coincides with the Left's sexual revolution and its ill effects on marriage and the family.

It's often said that the real problem facing Black Americans is a crisis of fatherhood. Google "crisis of fatherhood Black America" and you'll get multiple pages of articles lamenting the absence of Black fathers in the lives of their children.

True enough, but is it really an absence of fathers? According to the US Census Bureau, the overall percentage of children under

---

164 Douglas J. Besharov and Andrew West, "African American Marriage Patterns," pp. 95-113, quote p. 96. https://vdocuments.site/african-american-marriage-patterns.html?page=1.
165 Steven Pinker, *The Better Angels of Our Nature*, p. 108.

eighteen living with both parents in 1960 was 88 percent. But even then, Blacks were falling behind, with Black children under eighteen living with both parents at only 67 percent. By 1995, the overall percentage had fallen to about 69 percent, with the Blacks plummeting to 33 percent.[166]

Although this fall is often connected to the crisis of fatherhood, it's actually a crisis of *marriage*, fatherhood and motherhood in union, creating a home in which children can safely and healthily grow up. Again, to quote Pinker, "Young men are civilized by women and marriage," and that's why the connection between marriage and lower criminality "has become a commonplace of modern criminology."[167]

If you create a situation in which two-thirds of the young men are staying wild and single, and you add gangs and drugs, then it's predictable that the homicide rate will skyrocket to the levels seen in the Wild West. You're literally recreating the Wild West in a different form.

That brings us back to Black Lives Matter. We recall the now-deleted declaration on the BLM website that BLM wants to "disrupt the Western-prescribed nuclear family structure requirement" and "foster a queer-affirming network…with the intention of freeing ourselves from the tight grip of heteronormative thinking…." That's exactly what the Black community does *not* need—one more thing to further destroy marriage, the natural family, and fatherhood.

To return once again to the sanity of Pinker, "A famous study that tracked a thousand low-income Boston teenagers for forty-five years discovered that two factors predicted whether a delinquent

---

166 US Census Bureau, "Historical Living Arrangements of Children," December 2020, Table CH-1 Living Arrangements of Children under 18 Years Old: 1960 to Present, and Table CH-3 Living Arrangements of Black Children under 18 Years Old: 1960 to Present. https://www.census.gov/data/tables/time-series/demo/families/children.html.

167 Steven Pinker, *The Better Angels of Our Nature*, p. 106.

would go on to avoid a life of crime: getting a stable job and marrying a woman he cared about and supporting her and her children."[168] The effectiveness of getting a stable job is that it's aimed at caring for and supporting a man's wife and children.

If Black lives really matter, it's that simple—that's how you bring down the homicide rate, the crime rate, and the black victimization rate. But BLM isn't interested in what will fix the actual problems; like Antifa, it's simply a spokes-organization for the Far Left. So, what should real reform that really will save Black lives look like?

REAL CRIMINAL REFORM

I don't pretend to have all the answers, but I do agree with Pinker that being able to have a steady, respectable job will go a long way in reversing all these bad statistics, especially for incarcerated men, and being able to hold such a job will increase greatly the ability of young Black men in marrying a woman they care about and supporting their children. That's why, as a US Congressman, I introduced the SCORE Act[169] (with a Democrat, Florida's eminent Black Congresswoman Val Demings, Orlando's first female chief of police).

To quote from the bill, the "Second Chance Opportunity for Re-Entry Education Act of 2021" would "establish a grant program…to promote re-entry training programs and reduce recidivism to county jails for qualified non-violent inmates." The grant money would "be used to develop or manage an existing career training program at a county jail to provide training in welding,

---

168 Steven Pinker, *The Better Angels of Our Nature*, p. 106.

169 H. R. 3529. Available at https://www.congress.gov/bill/117th-congress/house-bill/3529/text?q=%7B%22search%22%3A%5B%22score+act%22%2C%22score%22%2C%22act%22%5D%7D&r=8&s=1.

heating ventilation, and air conditioning (HVAC), plumbing, or any other career training program determined to be an eligible project by the Director." These are real-life jobs that pay very good money and would give those who had been incarcerated a real sense of achievement working for the good of their community as members of the middle class. In other words, to focus on this chapter's theme, SCORE would help lift young incarcerated Black men out of poverty to be wage-earners who can support their families.

I realize, of course, that SCORE is directed to non-violent offenders, but it is a start, and a good way to keep non-violent offenders from become violent offenders later in life. But the problem stands: what do we do about the increase in violent crime and murder, especially among Blacks—because Black lives do matter, as do all lives. We've gotten a partial answer: encourage marriage and strengthen, rather than weaken, law enforcement.

Police departments also need to be positively related to the communities they serve, as I directed in Fort Bend. That means making real connections to the neighborhoods in which police officers serve.

But we've also got to do the obvious and undo the damage caused by the Defund the Police movement and the so-called "criminal justice reforms" put in place by Democrat mayors, city councils, and district attorneys. As of the time of this writing—February 2022—I'm happy to see that there are some Democrat-run cities that are finally realizing the harm such things have done and are trying to reverse course. Even Joe Biden and Nancy Pelosi are now pretending that they were never on board with the Defund the Police movement, which, however dishonest, might at least help push the political narrative in the right direction—away from the Democrat policies that have done so much harm for far too long.

CHAPTER 6

THE COVID CONSPIRACY

At the end of September of 2020, President Trump unveiled his Platinum Plan for Black Americans, outlining his commitment to Black Americans to make their lives better in concrete ways by creating better employment opportunities, by bringing about common sense criminal justice reform (as opposed to what the Left inflicted on Black communities) along with making Black neighborhoods safe again, by initiating much greater support for historically Black colleges and universities, and by stepping up investments in Opportunity Zones, among other things.[170]

But Trump wasn't reelected, so Black Americans weren't able to continue benefitting from what might have happened *if* Donald Trump had been declared the winner of 2020. In this chapter, we're going to look at one of the biggest reasons Democrats were able to get away with rigging the 2020 election: COVID. As we look at it in more detail, you'll see why I call it the COVID Conspiracy.

THE BIG IF

Think about the obvious. *If* the whole COVID-19 pandemic hadn't happened, then Democrats wouldn't have been able to rig

---

170 "The Platinum Plan: President Trump's Pillars," https://cdn.donaldjtrump.com/public-files/press_assets/president-trump-platinum-plan-final-version.pdf.

the election, and Donald Trump would have won the 2020 election. That's what I call the Big IF.

Everybody recognizes that truth, especially the Democrat Party. The economy was running strong in the last months of 2019. Trump's popularity among his base was higher and hotter than ever, and he was making significant inroads in gathering the Hispanic and Black vote. Trump was bringing back manufacturing to the US, successfully undoing the decades-long flood of manufacturing to China. He had negotiated historic deals in the Middle East to help bring peace to that region. He was intent on bringing the war in Afghanistan to a close, and he had forced our allies in Europe to pay for their own military protection rather than relying on billions of US dollars. All efforts by the Democrats to unseat Trump through drummed-up charges and sham impeachments had failed and were shown to be baseless.

And then the pandemic flared up in Wuhan, China, in November of 2019.

Was there a COVID-19 Conspiracy?

Yes, but it's far more complicated, and far deeper, than most would guess. But, for our purposes, everything begins with that Big IF. *If* there had not been a Wuhan virus, *then* Democrats wouldn't have been able to rig the election, and Donald Trump would have been re-elected in 2020.

A LOT OF SMALLER IFS

I'm now going to list a lot of smaller "ifs" so that you can begin to see how complex things really were (and are) once you start digging below the surface. I'd like you to think about each of them for a bit and then we'll see how they're connected to the Big IF.

If there hadn't been a COVID-19 worldwide epidemic, then big pharma's earnings would have been many tens of billions of dollars less.

If there hadn't been a COVID-19 worldwide epidemic, then Google's Larry Page and Sergey Brin wouldn't have had their wealth increase by over $40 billion dollars each, Facebook's Mark Zuckerberg wouldn't have been $35 billion dollars richer, Amazon's Jeff Bezos wouldn't have added $86 billion to his already immense pile of money, and Bill Gates wouldn't have increased his total wealth by an additional $22 billion.[171]

If there had been no COVID-19 lockdowns, then tens of thousands of small and medium sized businesses would still be thriving rather than being closed for good.

If there had been no COVID-19 worldwide epidemic, then most of us would never have heard of Anthony Fauci.

If there had been an inexpensive "magic pill" available in January of 2021 that significantly reduced both the symptoms and the death rates of COVID-19 by 80 percent, bringing them down even lower than a normal seasonal flu, then there would have been no need for vaccines, lockdowns, and mask mandates, and perhaps five hundred thousand lives could have been saved.

And related more directly to the Big IF, *if* there had been no COVID-19 lockdowns, then Donald Trump would have had many more massive campaign rallies, giving him an enormous advantage over Joe Biden in the presidential race.

If there had been no COVID-19 lockdowns, then Democrat candidate Joe Biden could not have hidden in his basement, and his deteriorating mental condition would have been obvious to everyone in multiple debates and campaign speeches.

---

171 Chase Peterson-Withorn, "How Much Money America's Billionaires Have Made During the COVID-19 Pandemic," *Forbes*, April 30, 2021. https://www.forbes.com/sites/chasewithorn/2021/04/30/american-billionaires-have-gotten-12-trillion-richer-during-the-pandemic/.

If there had been no COVID-19 lockdowns, then Democrats could not have pushed through their nationwide absentee ballot, vote-by-mail campaign, and other loosening of state election laws that (even according to Democrats themselves) brought them the extra votes needed to defeat Trump.

If there had been no COVID-19 lockdowns, and consequently Democrats were not able to rig the election against Donald Trump winning, there would not have been a Capitol Hill riot on January 6th.

Many more "ifs" could be added, but even with these we can begin to see how they are all connected, sometimes in quite illuminating ways.

So, as I pointed out, if there had been no lockdowns, Jeff Bezos would have earned billions anyway, but not $86 billion. When all the brick-and-mortar local stores were forced to close down for COVID, then everyone was ordering everything online, and Amazon sells nearly everything online. Happily for Bezos and Amazon, COVID wiped away a great swath of their competition from middle-size and small businesses. That was the general effect of COVID on the economy: big businesses that could ship online made mountains of money; the middle and little guys in actual stores across America were crushed. COVID made Bezos very wealthy and wiped out almost all remaining competition.

Pretty obvious. But what about making a connection that might seem rather far-fetched at first?

If there would have been an inexpensive "magic pill" widely available in January of 2020 that could drastically cut down the death rate, hospitalization rate, and suffering of COVID-19, then Donald Trump would have won the presidency in 2020.

How do we know that? It's not difficult to demonstrate. To begin with, even with all the obstacles thrown in his way by COVID, Donald Trump set a record in the 2020 election by getting the greatest number of popular votes for a presidential candidate in American history, over 74 million, beating the previous record set by Barack Obama's first term win of 69.5 million votes. That's over 4.5 million *more* votes than Obama got in 2008.

Somehow Joe Biden broke *that* record, getting a bit over 7 million more popular votes than Trump. As I noted, Biden won *only* because COVID allowed for an immense push for absentee voting (which, we repeat, opened up vast possibilities for voter fraud). But even setting aside the possibility of fraud, the numbers make clear the advantage for Democrats with increased absentee voting: 65 percent of Trump voters voted in person, whereas 65 percent of Biden voters voted by mail.[172] If mail-in voting had not been expanded so dramatically and the restrictions upon it loosened because of COVID—both things pushed fervently by the Democrats—millions of Biden votes would have been erased. Add to that the boost in votes Trump would have gotten from endless rallies and a booming economy and the negative effect of greater Biden exposure, and Biden's lead disappears. Recall as well that the Democrats had only *one* campaign strategy: repeat endlessly that Donald Trump's COVID's policies are killing millions of people.

Well, what if *in fact* there was not only one "magic pill" but several that would have had precisely the miraculous effects I've described, saving hundreds of thousands of lives in the US and millions worldwide, and bringing the epidemic to a quick close by March of 2020? Your obvious response would be—well then *why* wasn't it used?

As we'll see, it was because all the "ifs" noted above were connected. If there had been a "magic pill," then Trump would have won the 2020 election *and* big pharma, Google, Facebook, Bill Gates, and others would not have made their hundreds of billions.

---

172 See Ruth Igielnik, Scott Keeter, and Hannah Hartig, "Behind Biden's 2020 Victory," Pew Research Center, June 30, 2021. https://www.pewresearch.org/politics/2021/06/30/behind-bidens-2020-victory/.

You also probably wouldn't have heard of Anthony Fauci, director of the National Institute of Allergy and Infectious Diseases (NIAID) and medical advisor to both Donald Trump and Joe Biden.

How things all fit together is a bit of a mystery well worth solving. And if there was a collusion to keep a "magic pill" away from the public, and a half a million American lives were lost as a consequence, then it's a murder mystery.

THE MAGIC PILLS: A TIMELINE

Both hydroxychloroquine and ivermectin come in pill form, both have been around a very long time, both are completely safe, and both are inexpensive because they are not patented drugs. Most importantly, both are reportedly effective in combatting COVID (in combination with other readily available drugs and vitamins). But what is absolutely horrifying is that "a half a million excess deaths have happened in the United States through the intentional blockade of early treatment by the US government" of hydroxychloroquine and ivermectin.

Those are the words of Dr. Robert Malone, an internationally recognized scientist and physician and the original inventor of mRNA vaccination as a technology, DNA vaccination, and multiple non-viral DNA and RNA/mRNA platform delivery technologies. Dr. Malone also holds numerous fundamental domestic and foreign patents in the fields of gene delivery, delivery formulations, and vaccines, including for fundamental DNA and RNA/mRNA vaccine technologies.[173]

The statement that a half a million excess deaths could have been avoided if the US government, under the direction of

---

173   From Dr. Robert Malone's very valuable Substack, a non-censored platform that I highly recommend: https://rwmalonemd.substack.com/about.

Anthony Fauci, had not intentionally blocked the use of hydroxy-chloroquine and ivermectin comes from Dr. Malone's extensive interview with Joe Rogan. This interview was subsequently censored by Twitter and YouTube, once again proving that they don't work for their users but for big pharma, big media, liberal elites, and Anthony Fauci.

Because of the immense importance of what Dr. Malone had to say, and in support of freedom of speech, freedom of expression, and freedom of debate, I had the interview officially entered into the *Congressional Record* to preserve the podcast forever. Big tech may be able to censor information on their own platforms, but they cannot censor the *Congressional Record*.[174]

There wasn't only censorship but purposeful misinformation. It's likely you heard ivermectin is a kind of "horse-paste" deplorables and other anti-science, anti-vaxxers were eagerly ingesting and then getting horribly sick, and that hydroxychloroquine is some weird poisonous chemical that comes from fish-tanks that Donald Trump foolishly took when he got COVID. You also may have heard that Dr. Fauci, the FDA, every reputable scientist, and even your local pharmacist all heartily agree that ivermectin and hydroxychloroquine are harmful, and so are no substitute for approved vaccines.

If that's what you heard, then thank big tech, big pharma, and the mainstream media for a big dose of poisonous misinformation. Misinformation that, *all too conveniently*, fit with the Democrat agenda to beat Donald Trump by any means.

We can understand this by taking a closer look at the "magic pills" (and other effective non-vaccine treatments), using a timeline from the first recognition of the virus's appearance in Wuhan,

---

174 Congressional Record, January 3, 2022, pp. E1403-E1405 contains the beginning of the interview. The rest of the interview is available at my congressional website: https://nehls.house.gov/posts/joe-rogan-experience-1757-dr-robert-malone-md-full-transcript.

China, in November of 2019 to the fall presidential election on November 3, 2020.[175]

Mid-November of 2019: US intelligence receives news of a contagion sweeping through the Wuhan region of China, and for the rest of November and December the relevant bureaucratic, intelligence, and military policy-makers hold multiple meetings.[176]

January of 2020: A detailed account of the intelligence gathered about the outbreak of COVID in China is presented to Donald Trump in his Daily Brief.

January 20, 2020: The US has its first confirmed case of COVID.

January 30, 2020: Having confirmed over six thousand cases in China, the World Health Organization (WHO) declares COVID-19 a Public Health Emergency of International Concern (PHEIC).

Mid-January 2020: Responding to the health crisis, Dr. Paul Marik (Professor of Medicine and Chief of the Division of Pulmonary and Critical Care Medicine at the Eastern Virginia Medical School in Norfolk, Virginia) creates an effective protocol for COVID patients which directly reduces the inflammation that brings about Acute Respiratory Distress Syndrome in COVID patients, thereby rescuing them from having to go on a ventilator. The protocol is very simple, using inexpensive, readily available intravenous doses of hydrocortisone, ascorbic acid (vitamin C), and thiamine (vitamin B1).

March 3, 2020: The *Chinese themselves* published their own treatment protocol for COVID, based upon their collective experience of what worked for Chinese physicians who had been dealing

---

175   For the information in this section I am relying on the excellent and authoritative revelation of what the COVID pandemic is really about: Robert Kennedy, *The Real Anthony Fauci: Bill Gates, Big Pharma, and the Global War on Democracy and Public Health* (New York: Skyhorse Publishing, 2021), Chapter 1.

176   Josh Margolin and James Gordon Meek, "Intelligence report warned of coronavirus crisis as early as November: Sources," ABC News, April 8, 2020. https://abcnews.go.com/Politics/intelligence-report-warned-coronavirus-crisis-early-november-sources/story?id=70031273.

with the virus for four months. Their treatment protocol included "chloroquine (a cousin of hydroxychloroquine), antibiotics, anti-histamines, a variety of steroids, and probiotics to stabilize and fortify the immune system and apothecaries of traditional Chinese medicines, vitamins, and minerals, including a variety of compounds containing quercetin, zinc, and glutathione precursors."[177]

March 19, 2020: President Trump endorses the use of hydroxychloroquine.

April 3, 2020: Australian researchers publish an article, the title of which says it all: "Lab experiments show anti-parasitic drug, Ivermectin, eliminates SARS-CoV-2 in cells in 48 hours." The news creates a worldwide sensation.

April 2020: Other doctors, having learned of Dr. Marik's successful protocol, have banded together with Marik, creating the Front Line COVID-19 Critical Care Alliance (FLCCC) to collect and circulate more information on beneficial, readily available medicines and therapies effective against COVID. In the first week of April, the group sends "the protocol to the White House COVID-19 response team headed at the time by Jared Kushner."[178]

April 2020: Dr. Vladimir Zelenko in upstate New York dramatically reduces mortality of COVID patients using hydroxychloroquine.

April 2020: A team of Chinese scientists publish a study of a placebo-controlled trial of hydroxychloroquine, showing it to be effective in treatment of COVID.

May 8, 2020: Peru, besieged by COVID deaths, adopts the use of ivermectin. Deaths drop fourteen-fold wherever it's properly distributed.

---

177 Robert Kennedy, *The Real Anthony Fauci: Bill Gates, Big Pharma, and the Global War on Democracy and Public Health*, p. 13.

178 "The FLCCC Alliance Story," FLCCC Alliance, https://covid19criticalcare.com/about/the-flccc-alliance-story/.

May 2020: Looking at the available data, Dr. Harvey Risch, Yale Professor of Epidemiology, concludes that hydroxychloroquine is both a safe and effective treatment of COVID. Dr. Risch's credentials directly relate to the assessment of COVID. Not only is he Professor of Epidemiology in the Department of Epidemiology and Public Health at the Yale School of Public Health and Yale School of Medicine (he received his MD degree from the University of California San Diego), but he also has a PhD in mathematical modeling of infectious epidemics from the University of Chicago.

June 2, 2020: The American Association of Physicians and Surgeons publishes a comparison of death rates in countries that allow hydroxychloroquine and those that don't, showing that those that allow it for early treatment have far lower death rates.

June 9, 2020: Miami doctor Jean-Jacques Rajter publishes a paper describing the sharp rise in recoveries of COVID patients when a combination of ivermectin and hydroxychloroquine are used.

June 2020: Frustrated by the common practice of simply letting patients with COVID go untreated while everyone waited for a vaccine, Dr. Peter McCullough (a practicing cardiologist, and founder and current president of the Cardiorenal Society of America, an organization that brings cardiologists and nephrologists together to work on the emerging problem of cardiorenal syndromes) started contacting practicing physicians around the world to find out what protocols were working for them in each stage of the virus.

June 12, 2020: *The Journal of Antibiotics* publishes "Ivermectin: a systematic review from antiviral effects to COVID-19 complementary regimen." Going back over years of research the article's authors found that ivermectin was already proven to be highly effective against viruses such as Zika, dengue, yellow fever, and the

West Nile virus, thereby lending credibility to its use against the COVID virus as well.

July 1, 2020: Dr. Peter McCullough and his team publish their protocol in the prestigious *American Journal of Medicine*[179] based on what had been effective to treat COVID in each of its stages: the early replication of the virus, the deadly inflammation, and finally the blood clotting. They report the amazing effectiveness of hydroxychloroquine and ivermectin, especially if supplemented with other readily available medications such as azithromycin, zinc, vitamin D, Celebrex, bromhexine, vitamin C, and quercetin. The protocol works, they say, because hydroxychloroquine, ivermectin, and quercetin all facilitate zinc uptake in the cells that helps destroy the ability of the coronavirus to replicate.

July 23, 2020: A frustrated Dr. Harvey Risch publishes an article in *Newsweek*, "The key to defeating COVID-19 already exists. We need to start using it." In it, he begs US doctors to use hydroxychloroquine to save lives and stop the pandemic.

That's enough to make a very important point: *by July 2020 we had sufficient information to understand how we could significantly reduce the hospitalizations and death rate of COVID-19.* (I haven't included a long list of studies done outside the US.)

Moreover, there were other readily available, inexpensive drugs I didn't mention above that doctors discovered also significantly reduced COVID suffering and mortality, including fluvoxamine and famotidine, and the anti-inflammatories prednisone and budesonide. Physicians even found that saline nasal lavages could reduce viral loads and transmission.

A host of studies since the summer of 2020 have only reinforced our knowledge of the effectiveness of hydroxychloroquine, ivermectin, and a multitude of other drugs that could easily have

---

179 Peter McCullough, et al, "Pathophysiologic Basis and Clinical Rationale for Early Outpatient Treatment of SARS-CoV-2 (COVID-19) Infection," *American Journal of Medicine* 134, no. 1 (January 2021): 16-22. DOI: https://doi.org/10.1016/j.amjmed.2020.07.003.

been deployed to slow the pandemic in the early summer.[180] And that means—as Dr. Robert Malone said—we could have possibly saved hundreds of thousands of lives in the US alone.

Why didn't that happen? Three related reasons.

First, Anthony Fauci and big pharma (along with other major investors in vaccines like Bill Gates and Google) were set to make billions of dollars in revenue *if* the pandemic lasted until the vaccines were available. That's why Fauci made sure that any other solution was discredited, no matter what the cost in suffering and lives lost.

Second, if Trump were able to stop the epidemic months before the election with inexpensive, repurposed and readily available drugs, he would have been treated like a hero. But the Far Left couldn't allow that, so they worked with Fauci and big pharma to discredit all possible treatments and get Democrat governors to implement harmful lockdowns.

Third, if the COVID epidemic didn't run right up to the fall elections, then all the "emergency" voting changes, in particular the immense expansion of absentee and mail-in voting, would have been dropped. That expansion was known by the Democrats to be the key to rigging the election against Trump.

Adopting the use of hydroxychloroquine and ivermectin (along with supportive drugs and vitamins) for early treatment of COVID would have pulled the rug out from under the Democrats, Anthony Fauci, and big pharma.

To be more pointed, if Fauci and the medical establishment had adopted hydroxychloroquine on March 19, 2020, the day it was first touted by President Donald Trump, according to Dr. Robert Malone, hundreds of thousands of deaths could have been avoided because the other off-patent remedies like ivermectin

---

180 For a continually updated list of articles as well as charts and graphs that clarify relative effectiveness, see the website COVID-19 Treatment Studies. https://c19early.com/.

would then have been adopted, too, along with the other medicines readily available as part of known, effective protocols. The pandemic would have ended by the beginning of June 2020, long before the fall presidential election.

And Donald Trump would have been elected president in November of 2020.

It's not difficult to understand how continuing the pandemic—with its rising death toll numbers, deepening economic destruction, lockdowns that allowed mail-in voting and shut down Trump's rallies—benefitted the Democrats. But could the esteemed Anthony Fauci be capable of such a horrible thing? You need to meet the real Anthony Fauci.

THE REAL ANTHONY FAUCI

I'm purposely using the title of Robert F. Kennedy's smash bestseller, *The Real Anthony Fauci: Bill Gates, Big Pharma, and the Global War on Democracy and Public Health*, because everyone needs to read it in order to understand the year 2020, the year that COVID swallowed everything, defined everything, influenced everything, changed everything—including the most massive changes in how Americans voted in our country's history.

It was not (so far as I know, anyway) Anthony Fauci's goal to ensure that Donald Trump was not elected. But as Robert Kennedy makes clear, it was Fauci's goal to ensure that big pharma made billions and billions of dollars from new vaccines, and that meant that he had to make sure that any inexpensive, available medicines would be shunned, defamed, ridiculed, or declared ineffective or dangerous, *so that* Americans would believe that their only hope in battling the evil COVID virus was a yet-to-be created patented vaccine or vaccines that would earn big pharma untold profits in a worldwide epidemic (and enrich Fauci himself, as well as add to his already immense bureaucratic power).

Fauci was not conspiring to unseat Donald Trump with COVID; he was conspiring to enrich big pharma and himself. But the unintended effect was real nonetheless, and *that* is why Anthony Fauci was taken to be a hero, even a saint, by the Democrat Party.

I am not making the claim that Democrats knew what Fauci was up to, and so they were also willing to allow hundreds of thousands of Americans to die just so they could rid themselves of Trump. I think on the whole they genuinely believed what Anthony Fauci so convincingly said. They likely thought that they were on the side of angels in siding with Fauci. Yet, they also understood that Fauci's handling of the pandemic was extremely helpful to them politically.

In throwing such unquestioning *and politically strategic* support behind Fauci, they were indirectly the cause of a lot of needless suffering and death in their feverish desire to beat Donald Trump by any means. That's why they loved lockdowns, mask mandates, and waiting for vaccines (as long as they didn't arrive before November). That's why they hooted and howled in laughter when Trump suggested the use of hydroxychloroquine.

And that's why they love Fauci.

Anthony Fauci has been around in government bureaucracy for a long time, joining the National Institutes of Health (NIH) in 1968, and taking his current position as director of NIAID in 1984. As Kennedy makes clear in his detailed, well-documented account, Fauci's extraordinary bureaucratic career is built upon bringing about the "regulatory capture" of the nation's health-related agencies by big pharma—the NIAID itself, the NIH, the Food and Drug Administration (FDA), the Centers for Disease Control (CDC), and Health and Human Services (HHS). Regulatory capture means "the corporate seizure of America's public health agencies by the pharmaceutical industry,"[181] and that capture benefitted Fauci both in terms of money and immense bureaucratic power.

As Kennedy documents in detail, Fauci ensured that the federal agencies that were supposed to regulate industries were instead controlled by the industries they were supposed to regulate. Fauci's regulatory empire was built on a huge taxpayer-supplied budget and piles of money from big pharma, and all the power that money gave him over hospitals, doctors, research institutes, universities, and even medical journals. Even more, Fauci's power extends far beyond the US because the reach of American pharmaceutical interests stretches over the globe (especially when mixed with concerns about biological weapons, which brings in our defense and intelligence agencies).

Again, I ask readers, please, to read all of Robert Kennedy's *The Real Anthony Fauci* for an extremely detailed account of the many years and many ways that Fauci corrupted our health bureaucracy. Particularly insightful into his real character are the chapters detailing his oversight of the dangerous drug trials that caused the death of countless Africans (Chapter 8), his gross mishandling of the AIDS epidemic that caused thousands of unnecessary deaths and untold suffering (Chapters 4–6), and his barbaric and illegal experiments on foster children in New York (Chapter 7). All that is important, but our focus on this chapter is his handling of the COVID pandemic as it relates to the 2020 presidential election.

To do that most efficiently, I'll provide another timeline, one that could be superimposed on the one above.[182] As you'll see, I start much earlier than the above timeline to include key details.

---

181 Robert Kennedy, *The Real Anthony Fauci: Bill Gates, Big Pharma, and the Global War on Democracy and Public Health*, p. xxiii.
182 Based upon details provided in Robert Kennedy, *The Real Anthony Fauci: Bill Gates, Big Pharma, and the Global War on Democracy and Public Health*, Ch. 1.

KILLING THE MAGIC PILLS: ANOTHER TIMELINE

December 1980: The Bayh-Dole Act allows Fauci and the NIAID and other health-related government bureaucracies to file for patents on medicines and therefore collect enormous sums on medical products they have a hand in developing. This act will allow Fauci to use taxpayer money for medical research that will directly benefit him and big pharma financially, rather than oversee the pharmaceutical industry for the benefit of the public. That defined Fauci's approach as the head of NIAID for decades and thus his approach to COVID.

October 2004: Scientists report that hydroxychloroquine and the related chloroquine are effective in treating coronavirus. (Keep in mind COVID-19 is just one kind of coronavirus.)

August 2005: A CDC study published in the *Virology Journal* affirms the effectiveness of chloroquine as the title itself makes clear: "Chloroquine Is a Potent Inhibitor of SARS Coronavirus Infection and Spread." *Fifteen years before the pandemic kicked in, the CDC and Anthony Fauci already knew how to stop it.*

2016: Just after Donald Trump was elected, tech giant Google decides that it must do something to combat "misinformation," thus putting the full manipulative resources of Google behind ensuring that Donald Trump does not win a second term. The meeting was secretly videoed, and the video leaked to the public.[183] This sets the stage for big tech censorship during both the 2020 election and then the COVID pandemic.

2018: Google starts the Digital News Initiative to "support high quality journalism," focusing especially on battling "misinformation."

---

183 Allum Bokhari, "Leaked Video: Google Leadership's Dismayed Reaction to Trump Election," Breitbart, September 12, 2018. https://www.breitbart.com/tech/2018/09/12/leaked-video-google-leaderships-dismayed-reaction-to-trump-election/.

Summer 2019: The BBC creates the (ironically named) Trusted News Initiative to combat "fake news" about elections (especially focusing on the upcoming US election), and then adds that it will battle COVID "misinformation." According to its website, "The BBC's Trusted News Initiative is a partnership that includes organizations such as Facebook, Twitter, Reuters and The Washington Post. It is the only forum in the world of its kind designed to take on disinformation in real time."[184] Other members of the Trusted News Initiative reveal its left-wing bias: the Associated Press, AFP, CBC/Radio-Canada, European Broadcasting Union (EBU), Facebook, Financial Times, First Draft, Google/YouTube, The Hindu, Microsoft, and Reuters. As it turns out, COVID misinformation means anything that goes against the narrative of Anthony Fauci and big pharma, just political misinformation means anything that favors Donald Trump.

March 2020: Even before Trump's tweet on March 19th, there were so many doctors administering hydroxychloroquine, with positive results, that supplies were running low.

March 13, 2020: Michigan Doctor James Todaro tweets about the effectiveness of hydroxychloroquine and includes a link to a supportive Google document. Google's parent company, Alphabet, happens to own several vaccine companies and has multimillion-dollar partnerships with other vaccine companies. Big tech reveals itself to be the censor for big pharma and Fauci, as well as the Democrat Party, by censoring this information.

March 25, 2020: Fauci is asked directly at a news conference whether there is any evidence to suggest that hydroxychloroquine and chloroquine would be effective against COVID. He bluntly states, "The answer is no."

Late March 2020: As CNN itself reported, "The government started stockpiling hydroxychloroquine in late March, after

---

184 See its website: https://www.bbc.com/beyondfakenews/trusted-news-initiative/.

President Trump touted it as 'very encouraging' and 'very power-ful' and a 'game-changer.'"[185] To be more exact, in March, Health and Human Services (HHS) requested several large pharmaceutical companies to "donate" their inventory of hydroxychloroquine and chloroquine to the Strategic National Stockpile. Stockpiling it was a way to remove it from circulation (allegedly because these super-safe drugs that had been around for decades were suddenly "danger-ous"). As Kennedy makes clear, the FDA's reasoning for consider-ing the decades-old, entirely safe drug to be suddenly harmful were purposely fraudulent studies (funded directly or indirectly by Bill Gates, who is heavily invested in big pharma and stands to make countless millions) in which toxic levels of hydroxychloroquine were purposely given to patients, beginning with six times the stan-dard dose, and were given too late to have a positive effect.[186]

April 10, 2020: To combat the worldwide attention given to the Australian study (see previous timeline, April 3, 2020) and the work of Dr. Jean-Jacques Rajter (June 9, 2020) that affirmed the immense positive effects of using ivermectin, the FDA declared that additional testing is needed to determine if ivermectin is actu-ally safe (this, despite the fact that it already declared ivermectin safe and effective in 1996, and indeed a kind of "miracle drug").

May 1, 2020: The prestigious *New England Journal of Medicine* publishes a study purporting to show that hydroxychloroquine is both ineffective and dangerous. The study is based upon data from the Surgisphere Corporation. Reputable scientists immediately dis-covered that the Surgisphere database didn't exist, and the com-pany itself was a sham. The article was then retracted on June 25, 2020.[187] As Kennedy notes, Fauci controls the journal.

---

185 Elizabeth Cohen and Wesley Bruer, "US stockpile stuck with 63 million doses of hydroxychlo-roquine," CNN, June 18, 2020. Available at https://cnnphilippines.com/world/2020/6/18/US-hydroxychloroquine-stockpile-FDA.html.

186 Robert Kennedy, *The Real Anthony Fauci: Bill Gates, Big Pharma, and the Global War on Democracy and Public Health*, pp. 26-29.

187 For the retraction notice see https://pubmed.ncbi.nlm.nih.gov/32501665/.

May 22, 2020: The prestigious medical journal *The Lancet* also publishes a study allegedly showing that hydroxychloroquine is both ineffective and dangerous. The study is also based upon data from the sham Surgisphere Corporation. This article was then retracted on June 13, 2020.[188] Fauci also controls the journal as well.

May 25, 2020: Based upon the yet-to-be retracted, fraudulent studies in *The New England Journal of Medicine* and *The Lancet*, the World Health Organization (WHO) halts trials of hydroxychloroquine over "safety fears." According to Kennedy, Fauci has immense power over WHO, as does Bill Gates (through his millions in donations).

June 15, 2020: Basing its actions on the fraudulent Gates-funded studies in March, and the fraudulent studies in *The New England Journal of Medicine* and *The Lancet*, the FDA revokes permission for hydroxychloroquine to be distributed to COVID patients, thereby ensuring that big pharma would get its billions, and, as Dr. Robert Malone said, a half a million excess deaths would occur in the United States through the intentional blockade of early treatment by the US government.

By the November 2020 election, interest in ivermectin use among doctors and the public against COVID picked up substantially, and the Front Line COVID-19 Critical Care Alliance (FLCCC) judged that the evidence was significant enough to add ivermectin to its protocol against COVID. The evidence for the effectiveness of ivermectin continued to grow after the election, with positive effects being reported in ever more studies worldwide.[189]

Rather than accept the good news, Fauci's FDA and WHO issued statements against using ivermectin in March 2021, and on

---

188   For the retraction notice see https://pubmed.ncbi.nlm.nih.gov/32511943/.
189   For an extended account of ivermectin see Robert Kennedy, *The Real Anthony Fauci: Bill Gates, Big Pharma, and the Global War on Democracy and Public Health*, pp. 37-62.

August 16, 2021, Fauci's CDC ordered doctors to stop prescribing ivermectin. It took longer to suppress the use of ivermectin than it did hydroxychloroquine, but it happened for the same reason: effective low-cost, readily available drugs would prove the ruin of big pharma's profits and hence Fauci's bureaucratic empire.

That's enough for us to see several things very clearly. Four decades before the COVID-19 pandemic, the Bayh-Dole Act of 1980 set up our federal health bureaucracy to be corrupted by big pharma because federal regulators and regulatory agencies themselves were thereby permitted to use tax dollars to reap profits by developing and patenting drugs (in collusion with big pharma) that they also regulated. The fox was thereby put in charge of the henhouse, and Fauci has been the chief fox of NIAID since 1984.

Second, Anthony Fauci (and those under him) did everything they could to undermine the acceptance of hydroxychloroquine, ivermectin, and every other non-patented, readily available medicine, and continue to do so right up to the present. We know that both hydroxychloroquine and ivermectin are immensely effective in treating COVID, and our own government won't let us have them. Industry profits are more important than saved lives.

Third, Google's Digital News Initiative and the BBC's Trusted News Initiative were formed, in a collusion between big tech and the mainstream media, to control the news and the internet so that Trump would not win the 2020 election, and they also turned their resources to undermine the legitimacy and effectiveness of hydroxychloroquine, ivermectin, and other medicines.

Fourth, the Democrat Party knew its only hope against Trump was COVID, and so they gladly affirmed Fauci and big tech censorship, booed hydroxychloroquine, and laughed at ivermectin.

That political strategy, according to Dr. Robert Malone, came at the cost of hundreds of thousands of lives.

Remember the daily COVID death toll the mainstream media insisted on displaying during every newscast? Well, as it turns out, that was really a condemnation of the Democrat Party, not Donald Trump.

A FINAL TIMELINE: LOCKDOWN MANIA

There's one final aspect of the pandemic that we need to touch on, the lockdowns. The supposed goal of lockdowns is to contain the spread of the virus. Setting aside the question of whether they were effective in doing that or not, we know that they achieved three things related to what we've discussed so far.

First, lockdowns meant that Democrats, under the guise of a national health emergency that "demanded" quarantines, could invoke the executive powers of governors and state bureaucrats to loosen voting restrictions, especially in regard to absentee voting, which we know (from Chapter 3) is the easiest kind of voting to corrupt and has been used by Democrats to commit fraud in elections reaching all the way back to the presidential election of 1864.

Second, lockdowns wrecked the economy, which was one of President Trump's strongest points going into the 2020 election cycle.

These two things alone reveal why Democrat politicians and Democratic voters were such enthusiastic cheerleaders of lockdowns, and the mainstream media was such a fervent fearmonger about COVID. These two aspects were mutually reinforcing: Democrat voters watched the mainstream media, which kept them in continual fear of lifting lockdowns.

Third, lockdowns coupled with Fauci's insistence on denying the effectiveness of hydroxychloroquine, ivermectin, and other off-patent drugs ensured Americans would have to wait in fear, huddled in their homes, until the vaccines appeared, and big pharma could reap its profits.

But there's a final, devastating thing we must consider: the actual cost of lockdowns. As even the mainstream media and the Left began to admit after the election, the lockdowns had devastating effects on the mental and physical health of Americans. As a *New York Times* article of March 27, 2021, stated in its elongated title and teaser, "Suicide and Self-Harm: Bereaved Families Count the Costs of Lockdowns. As more people are vaccinated, and communities open up, there is a tally that experts say is harder to track: the psychological toll of months of isolation and global suffering, which for some has proved fatal."[190]

While people were forced to hide in their homes, and the fear-mongering press continued its daily death counts, deaths occurred through another means. As an astute *City Journal* article warned all the way back in July of 2020, "People delayed needed medical care because they were instructed to shelter in place, were too scared to go to the doctor, or were unable to obtain care because of limitations on available care, including a moratorium on elective procedures."[191]

I use the *City Journal* article because it shows that the destruction caused by lockdowns was known in the late spring and summer of 2020 (and that means decisions to continue lockdowns were done while we knew the heavy cost). Some important statistics from this article, well-worth quoting at length:

> *Inpatient admissions nationwide in VA hospitals, the nation's largest hospital system, were down 42 per-*

---

190 Elian Peltier and Isabella Kwai, "Suicide and Self-Harm: Bereaved Families Count the Costs of Lockdown," *New York Times*, April 15, 2021. https://www.nytimes.com/2021/03/27/world/europe/suicide-self-harm-pandemic.html.

191 Joel Zinberg, "Death by Policy: Mortality statistics show that many people have died from lockdown-related causes, not from Covid-19," *City Journal*, July 9, 2020. https://www.city-journal.org/deadly-cost-of-lockdown-policies.

cent for six emergency conditions—stroke, myocardial infarction (MI), heart failure, chronic obstructive pulmonary disease, appendicitis, and pneumonia— during six weeks of the Covid-19 pandemic (March 11 to April 21 [2020]) compared with the six weeks immediately prior (January 29 to March 10 [2020]). The drop was significant for all six conditions and ranged from a decrease of 40 percent for MI to 57 percent for appendicitis. No such decrease in admissions was found for the same six-week period in 2019. These emergency conditions did not become any less lethal as a result of the pandemic; rather, people simply died from acute illnesses that would have been treated in normal times.

[T]he five states with the most Covid-19 deaths from March through April [2020] (Massachusetts, Michigan, New Jersey, New York, and Pennsylvania), experienced large proportional increases in deaths from non-respiratory underlying causes, including diabetes (96 percent), heart diseases (89 percent), Alzheimer's disease (64 percent), and cerebrovascular diseases (35 percent). New York City—the nation's Covid-19 epicenter during that period—experienced the largest increases in non-respiratory deaths, notably from heart disease (398 percent) and diabetes (356 percent).

The lockdowns led to wide unemployment and economic recession, resulting in increased drug and alcohol abuse, in domestic abuse and suicide. Most studies in a systematic literature review found a positive association between economic recession and increased suicides. Data from the 2008 Great Recession showed

*a strong positive correlation between increasing unem-
ployment and increasing suicide in middle aged (45–
64) people. Ten times as many people texted a federal
government disaster mental-distress hotline in April
2020 as in April 2019.*

That is horrifying data, and again, it was available in the early summer of 2020, but the Democrat Party, Anthony Fauci, big pharma, big tech, and the mainstream media continued to push lockdowns and ignore the "inconvenient," significant collateral damage. Like COVID itself, lockdowns had to last until the election was over.

That brings us to our third and final timeline, and it's a short one, but still needs to be understood in light of the two we've just been over.

March 19, 2020: The first lockdown order in the US by Governor Gavin Newsom. Multiple states follow.

July 9, 2020: *City Journal* article above makes the bad effects of lockdowns clear to the public.

October 4, 2020: The *Great Barrington Declaration* is made public. The declaration is first signed by its originators, three of the most respected and qualified doctors in the world: Dr. Martin Kulldorff, professor of medicine at Harvard University, a biostatistician, and epidemiologist with expertise in detecting and monitoring infectious disease outbreaks and vaccine safety evaluations; Dr. Sunetra Gupta, professor at Oxford University, an epidemiologist with expertise in immunology, vaccine development, and mathematical modeling of infectious diseases; and Dr. Jay Bhattacharya, professor at Stanford University Medical School, a physician, epidemiologist, health economist, and public health policy expert focusing on infectious diseases and vulnerable populations. Other prominent doctors soon sign the declaration as well. In it, these eminent scientists declare the following:

Current lockdown policies are producing devastating effects on short and long-term public health. The results (to name a few) include lower childhood vaccination rates, worsening cardiovascular disease outcomes, fewer cancer screenings and deteriorating mental health – leading to greater excess mortality in years to come, with the working class and younger members of society carrying the heaviest burden. Keeping students out of school is a grave injustice. Keeping these measures in place until a vaccine is available will cause irreparable damage, with the underprivileged disproportionately harmed.

Instead of blanket lockdowns, they assert that "the most compassionate approach that balances the risks and benefits of reaching herd immunity, is to allow those who are at minimal risk of death to live their lives normally to build up immunity to the virus through natural infection, while better protecting those who are at highest risk. We call this Focused Protection."

Focused Protection as a policy would mean that there would be no need for lockdowns, and "those who are at minimal risk of death" (i.e., everyone but "the old and infirm") would be free "to live their lives normally"—and, we should add, to vote in person.[192]

October 8, 2020: Dr. Francis Collins, the head of the NIH, sends an email to Anthony Fauci and other senior staff of his agency.[193] (These emails were not publicly known until they were obtained in late December, 2021, through the Freedom of Information Act.) The content of the first email:

---

192 Great Barrington Declaration, https://gbdeclaration.org/.
193 For the backstory and actual emails see Phillip Magness, "Fauci, Emails, and Some Alleged Science," American Institute for Economic Research, December 19, 2021. https://www.aier.org/article/fauci-emails-and-some-alleged-science/.

Hi Tony and Cliff,

See https://gbdeclaration.org. This proposal from the three fringe epidemiologists…seems to be getting a lot of attention—and even a co-signature from Nobel Prize winner Mike Leavitt at Stanford. There needs to be a devastating and quick published take down of its premises. I don't see anything like that online yet—is it underway?

Francis

Fauci writes Collins back that evening that "I am pasting in below a piece from *Wired* that debunks this theory." (The article was by Matt Reynolds, called, "There is no 'scientific divide' over herd immunity," October 7, 2020.[194])

October 9, 2020: Collins writes another email to Fauci, touting a second takedown piece entitled "Focused Protection, Herd Immunity, and Other Deadly Delusions," by Gregg Gonsalves.[195]

October 14, 2020: In a *Washington Post* article Francis Collins says of the Great Barrington scientists, "This is a fringe component of epidemiology. This is not mainstream science. It's dangerous. It fits into the political views of certain parts of our confused political establishment…. I'm sure it will be an idea that someone can wrap themselves in as a justification for skipping wearing masks or social distancing and just doing whatever they damn well please."[196]

---

194 Matt Reynolds, "There is no 'scientific divide' over herd immunity," Wired, July 10, 2020. https://www.wired.co.uk/article/great-barrington-declaration-herd-immunity-scientific-divide.

195 Gregg Gonsalves, "Focused Protection, Herd Immunity, and Other Deadly Delusions," *The Nation*, October 8, 2020. https://www.thenation.com/article/society/covid-jacobin-herd-immunity/.

196 Joel Achenbach, "Proposal to hasten herd immunity to the coronavirus grabs White House attention but appalls top scientists," *Washington Post*, October 14, 2020. https://www.washingtonpost.com/health/covid-herd-immunity/2020/10/10/3910251c-0a60-11eb-859b-f9c27abe638d_story.html.

October 16, 2020: Fauci emails Deborah Birx, White House Corona Response Coordinator and friend of Fauci, noting that, "Over the past week I have come out very strongly against the 'Great Barrington Declaration'." The implication is that should be her response as well, even though it goes against President Trump's long-standing opposition to lockdowns and his early affirmations of herd immunity.

October 22, 2020: The three eminent epidemiologists of the Great Barrington Declaration publicly assert (using the CDC's own statistics) that "the COVID-19 lockdown strategy has led to more than 222,000 deaths, with the working class carrying the heaviest burden."[197] This includes not only suicides but deaths caused by shutting off life-saving medical tests and treatments.

The November election was in less than a month. The Great Barrington Declaration would affirm President Trump's original approach to the pandemic, repeated from February 2020 onward, that we should treat COVID more like the seasonal flu, avoid lockdowns, and try to achieve herd immunity while we wait for the development of the vaccines (a project which he energetically drove forward at "warp speed"). Big tech, the mainstream media, big pharma and its medical dependents, and as we've just seen, Francis Collins and Anthony Fauci all banded together—with the Democrat Party in chorus—to dismiss and disparage the Great Barrington Declaration and characterize the growing list of eminent doctors as fringe lunatics.

And so I repeat, not just Anthony Fauci but the Democrat Party must share the blame for the horrendous collateral damage of championing lockdowns. That's another two hundred thousand

---

197 Martin Kulldorff, Sunetra Gupta, and Jay Bhattacharya, "Our COVID-19 plan would minimize mortality and lockdown-induced collateral damage," USA Today, October 22, 2020. https://www.usatoday.com/story/opinion/todaysdebate/2020/10/22/covid-plan-would-minimize-mortality-lockdown-induced-damage-editorials-debates/3735800001/.

plus deaths to add to the half a million caused by withholding effective readily available drugs.

Now those who championed lockdowns have had to admit the terrible effects. The CDC revealed on June 11, 2021, that, "Compared with the rate in 2019, a 31 percent increase in the proportion of mental health–related emergency department (ED) visits occurred among adolescents aged 12–17 years in 2020." To be more exact, "In May 2020, during the COVID-19 pandemic, ED visits for suspected suicide attempts began to increase among adolescents aged 12–17 years, especially girls." The insistence on continued lockdowns took its toll the next year as well. "During February 21–March 20, 2021, suspected suicide attempt ED visits were 50.6% higher among girls aged 12–17 years than during the same period in 2019; among boys aged 12–17 years, suspected suicide attempt ED visits increased 3.7%."[198] That wasn't the only collateral damage. During lockdowns, drug overdose rose over 30 percent.[199] Domestic abuse calls rose immediately, in the first five weeks of the pandemic, up almost 10 percent.[200]

And witness another press release from the CDC on June 30, 2021, revealing that during January to June 2020, "Declines in breast cancer screening varied from 84% percent among Hispanic women to 98% among American Indian/Alaskan Native women." In addition, "Declines in cervical cancer screening varied from 82% among Black women to 92% among Asian Pacific Islander women." Finally, "In April [2020], the number of screening tests

---

198 Ellen Yard, Lakshmi Radhakrishnan, Michael F. Ballesteros, et al, "Emergency Department Visits for Suspected Suicide Attempts Among Persons Aged 12–25 Years Before and During the COVID-19 Pandemic — United States, January 2019–May 2021," *Morbidity and Mortality Weekly Report* 70, no. 24 (June 2021): 888-894. DOI: http://dx.doi.org/10.15585/mmwr.mm7024e1.

199 Julie Steenhuysen and Daniel Trotta, "U.S. drug overdose deaths rise 30% to record during pandemic," Reuters, July 14, 2021. https://www.reuters.com/world/us/us-drug-overdose-deaths-rise-30-record-during-pandemic-2021-07-14/.

200 Emily Leslie and Riley Wilson, "Sheltering in Place and Domestic Violence," National Commission on COVID-19 and Criminal Justice, August 2020. https://covid19.counciloncj.org/2020/08/18/domestic-violence/.

for breast cancer declined in metro (86%), urban (88%), and rural (89%) areas compared to the respective five-year averages. The decline for cervical cancer screening tests was 85% and 82% for metro and rural areas, respectively, and 77% for urban areas."[201] A May 17, 2021, study in the online journal *Frontiers in Oncology* reported that "cancer screening programs have been clearly interrupted since the onset of the COVID-19 disease. The anticipated outcomes include delayed diagnosis and marked increases in the numbers of avoidable cancer deaths."[202]

The Democrats were big on lockdowns; they took it as a point of political pride. Democrat governors were the most aggressive in using their executive powers to enforce lockdown mandates. And so, given all the harm we now know occurred because of lockdowns, the Democrats have to answer this question: *Was it worth it, just to beat Donald Trump?*

Oh, I almost forgot to add one more date to the timeline, January 2022. That's when Johns Hopkins University released a meta-analysis (that is, a kind of gathering of all the studies done on a particular topic) on the efficacy of lockdowns.[203] The results, bluntly stated, "Lockdowns have had little to no effect on COVID-19 mortality."[204] As they state in the Conclusion, "In the early stages of a pandemic, before the arrival of vaccines and new treatments, a society can respond in two ways: mandated behavioral changes or voluntary behavioral changes. Our study fails to

---

201 CDC Newsroom, "Sharp Declines in Breast and Cervical Cancer Screening:

Prolonged delays in cancer screening due to the COVID-19 pandemic threaten to increase existing health disparities," https://www.cdc.gov/media/releases/2021/p0630-cancer-screenings.html.

202 Ibrahim Alkatout, et al, "Has COVID-19 Affected Cancer Screening Programs? A Systematic Review," *Frontiers in Oncology*, May 17, 2021. https://www.ncbi.nlm.nih.gov/pmc/articles/PMC8165307/.

203 Jonas Herby, Lars Jonung, and Steve H. Hanke, "A Literature Review and Meta-Analysis of the Effects of Lockdowns on COVID-19 Mortality," January 2022. https://sites.krieger.jhu.edu/iae/files/2022/01/A-Literature-Review-and-Meta-Analysis-of-the-Effects-of-Lockdowns-on-COVID-19-Mortality.pdf.

204 Jonas Herby, Lars Jonung, and Steve H. Hanke, "A Literature Review and Meta-Analysis of the Effects of Lockdowns on COVID-19 Mortality," p. 2.

demonstrate significant positive effects of mandated behavioral changes (lockdowns)."[205]

So, not only were the lockdowns causing significant harm, they actually weren't doing anything to stop COVID anyway.

Harmful and useless.

I end with the very powerful words of this study that must never be forgotten precisely because lockdowns proved to have one significant "benefit," at least for certain people inclined toward totalitarianism: they allowed enormous political power to be exercised by people who were all too eager to use it.

> *The use of lockdowns is a unique feature of the COVID-19 pandemic. Lockdowns have not been used to such a large extent during any of the pandemics of the past century. However, lockdowns during the initial phase of the COVID-19 pandemic have had devastating effects. They have contributed to reducing economic activity, raising unemployment, reducing schooling, causing political unrest, contributing to domestic violence, and undermining liberal democracy. These costs to society must be compared to the benefits of lockdowns, which our meta-analysis has shown are marginal at best. Such a standard benefit-cost calculation leads to a strong conclusion: lockdowns should be rejected out of hand as a pandemic policy instrument.[206]*

205 Jonas Herby, Lars Jonung, and Steve H. Hanke, "A Literature Review and Meta-Analysis of the Effects of Lockdowns on COVID-19 Mortality," p. 43.

206 Jonas Herby, Lars Jonung, and Steve H. Hanke, "A Literature Review and Meta-Analysis of the Effects of Lockdowns on COVID-19 Mortality," p. 43.

CHAPTER 7   *TIME* (BOMB) ARTICLE

We move now from the COVID Conspiracy to a political conspiracy that worked at the same time to ensure the election was rigged against Trump. We know about this conspiracy because the conspirators admitted it in an article in *Time*.

When Molly Ball's article appeared in *Time* on February 4, 2021, it caused a huge shock of surprise among those who believed that there had been a deep state, multipronged, massive effort to orchestrate the election of Joe Biden behind the scenes. Why? Because she—a member of the mainstream media and Democrat supporter—proudly revealed in her rather brash article, "The Secret History of the Shadow Campaign That Saved the 2020 Election," that there actually had been a deep state, multipronged, massive effort to orchestrate the election of Joe Biden behind the scenes.[207]

If you haven't read this article, you need to get it immediately and read it twice. It's that important—not just because it tells you about the "Shadow Campaign" that worked behind the scenes, but also because you'll realize that there will be even greater shadow campaigns in the 2022 and 2024 elections.

The response from the Right upon reading this Time Bomb article was, "What? After calling us tin-hat, irrational conspiracy

---

207 Molly Ball, "The Secret History of the Shadow Campaign That Saved the 2020 Election," *Time*, February 4, 2021. https://time.com/5936036/secret-2020-election-campaign/.

theorists for saying this very thing for the last half year, *you have the gall to proudly admit it*!"

Yes.

In her words, "There was a conspiracy unfolding behind the scenes" in the year leading up to the election of 2020 that was "the result of an informal alliance between left-wing activists and business titans," the architect of which was Michael Podhorzer (progressive activist and long-time senior adviser to the president of the AFL-CIO). The conspirators now "want the secret history of the 2020 election told, even though it sounds like a paranoid fever dream—a well-funded cabal of powerful people, ranging across industries and ideologies, working together behind the scenes *to influence perceptions, change rules and laws, steer media coverage and control the flow of information*."

Many conservative commentators have pointed to this article as proof-positive that the election was rigged. But then they tend to drop it for the next hot-button issue popping up in the never-ending political turmoil that churns up the media cycle.

I think we really need to slow down and examine this article because it gives us real insight into two things: how the election was stolen in 2020, and how it might be stolen in 2022 and 2024. This deeper examination, using what we've learned in the previous chapters, will prepare us to look at the details of the 2020 election itself in the next chapter.

IF THERE HAD BEEN NO SHADOW CONSPIRACY...

Molly Ball, writing on behalf of the conspiratorial cabal, claims that the aim of the "extraordinary shadow effort" was "dedicated not to winning the vote but to ensuring it would be free and fair, credible and uncorrupted." It was not, she assures readers, attempting "to stop…a Trump victory." The conspirators "were not rigging the election; they were fortifying it."

The problem with that claim is that, by their own admission, their "work touched every aspect of the election." And they really mean *every* aspect. When you read through what they admit to doing, it brings us back to the obvious point: *if* they had not done these things, *then* Trump would have won. See for yourself what the conspirators claim to have done:

> *They got states to change voting systems and laws and helped secure hundreds of millions in public and private funding. They fended off voter-suppression lawsuits, recruited armies of poll workers and got millions of people to vote by mail for the first time. They successfully pressured social media companies to take a harder line against disinformation and used data-driven strategies to fight viral smears. They executed national public-awareness campaigns that helped Americans understand how the vote count would unfold over days or weeks, preventing Trump's conspiracy theories and false claims of victory from getting more traction. After Election Day, they monitored every pressure point to ensure that Trump could not overturn the result.*

We're going to go into each of these activities in some detail, but just picking out one is sufficient to realize that the actual aim of the conspirators was the election of Joe Biden, not a free and fair election: *getting states to change voting systems and laws so that millions of people would vote by mail rather than in person.*

As we've noted already, Republicans are far more inclined to vote in person, while Democrats are more inclined to vote by mail, something that was known in advance of the 2020 election.

Changing existing voting laws leading up to the election (aided by COVID) helped to shift the results through immensely increased absentee and mail-in voting that greatly increased the Democrat vote. In fact, we know that the "hundreds of millions in public and private funding" was spent almost completely on getting out the *Democrat* vote.[208] *That* was the aim of the shadow conspiracy—or better, one of its main strategies to beat Trump.

Other aspects of the conspiracy make sense in terms of this strategy. Because voting by mail heavily favors Democrats, Democrats considered any laws restricting mail-in voting to be a kind of "voter suppression," and so the conspirators fought to change them. Any legal challenges by Republicans to the changes were then considered "voter suppression lawsuits." Big tech then did its part by censoring any information that brought up questions about the integrity of mail-in voting, labeling it "disinformation."

Since Republicans tended to vote on election day (65 percent, as it turned out, in 2020), and Democrats voted by mail (65 percent in 2020), then it would appear Donald Trump won on election day. Counting all those extra Democrat mail-in votes could take "days or weeks" after election day, so there had to be "national public-awareness campaigns" to convince people that November 3rd was not really election day (therefore, Trump couldn't claim victory that night, as presidential victors almost invariably have done).

If that's all there were to it, then perhaps Republicans wouldn't have much they could object to, except that they were out-maneuvered strategically by Democrats. For whatever reason, Democrats like to vote by mail; increasing the way they like to vote caused more Democrats to vote, and they voted for Biden. Biden won. All those Democrat votes were entirely legitimate. They just came through the mail!

---

208 Mollie Hemingway, "Facts about Zuck Bucks: How he helped swing the electorate in 2020," *New York Post*, October 13, 2021. https://nypost.com/2021/10/13/how-mark-zuckerberg-helped-swing-the-electorate-in-the-2020-election/.

That's the tone of Molly Ball's article. She presents Trump and his supporters as sore losers who simply don't like it when more Democrats vote. They tried to deprive Democrat voters of expanded opportunities, thereby fighting against democracy itself, where every vote should count whether it's done in person or through the mail. The choice of kinds of voting is really no different than, say, buying a shirt at a store in person, or ordering one online and getting it through the mail. What's the problem?

The problem was really "President Trump [who] spent months insisting that mail ballots were a Democratic plot and the election would be rigged," and he therefore wouldn't accept the election as free and fair. Trump's tyrannical temper tantrum threatened democracy itself, and the brave conspirators were rushing in to save our country.

That's the picture Molly Ball paints. Democrats were innocently changing unjust voting restrictions in states to allow much greater mail-in voting because of COVID and to get out more people to vote, and Donald Trump was, for no reason, claiming that mail-in ballots would invite widespread fraud on the part of the Democrat party and therefore undermine the integrity of the election.

The obvious question should be this: Are absentee and mail-in ballots far more subject to fraud than in-person voting? If so, then Trump's fear of fraud was entirely justified. Given what we've seen in Chapter 3, we know that Trump was right. He wasn't throwing a temper tantrum; he was taking a clear-eyed view of history and therefore knew exactly what the conspirators were up to.

ABSENTEE AND MAIL-IN BALLOT FRAUD... TRUMP WAS RIGHT

Now that we've worked through a good amount of the history of voter fraud in Chapter 3, we know that absentee and mail-in balloting are rife with fraud. Let's begin with a bit of clarification. Technically speaking, mail-in ballots are not the same as absentee ballots.

Absentee ballots are used for people who cannot make it to their assigned polling place on election day (e.g., military personnel, college students living out of state, the infirm in nursing homes), and therefore are given specific permission, upon request to the state of their residency, to vote using an absentee ballot. A ballot is then mailed to them, and they return the completed ballot (of course) by mail.

Mail-in ballots are just that, ballots that anyone can send through the mail, thereby avoiding having to vote in person. For the 2020 elections, nine states (Vermont, Nevada, California, New Jersey, Colorado, Hawaii, Utah, Washington, Oregon) and Washington, DC, sent out ballots automatically to all voters on the registration rolls (living, dead, or moved). Joe Biden won all those states but Utah.

Technically speaking, absentee voting is much stricter than mail-in voting; or, to put it the other way, mail-in balloting is much more lax, and hence even more subject to fraud, than absentee voting. But, due to both COVID and the shadow conspirators' efforts to expand mail-in voting, thirty-five states smeared the difference between the two by allowing even the *fear* of COVID to count as a legitimate excuse to request an absentee ballot. So, in the 2020 election, the two became much the same thing.

Given all that, the point is that *both* are historically subject to fraud, as we've found in Chapter 3. Democrats have a long history of abusing them, all the way back to the 1864 presidential election where Republicans discovered widespread fraud in regard to the absentee soldier vote, involving thousands of forged registration papers, as well as numerous sick, disabled, and dead soldiers illegally registered.

And remember the long list of fraud using absentee ballots I listed in that chapter—filling out of absentee ballots for people in nursing homes who had no idea what was happening, absentee ballots being cast by fictional and dead voters, or by non-citizens. It's no wonder (as I mentioned before) that Mary Frances Berry, an African American by the way, remarked that "absentee ballots have proven particularly susceptible to vote buying because campaign workers collaborate with county clerks and voting registrars to accept ballots signed and submitted in bulk." And don't forget historian James Merriner's words, written in 2004, in regard to corruption in Democrat-dominated Chicago, "The favored techniques of fraud now occur not in the polling place but in manipulations of absentee voting."

Let's add to what we've already heard in Chapter 3, historian Tracy Campbell's assessment that "absentee-ballot fraud" is a "modern and effective device for fraud, especially in rural counties," and that vote buyers "prefer absentee ballots" because they "can mark the ballots themselves after payment, making certain that the bought voter voted correctly."[209] Absentee ballot fraud isn't just a big-city, Chicago, or New York thing.

There was also the famous Miami mayor's race in 1997, pitting Republican Joe Carollo against Democrat Xavier Suarez. Interestingly, Democrat candidate Suarez won 61 percent of the absentee vote. The absentee vote was 11 percent, which was well over twice its normal level, with one district registering 25 percent of its votes in absentees. The reason? As it was soon discovered, massive voter fraud on the part of Democrat Suarez. The cause of the rise in fraud through absentee ballots should sound somewhat familiar. As Tracy Campbell reports,

---

209 Tracy Campbell, *Deliver the Vote*, p. 281.

In an attempt to accommodate Florida's elderly pop-
ulation, the state legislature had written some of the
most lax absentee-ballot regulations in the nation, reg-
ulations that allowed great latitude to unscrupulous
brokers [of votes]. Brokers could call the elections office
and order ballots, so long as they could provide names,
address, and Social Security numbers of those suppos-
edly needing a ballot. When the ballots arrived, all the
broker needed to do was mark the ballot, sign it as a
witness, and send it back.[210]

In this instance, the fraud was detected and prosecuted. "In February 1998, a grand jury found that absentee-ballot brokers were essentially 'thieves who steal democracy,' and concluded that fraud had 'tainted' the election results."[211] Absentee ballots make it simple to steal elections, a problem which, obviously, could only be made far worse by mail-in ballots, and even worse yet by lax mail-in ballot regulations such as the Democrats successfully pushed to get in place during COVID.

Perhaps for this very reason, absentee balloting grew ever more popular as the 20th century drew to a close and the 21st began. Campbell quotes an important study of this trend conducted by Caltech and MIT: "The convenience that on-demand absentees produce is bought at a significant cost to the real and perceived integrity of the voting process."[212] Summing up his research on the growing trend of absentee voting—and his book was written fifteen years before the 2020 election—Campbell concludes, "In terms of effectiveness, absentee ballots remain the easiest way of buying votes in advance, or swinging them after the results are in,

---

210 Tracy Campbell, *Deliver the Vote*, pp. 286-288.
211 Tracy Campbell, *Deliver the Vote*, p. 289.
212 Tracy Campbell, *Deliver the Vote*, p. 291.

whichever way works."[213] Again, whatever is true with absentee ballots is a hundred times more so with mail-ins.

I use Campbell's assessment of absentee voting for two reasons: first, he's not a fan of the Republican Party, as his treatment of the Bush-Gore election makes clear, and two, it was written a decade and a half *before* the 2020 election (so we know that the problems with widespread absentee ballot fraud were real and known for a good fifteen to twenty years before Trump and Biden faced off).

So, as it turns out, given the history of Democrat Party fraud in regard to absentee ballots alone, Trump was rightly suspicious. Add to that the immense loosening of restrictions in mail-in ballots, and he would have been a fool not to object and not to have litigated in advance to do everything he could to stop the Democrat campaign from loosening up election rules that would allow massive absentee and mail-in voting.

We'll see what Democrats actually did in the 2020 election in the next chapter, but let's stick with Ball's account of the shadow campaign.

THE EARLY MORNING BLUE TSUNAMI

As noted above, there was another, related aspect of the shadow campaign's efforts to transform the elections by drastically increasing the absentee and mail-in vote. Of course, people could mail in their votes early, but the questions is not when they mail them, but when they are actually counted. If a state's election laws demand that the counting not begin until election day, and there's a really big stack of mail-in ballots, then "the vote count would unfold over days or weeks" before a winner could be declared. Voters had to understand that, so the Democrats said. And since Democrats

---

213 Tracy Campbell, *Deliver the Vote*, p. 333.

were expected to be much, much more likely to use mail-in voting, and Republicans much more likely to vote in person, political pundits and voters alike had to accept the fact that, although it might appear that Trump won on November 3rd, the Democrat mail-in votes could (or would) cause a "blue shift," and swing the election to give a late victory to Biden as the mail-in votes were counted in the days and weeks after November 3rd.

I emphasize "days and weeks" because that makes some sense if there are a big stack of entirely legitimate mail-in votes to be counted (just as it always takes time after every election day to count in all the absentee votes from the military).

That's the message that was pushed by the shadow conspirators and echoed by the mainstream media and big tech. But, as with the history of absentee voting, we know from the history of voter fraud in regard to the "early morning vote" that a sudden early morning surge in votes is a sure sign of election stealing. Remember how Mayor Daley magically made all those votes appear in the wee hours of the morning so that Kennedy could beat Nixon? Remember also that this trick—one of the oldest tricks in voter fraud—is necessary because the fraudster has to provide just enough votes to beat his opponent but not so many as to make the fraud obvious. That's how he gets that early morning, surprise victory.

Now if what Molly Ball says is correct, then we would expect Joe Biden's victory to have been slowly won in the days and weeks after the election as the mail-in votes gradually shifted the victory from Trump to Biden, a kind of slow-rising Blue Tide. We would *not* expect a Blue Tsunami of votes all at once in the early morning of November 4th, just enough to surpass Trump's November 3rd election day victory. The latter would be a sure sign of foul play. As we'll see in the next chapter, the Blue Tsunami was a carefully timed surge of votes in key states, giving Biden the needed votes to surpass Trump and declare victory as the sun came up.

But even within Ball's article, we can see that something was deeply suspicious. The so-called architect of the shadow conspiracy, Michael Podhorzer, warned his co-conspirators and fellow activists that "polls were underestimating Trump's support," so that they really hadn't "comprehended how much better Trump was likely to do on Election Day."

The result was that "election night began with many Democrats despairing. Trump was running ahead of pre-election polling, winning Florida, Ohio and Texas easily and keeping Michigan, Wisconsin and Pennsylvania too close to call." By 11:00 p.m., his fellow Democrats were "freaking out." Podhorzer was, by contrast, "unperturbed," because "he could tell that as long as all the votes were counted, Trump would lose."

Really? That would mean that Podhorzer would have to know that the mail-in votes counted in the days after the election would indeed be enough to overcome Trump's surprisingly strong support. How strong? Trump was on his way to collecting more popular votes than any other president in history, almost seventy-five million! That would mean that Biden would have to surpass the all-time record, and Biden was an exceedingly weak candidate.

Yet, as Ball reports, Podhorzer remained strangely calm. Did Podhorzer know that there would be a Blue Tsunami surge of Biden votes within a few hours? Or more exactly, like Mayor Daley, did he know that "the machine" could provide enough votes to win, no matter how many were needed?

We'll try to answer this question in the next chapter. Suffice it to say here that the history of voter fraud in America leads us to be rightly suspicious of absentee and mail-in voting, as well as early morning election surges. That much could be known far in advance of the election.

THE DEMOCRAT PARTY AND BIG TECH DISINFORMATION CAMPAIGN

But that accurate historical information about voter fraud would obviously not benefit the Democrat Party, and Trump was certainly aware of the dangers of voter fraud and not shy about making his worries known.

According to Molly Ball, the task facing the shadow conspirators was battling such *disinformation*. First of all, they needed to tell Americans that, regardless of what Trump or anyone else was saying, "mail-in votes weren't susceptible to fraud…." As we now know, historically that's simply a *false statement*.

For the conspirators, the actual, historical truth had to be treated like disinformation and censored, and so they had to push "social media platforms to take a harder line…." That meant drawing Facebook's Mark Zuckerberg and Twitter's Jack Dorsey "and others" into the shadow conspiracy, along with Google, to censor the historically correct information that absentee and mail-in voting are highly subject to fraud and have been since their inception.

And as we've just seen, an important thing to censor was the notion that there was something fishy about not concluding the election *on* election night. The successful push for drastically increasing mail-in voting meant that it would take some time beyond November 3rd to count the votes. Big tech rose to the challenge. As Ball notes, the efforts of "Twitter, Facebook, Instagram and Tik Tok" were successful: "The percentage of the public that didn't expect to know the winner on election night gradually rose until by late October, it was over 70%." But would they then be ready for Biden to suddenly find enough votes to win in the early morning hours of November 4th?

But that's not all big tech did for the Democrat Party—and *this point cannot be emphasized enough*. Big tech engaged in changing the minds of its users, not just by purposely hiding pro-conservative views, but by psychologically nudging people toward the Democrat Party. As Mollie Hemingway reports in her *Rigged: How the Media, Big Tech, and the Democrats Seized Our Elections*, this was proven by psychologist Robert Epstein, the former editor in chief of *Psychology Today*. Dr. Epstein is a very honest and brave liberal with a PhD from Harvard who did the research and dared to publish the results. He showed that in the 2016 election Google's purposeful bending of search results was biased toward Hillary Clinton, so much so that he estimated it brought Hillary an additional 2.6 million votes. So much for her bragging point about her big win of popular vote. When Epstein monitored Google in 2020, it found the same bias toward the Democrat cause could easily have shifted over six million votes to Biden.[214] Take big tech's concerted manipulation away, and Trump would have won.

CALLING ALL RIOTERS

Another very suspicious aspect of the shadow conspiracy was the use made of rioters. Ball begins her article by noting that on the day after the November 3rd election, "a weird thing happened." Riots did not break out. "The nation was braced for chaos. Liberal groups had vowed to take to the streets, planning hundreds of protests across the country. Right-wing militias were girding for battle. In a poll before Election Day, 75% of Americans voiced concern about violence. Instead, an eerie quiet descended."

It wasn't "Right-wing" groups that worried Americans but the real threats by Antifa, Black Lives Matter, and other "Liberal groups" that if Trump won, then the riots on November 4th would be far more destructive than those that tore apart so many cities in

---

214 Mollie Hemingway, *Rigged: How the Media, Big Tech, and the Democrats Seized Our Elections* (Washington, D.C: Regnery, 2021), pp. 197-198.

2020.[215] In short, these groups were engaged in real *voter intimidation*, one of the main tools of Democrats after the Civil War.

These riots, which the Democrat Party refused to disown, and the media consistently mischaracterized as peaceful, came in handy as part of the strategy to rig the election against Trump: if Trump wins, there will be nonstop rioting for 2021 and beyond. As with Democrats threatening southern Blacks if they voted for Republicans—something that, through cultural intimidation, Democrats still do to any Blacks thinking of voting Republican—the threat of violence was real.

As Ball reports, "Activists began preparing to reprise the demonstrations if Trump tried to steal the election." *Trump actually winning the election, fair and square, was not considered a real possibility by the activists.* If he won, it could only be that he stole the election. But the same was true for the shadow conspirators: Trump actually winning was not considered a possibility. In Ball's words, they considered the only real options to be two: "Trump losing and refusing to concede, and Trump winning the Electoral College (despite losing the popular vote) by corrupting the voting process in key states." In their eyes, Trump couldn't possibly win, so if he did, the violent rioting was the proper response, one that the conspirators not only encouraged but facilitated through networking.

Rioters were a big threat. "More than 150 liberal groups, from the Women's March to the Sierra Club to Color of Change, from Democrats.com to the Democratic Socialists of America, joined the 'Protect the Results' coalition," which certainly also included Antifa and Black Lives Matter. They set up in advance "400 planned post-election demonstrations, to be activated via text message as soon as Nov. 4." To stop the coup they feared, the Left was ready to flood the streets.

---

215 See, for example, Katy Grimes, "BLM, Antifa, Far Left Promise Rioting if Trump Wins," *California Globe*, October 23, 2020. https://californiaglobe.com/articles/blm-antifa-far-left-promise-rioting-if-trump-wins/.

This fear, interestingly enough, allowed for a strange alliance between Podhorzer's AFL-CIO and the Chamber of Commerce—labor and business. Why? Because "the business community" was "anxious…about how the election and its aftermath might unfold. The summer's racial justice protests had sent a signal to business owners too; the potential for economy-disrupting civil disorder." They understood the threat very clearly: if Trump wins, we'll burn your businesses down again.

But a funny thing happened; there were no riots when the sun rose on November 4, 2020. The needed votes for Biden had miraculously appeared overnight. And so protestors had nothing to protest. "Activists reoriented the Protect the Results protests toward a weekend of celebration" calculated to affirm Biden's amazing early-morning victory and show the American people that the great tide of Democrat support had spoken and legitimized the election.

But, beneath the revelry was the warning: *if* Trump, the Republicans, Congress, the Supreme Court, or Trump supporters tried to contest the Democrat win, the revelry would turn back into riot.

AND THEN JANUARY 6TH HAPPENED

Molly Ball confides that the last obstacle the shadow campaign had was the affirmation of the electoral votes by Congress on January 6th, 2021. Liberal activists stayed away, we are told, and let Trump's rally proceed unimpeded by counterprotests. Somehow, the peaceful protest on January 6th turned into a riot at the Capitol, which only further cemented Biden's victory, a perfect ending to their strategy.

One wonders if the shadow conspiracy somehow knew that would happen.

CHAPTER 8

THE 2020 WIN BY ALL MEANS ELECTION

On January 6, 2021, tens of thousands of Trump supporters came to Washington, DC, to protest against what they sincerely believed . was a stolen election. That protest should have been—and was meant to be—a peaceful protest, fully in conformity with our constitutional "right of the people peaceably to assemble, and to petition the Government for a redress of grievances." If the vote was stolen, they had a right to be angry.

Again, I am not defending the breach of the Capitol that occurred that day, and we're going to spend the next chapter looking at January 6th again in more detail to figure out exactly what happened. But in this chapter, we need to ask the question: Was their anger justified? Did they have good reason to believe that the election had indeed been stolen? As you'll see, the work we've done so far in this book will help us to answer that question.

GOOD REASONS TO BE SUSPICIOUS OF THE DEMOCRATS FROM THE HISTORY OF PRESIDENTIAL ELECTIONS

As we've seen, Democrats actually have a long history of winning presidential elections by voter fraud, suppression, and intimidation. Again, the first verified voter fraud in a presidential election was perpetrated by Democrat Andrew Jackson who shipped in voters from one state to another to vote using the names of the dead. Democrat James Polk won the 1844 presidential election thanks to the corruption of Tammany Hall (not to mention the fact that Black Americans, as slaves, couldn't vote at all). Democrat James Buchanan won in 1856 for the same reasons. Democrat Grover Cleveland barely won the 1884 election, pulling off a victory through the combination of New York City's fraudulent immigrant vote and the suppression of the Black Republican vote in the Democrat Jim Crow South. And, of course, we have the victory of Democrat John Kennedy in 1960, thanks to the corruption of Daley's Chicago political machine and the typical corruption in LBJ's Texas.

We also don't want to forget the number of presidential elections where Democrats tried to win by massive fraud but were unsuccessful. This happened in both the first and second elections of Republican Abraham Lincoln, as well as in the famous Hayes-Tilden race (where Democrats won the popular vote by suppression of the Black Republican vote but not the electoral college vote).

So, one thing we know: it would not be historically out of character for the Democrats to resort to election fraud and voter suppression and intimidation in the 2020 presidential election. But we have more to learn from history, as the previous chapters have shown.

THE HISTORY OF ELECTION-STEALING TACTICS

It's important to go over the kinds of tactics that the Democrats have used historically to steal elections because it sets a pattern of behavior that would alert us to suspicious activities in the 2020 election. Let's recall what we've learned.

To repeat, Andrew Jackson shipped in out of state voters, having them cast ballots in the name of the dead. For decades after the Civil War, Democrats intimidated freed Black Americans with violence if they dared to vote Republican, working literally for the extinction of Black Republicans (and they still are, through intimidation). Post-Civil War Democrats also used the poll tax for the same reason, charging Black Americans if they tried to vote Republican. After the Civil War, Democrats realized that election oversight institutions also "needed to be reconfigured along the lines of Democratic preferences" to ensure that they controlled the vote in the South. Ballot boxes were stuffed in the Solid South and in the northern big-city political machines. Democrats have used almost every way imaginable to steal elections: padding the voter roles with illegal voters, using paid repeat voters, shuttling out the inmate vote, bribing vagrants to vote, churning out countless brand-new citizens from immigrant naturalization scams, driving out poll watchers, voting under fictitious names, corrupting the absentee voting system in every way imaginable, chain voting, discarding Republican votes, four-legged voting, spoiling Republican ballots through the short-pencil technique, "helping" residents of nursing homes to vote, finding just enough votes in the wee hours of the morning to win, and discovering yet-to-be counted boxes of votes in the days after the election. I urge you to read Chapter 3 again, so the long history of voter fraud is fresh in your mind.

We also recall the signs that voter fraud has occurred or will occur. When the voter turnout in a particular area exceeds the actual number of eligible voters or is unusually high, that's suspicious. When one party refuses to clear the voting rolls of non-resident and deceased voters, that's suspicious. When one political party is intensely interested in a fast-track naturalization process for immigrants who just happen to always vote for that party, that's suspicious. When one party controls the local and state offices that do the vote counting, that's suspicious. When one party drives away election inspectors and poll watchers of the other party, that's suspicious. When one party relies heavily on the absentee vote, that's suspicious. When one party is an avid opponent of voter ID laws that would stop voting under fictitious names, dead and non-resident voting, repeat voting, and non-citizen voting, that's suspicious. When a party finds that it just happens to have the right number of votes to win an election, something they discover very early in the morning after their political opponent's votes have been counted last night, that's suspicious. When a box of uncounted votes—just enough to win the election—is suddenly discovered after the election or arrives in the middle of the night, that's suspicious. When officials from one party are found running ballots through machines multiple times, that's suspicious. When completed ballots are submitted in bulk by party operatives, that's suspicious. As we know from Chapter 3, the Democrats have used all these tactics to win elections.

Why wouldn't we be suspicious in 2020 if we see history repeating itself? And why shouldn't we be very worried about such tactics being used in the 2022 and 2024 elections?

Before getting into our analysis, I need to make everyone aware of a new way of stealing elections, one that has been almost entirely overlooked (in part, because the more obvious ways of stealing elections were so evident).

When computers entered into the election process, it opened up a way of stealing elections from inside that is almost indetectable—and that's why it's used. It shouldn't surprise us, given how sophisticated computer programming has become, that it's not difficult to set up a computer program to add needed votes—just enough votes, not too many, not too few—as the election unfolds, updating its formula in response to live updates of the vote count.

Such a program, since it's connected to outside sources, can update manufactured ballot images to cover the scam. Former state senator from Michigan Patrick Colbeck offers an in-depth analysis that everyone concerned with election integrity *needs* to read.[216] It's extremely hard to detect precisely because it's designed to remain hidden (like, for example, the algorithms that Google embeds to manipulate search results), and so it's not the kind of fraud that people are generally looking for.

Pat Colbeck believes that signs of this new kind of fraud were indeed detectable in the Michigan election, but the reasoning is so technical that I'm going to leave it aside in our assessment of fraud in this chapter—and, we have enough to show that the election was stolen without it. But I am very sure that, even if it wasn't used in the 2020 election, this way of stealing elections is the way of the future (and by future, I mean 2022 and 2024).

Let's begin our analysis of the 2020 election by looking at Biden's suspiciously big and strange victory.

THE SUSPICIOUSLY BIG AND STRANGE BIDEN VICTORY

Again, Joe Biden didn't just allegedly beat Trump by a few extra votes in tight state races. He won the popular vote by over seven million votes, gathering a total of about eighty-one million votes to Trump's seventy-four million.

We need to understand how extraordinary these 2020 popular vote totals are.[217] Prior to the 2020 election, the greatest number of popular votes for a president in American history was Barack Obama's first-term win with 69.5 million votes. In 2020, Donald

---

216 Patrick Colbeck, "Election Control System: Did 2020 Election Get an ECO Boost?" Let's Fix Stuff, September 29, 2021. https://letsfixstuff.org/2021/09/election-control-system-did-2020-election-get-an-eco-boost/.

217 For most of the statistics in this chapter, I've used the very helpful Atlas of U.S. Presidential Elections site: https://uselectionatlas.org.

Trump beat Obama's record, getting over 4.5 million *more* votes than Obama did in 2008. Yet, even though Trump set a new popular vote record, he still lost the election to Biden who managed to beat Obama's record by well over 11.5 million votes—a 16.5 percent increase in the popular vote! Because Joe Biden's popular vote was so surprisingly large, it easily translated into an electoral college victory, 306 to 232.

But that unprecedented increase in the popular vote is a clear warning sign, given the actual nature of the 2020 presidential election. Donald Trump was a hugely popular candidate with his base, and he was very active in campaigning for office (although hugely and conveniently hampered by COVID). It paid off handsomely when Trump broke the all-time record of the popular vote, something that was evidently very startling to Democrats as the numbers rolled in on election night. Joe Biden was about as lackluster and unpopular a candidate as the Democrats could bring forth, a man who used the COVID-19 pandemic to avoid appearing in public at all, yet he shattered the all-time popular vote record set by Trump in the very same election.

Voters were right to think that something was fishy. Could that many people *really* have voted for Joe Biden? Was the barely functional Biden really more glamorous than John Kennedy? More charismatic than Bill Clinton or Obama?

In regard to the percentage of the vote won in each state, Biden beat Obama's vote in only twelve states: Alaska, Arizona, California, Colorado, Georgia, Maryland, Massachusetts, New Jersey, Texas, Utah, Virginia, and Washington (three of which Biden lost to Trump: Alaska, Texas, and Utah). So, somehow Biden had to make up a lot of votes to have beaten Obama's record by so much.

That's not all. Statisticians love to note patterns in elections, and not just because they are interesting. Long-standing patterns are reliable predictors of elections. A single exception, or anomaly, in a long-standing pattern is a little red flag. Multiple exceptions are a big red flag that something really abnormal and suspicious has occurred.

When something that violates the usual patterns occurs, it's a clue. The exceptions (the *effects*) are signs of what *caused* the exceptions.

Because we know the expected patterns, and what might cause them to be violated, that allows us to make predictions; "What *effects* would you expect to see *if*...."

I'm going to fill in the "if."

What *effects* would you expect to see *if* Democrats, caught by surprise with the election of Donald Trump in 2016, were determined to win the 2020 presidential election by the most efficient means possible, both in terms of money and time?

The most efficient way to do that would be drop big piles of "extra" votes in a few, strategically important cities and neglect everywhere else. How big? Big enough to win the cities, and hence the state's electoral votes, and to win the overall popular vote as well.

If that's what happened, what effects would we expect to see, especially if Donald Trump was a very popular candidate?

You'd expect to see multiple signs conforming to long-standing historical patterns, all pointing to a Trump victory, even though Biden won. Why? Because when you drop enormous numbers of votes in only a few places, rather than win the election fair and square, you disregard the larger set of normal patterns so they still point to the legitimate winner.

Remember that Donald Trump won more popular votes than any presidential candidate in American history, beating Obama's record by 4.5 million votes. He increased his own 2020 popular vote tally from 2016 by over 11 million votes. In all American history there has been only *one* other president who increased the number of votes when he ran for a second term but lost anyway—

Grover Cleveland in 1888. (And Trump increased his vote by 17.8 percent, while Cleveland's only went up by 12.6 percent.) Even more, there have been a total of seventeen presidents who have been elected twice (as opposed to two-term presidents who came into office because of the death of a president rather than being elected twice). Trump increased his popular vote by a greater percentage than half of them.

The overwhelming pattern points to a Trump victory. If you knew all those statistics about Trump's popular vote in 2020 but didn't know that he'd lost, you would predict that he'd be the winner. If you then found out that Biden won, then you'd expect he'd have to do it by some kind of wildly improbable increase in votes that caused suspicious violations of deeply set historical patterns.

And so he did, and not only the ones I've just mentioned. There were other wildly improbable exceptions, such as what happened with the famous bellwether counties. Of the over three thousand counties in the US, there are a handful called bellwether counties, so called because they provide statistically reliable indications of who will be elected president.

From 1980–2016 (from Reagan's first term forward) there were nineteen counties that voted for the presidential winner every time, whether it was a Republican or Democrat. One of these counties, Ottawa County (OH), backed every presidential winner from 1964 onward (i.e., from Lyndon Johnson). Valencia County (NM) has done even better, correctly picking the winner since 1952, Dwight Eisenhower's first term. Trump won a whopping eighteen of the nineteen bellwether counties, including Ottawa and Valencia.

Again, if you didn't know the actual outcome of the election, you would predict that Trump would be the winner in 2020. If you found out that Biden somehow won, then you'd be looking for an explanation.

How could Biden win when Trump won eighteen of the nineteen bellwether counties? The answer is simple. Bellwether counties are spread all over the US map. The Democrat plan was to dump enormous piles of votes in a few key cities, and that strategy neglected all those far-flung counties, so that they continued to show the pattern of the true winner of the election.

There are also bellwether states. Ohio has chosen the presidential winner every time since 1896, with two exceptions: it chose Dewey in 1944 and Nixon in 1960. Since we know that Nixon lost to Kennedy because of the Daley machine in Chicago, then it's only been wrong once in 124 years. Florida has picked the presidential winner since 1928, also with two exceptions: it chose Nixon in 1960, and Bush in 1992. Again, since the election was stolen in 1960, Florida has only been wrong once. That, by the way, is confirmation of the importance of the pattern: a stolen election violated the bellwether status of both states.

Well, Trump won both Ohio and Florida in 2016 and 2020. Again, if you knew that and nothing else, you'd predict he'd win the presidency in 2020. If you added all the other predictive patterns we've just been over, then you'd bet all your money on a Trump victory. But Biden won the presidency without winning either state.

What would explain that? Again, that's exactly what you would expect if the Democrats won by dumping an enormous number of ballots in a few key cities in other states. The long-established pattern of Ohio and Florida would remain intact, still indicating the real winner.

We'll add to this another suspicious record set by Biden. Biden set the all-time presidential vote record with eighty-one million votes. He did it even though he beat Obama's record of the *lowest* number of counties won by a victor in the presidential election. Obama had the previous records of winning elections by winning the *fewest* number of counties. In 2008, he set the record by winning only 875 counties (28 percent of the total number of counties). Obama then beat his own record in 2012, winning with a new record low of 689 counties (22 percent). Biden smashed both records by winning with only 509 counties (16.7 percent).

Again, this makes sense if the Democrat strategy was to dump an enormous load of ballots in a few key states, in fact, a few key cities in those states. He'd win in the few key cities, even while neglecting even more of the nation's counties.

Violating one of the long-standing historical patterns in a presidential election is, as I said, a little red flag. Violating multiple patterns is a big red flag. In order to understand this even more clearly, we need to look at the actual vote dumping strategy that caused these anomalies.

THE STRATEGIC STATES DEMOCRATS HAD TO WIN

To understand the Democrats' strategy in the 2020 election, we need to look at the popular vote margins of the 2016 election in particularly important states.

In 2016 Trump ended up with 304 electoral votes to Clinton's 227 (even though he didn't win the popular vote). His victory came from winning key states: Arizona by 91,234 (thereby receiving eleven electoral votes); Michigan by 10,704 (sixteen electoral votes); Pennsylvania by 44,292 (twenty electoral votes); Wisconsin by 22,748 (ten electoral votes); and Georgia by 211,141 (sixteen electoral votes).

The Democrats understood very clearly that they needed to flip these states in order to beat Trump in 2020. If Trump won them all, he would have the presidency. (Or, to put another way, if Trump had won them in 2020, he would have had the electoral vote, 304 to Biden's 234.)

That defined the Democrats' strategy and of course the greater shadow conspiracy: throw *everything* into winning these key states, or more exactly, the key cities in these states, and neglect pretty much everything else.

In order to make the win appear legitimate, however, Democrats would have to win the overall popular vote as well. That would mean that they not only needed to have enough votes in the key cities to win the states but a whole lot more, a disproportionately high number in order to win the popular vote as well.

What happened in 2020? Let's go through the five states we just mentioned.

Setting aside Bill Clinton's win in Arizona, Republicans won Arizona in every election since 1952. Trump had every reason to believe that he would win it in 2020 as well, given his significant margin of victory in 2016. Yet, Joe Biden somehow managed to pull off a victory, with a margin of only 10,457 more popular votes than Trump. That was a really big overall increase for Biden as a Democrat candidate: 637,436 more votes than Obama got in Arizona in 2008 and 510,976 more votes than Hillary got in 2016. In fact, Arizona was one of the few states that Biden got a larger percentage of the state vote than Obama had in 2008 (49.36 percent, as compared to Obama's 45.1 percent). I use Obama's record-setting vote as a kind of benchmark that allowed the Democrats to understand how many more votes they needed and allows us to see more clearly how absurd Biden's larger numbers were. So Biden's numbers in Arizona were more than a bit suspicious.

Biden won Michigan by 154,188 votes in 2020. The Democrats had won Michigan since Clinton was elected in 1992, and so they desperately wanted to overturn Trump's slim margin of victory in 2016. Biden was able to beat Trump in Michigan, despite the fact that he did it with 68,539 *fewer* votes than Obama did in 2008.

Pennsylvania had likewise gone to Democrats since Clinton's 1992 victory, and so was considered another state Democrats had to flip back after Trump's surprise win in 2016. Biden won by 80,555 votes, erasing Trump's big election night lead.

Democrats had won Wisconsin since 1988, and so likewise believed that they could flip it back after Trump's slim victory of 2016. Biden won by only 20,467 votes, even though he did it with 46,345 *fewer* votes than Obama had in 2008. Interesting.

Republicans won Georgia every year going back to 1996, and since Trump won there in 2016 by a significant margin, he had no reason to think Biden would be able to beat him. Yet, Biden was able to win with a slim margin of 12,636 votes. He did it by getting an astounding 629,496 more votes in Georgia than Obama had in 2008. Again, rather suspicious.

Some other states are worth taking a quick look at, even though they aren't considered swing states in the 2020 election, but remember, we're looking for how it was that Biden was able to smash the all-time record for the popular vote. Where did all those votes come from?

California is now as blue a state as you get. No wonder Obama won it in 2008 with a total of 8,274,473 votes. The lackluster Biden was somehow able to get 2,835,777 *more* votes than Obama had in 2008. That's a nearly miraculous increase of more than 34 percent. Biden got an even bigger increase in Colorado, 40 percent. In Maryland, Biden had a 21.8 percent increase over Obama and a 25.1 percent increase in Maryland. And here's an interesting one. Even though neither Obama nor Biden won Texas, Biden was able to gather 1,730,493 more votes than Obama had in 2008, an astounding 49 percent increase!

If there were going to be election irregularities and questionable activities on the part of Democrats, one would know where to look—the key states Democrats needed. If, likewise, we wanted to find out where and how Biden picked up all those extra record-setting popular votes, we'd know where to look. Let's look at the key states.

THE KEY TO THE DEMOCRATIC WIN: ABSENTEE AND MAIL-IN BALLOTS

How could they find all the needed votes, not just enough to win the key cities in Arizona, Pennsylvania, Wisconsin, Michigan, and Georgia, but also the popular election?

We already know from Chapter 7 that the Democrat Party has a long history of absentee ballot fraud, and that for the last twenty years (at least), "The favored techniques of fraud now occur not in the polling place but in manipulations of absentee voting." We also know that the greatest efforts of the massive, behind-the-scenes shadow conspiracy were spent in changing election laws, under cover of COVID, and ensuring that there was a massive increase in the use of absentee and mail-in ballots. Finally, we know that this effort was immensely successful *for the Democrats*: 65 percent of Trump voters voted in person, whereas 65 percent of Biden voters voted by mail. To put the massive shift in perspective, it's estimated that only 21 percent voted by mail or absentee ballot in 2016, and 60 percent voted in person on election day, while in 2020 a whopping 46 percent voted by mail or absentee ballot, and only 28 percent voted on election day (the rest voted early).[218]

How should we understand this great shift? As fitting into the history of Democrat vote fraud. If you know in advance that absentee and mail-in ballots offer the easiest way to increase the vote through fraud, then as a strategy, you'd want to drastically increase

---

218 Nathaniel Rackich and Jasmine Mithani, "What Absentee Voting Looked Like in All 50 States," FiveThirtyEight, February 9, 2021. https://fivethirtyeight.com/features/what-absentee-voting-looked-like-in-all-50-states/.

the opportunities for absentee and mail-in ballots. You'd also want to loosen the restrictions to maximize the number of votes you could manufacture without being detected. And since you knew these votes were going to come in after the in-person votes, you'd spend a lot of effort trying to convince people that they'd have to wait to know who won while you "found" enough votes to beat your opponent.

WHAT HAPPENED IN PENNSYLVANIA

Again, Biden won Pennsylvania by only 80,555 votes. Even though Biden got 181,866 more votes in Pennsylvania in 2020 than Obama did in 2008, he actually had a smaller percentage of the vote (50.01 percent) than Obama (54.3 percent)—and yet, he managed to win Pennsylvania and beat Obama's all-time popular vote record set in 2008. Suspicious.

That means we should be able to pinpoint where Biden increased the percentage of his vote, if we do a county-by-county analysis. His increase over Obama and win in Pennsylvania is even more astounding because he actually had *fewer* votes than Obama in forty-three of sixty-seven counties. That can only mean one thing—and it is consistent with the concentration of ballot fraud in a few key places—that the Democrats focused their victory efforts on only a few, strategic counties: Chester (where the Democrat vote rose by 35 percent since Obama's victory), Cumberland (where it rose 37 percent), Delaware (21 percent), and Montgomery (28 percent). That's a total of 169,604 votes. Adding the votes from another likely hotspot, Philadelphia County (which rose by 5 percent since Obama), and the vote total over Obama's is 198,464.

Of course, I'm not saying that all two hundred thousand votes over and above Obama's are the result of voter fraud. But since these are the only counties that had significant increases, significant enough to boost Biden to surpass Obama's votes and Trump's as well, that's where the cheating would likely have taken place.

But in order to pull off that kind of a victory, Pennsylvania's voting laws would have to be changed to allow for the needed fraud. That brings us to a constitutional issue.

The foremost problem for me was that Pennsylvania directly violated the constitutional demand that *only state legislatures* can define the requirements of national elections (Article II, Section 1). But on September 17, 2020, the Pennsylvania Supreme Court extended the deadline for mail-in ballots to three days after the election, mandated that ballots mailed without postmarks were acceptable, and allowed drop boxes for vote collection. On October 23, 2020, it ruled that no authentication of signatures was mandatory on mail-in ballots.[219]

Why is that constitutional requirement there, and why is it so important? The state legislatures are answerable to the people who elected them. They are the ones who make the laws for each state, not single individuals in other branches of the state government like governors, secretaries of state, attorney generals, judges, or bureaucratic officials. The Pennsylvania state legislature had debated and passed election laws to ensure the integrity of its voting. The state supreme court simply overrode them, thereby directly violating the Constitution and the laws of its own state—*and did so to loosen up laws designed to keep election fraud from happening.*

It isn't just the fact that there was a direct violation of the Constitution. It's that the court did exactly what anyone rigging an election would want. Extending deadlines means that there is more time to "find" enough votes to swing the election *after* the election. We know that absentee and mail-in voting are the easiest kinds of

---

219 See the Testimony of Pennsylvania State Representative Francis Ryan, December 16, 2020. https://www.hsgac.senate.gov/imo/media/doc/Testimony-Ryan-2020-12-16.pdf.

votes to corrupt. Extending the deadline for mail-in ballots is a variation of "one of the oldest election tricks in the book," allowing time for adding needed votes in the wee hours of the morning—except here, the time available for finding those needed votes was extended to three days! Trump was leading by a huge margin in Pennsylvania the night of the election; it took sixty-one hours *after* the close of the polls for Biden to surpass Trump.[220]

Where did those extra votes come from? On source was drop boxes. Drop boxes for ballots are an open invitation to fraud, a way of ballot collection that removes almost all oversight into what goes into the box. Simply put, it allows for ballot box stuffing on a level that would make Boss Tweed blush. The Pennsylvania Supreme Court simply bypassed the legislature and gave Democrats an immense opportunity for fraud by allowing drop boxes.

My friend Dinesh D'Souza (in cooperation with the voting integrity watchdog organization, True the Vote) will be coming out with a movie in the late summer of 2022, called *2000 Mules*, that will reveal extensive footage of "mules," the many individuals paid to stuff ballots in drop boxes in all the key swing states. These mules had to take a selfie of themselves stuffing the ballot boxes in order to be paid, and little did they know that they were being filmed in mid-fraud. Pennsylvania is just one of the many states with paid Democrat mules stuffing drop boxes full of ballots by the fistful.[221]

Finally, signature authentication is used throughout our legal system to ensure that the person entering into a contract, or signing a check, or using a driver's license as identification is the per-

---

220 Laura Bronner, Anna Wiederkehr, and Nathaniel Rakich, "What Blue and Red Shifts Looked Like in Every State," FiveThirtyEight, November 12, 2020. https://fivethirtyeight.com/features/where-we-saw-red-and-blue-mirages-on-election-night/.

221 Randy DeSoto, "Conservatives Buzzing After D'Souza Drops Must-See Trailer for Explosive Election Fraud Movie – Watch," *Western Journal*, January 31, 2022. https://www.western-journal.com/conservatives-buzzing-dsouza-drops-must-see-trailer-explosive-election-fraud-movie-watch/.

son he says he is. There is no reason to drop that requirement for voting, one of the most important acts of self-government—except making voting fraud much easier.

No wonder that Pennsylvania State Representative Francis Ryan stated that, "The mail in-ballots system for the general election of 2020 in Pennsylvania was so fraught with inconsistencies and irregularities that the reliability of the mail-in votes in the Commonwealth of Pennsylvania is impossible to rely upon."

For example, the official state data site reported on November 2, 2020, that it had sent out a total of 2.7 million mail-in ballots, but two days later, it stated that 3.1 million ballots had been sent out. That's a big difference, about four hundred thousand, and creates a lot of space for voter fraud.

To add to Rep. Ryan's account, accessing the site[222] at a later date (1/28/2022) shows that "the number of individual voters who requested a mail-in or absentee ballot for the 2020 general election" was 3.08 million. But the site breaks it down by date, making it even more clear why the vote was "so fraught with inconsistencies and irregularities." As of October 6, 2020 (a month before the election), the total of requested ballots was 2.46 million. By October 27, the total was 3.08 million (with over twice as many requested by Democrats as Republicans). That's a total of 620,000 absentee and mail-in ballots flooding out in a three-week block in the month before the election. That's not suspicious?

What else? The good thing about the internet is that concerned citizens have access to the election data as it is released and can note glaring discrepancies and irregularities that raise red flags. Here's a selection from the *very* concerned citizens who started AuditTheVotePA.com.[223]

---

222 "2020 General Election: Mail Ballot Application Statistics," https://data.pa.gov/stories/s/2020-General-Election-Voting-Story/kptg-uury.

223 "Election 2020 Pennsylvania Voter Data Analysis," September 14, 2021, October 3, 2021, https://static1.squarespace.com/static/60a8b01a8bac0413e6ac618e/t/61679dc8ef92ad-528a659cef/1634180553080/VotingAnalysis.pdf.

There were 485,284 voters purged from the voter rolls between 11/23/2020 and 08/02/2021. Among those purged voters, at least 61,067 voted in the 2020 general election. It's pretty unlikely that 61,067 people legally voted on 11/03/2020, and then died or moved away in the next ten months. Some, yes, but not that many.

During that same period 107,001 voters were added to the voter rolls—nothing wrong with that. The problem was that at least 546 voters had voted in the 2020 general election before they were added.

Inactive voters are those who have not voted in the last 4 years, and all official election materials mailed to them (for example, an absentee ballot, a voter registration card, a precinct change notification) have been returned as undeliverable. As of 11/23/2020 (i.e., two weeks after the election), there were about 2,261,000 inactive voters on the voter rolls in Pennsylvania, but over 558,000 of them had voted in the 2020 general election. If they voted, their status would have been changed to active. That's pretty suspicious. Moreover, voting must have really made some of these voters unusually active, since according to the data, 2223 of them were over 90 years old.

There are yet more reports of fraud, such as the truck driver subcontracted to the US Postal service who brought in huge boxes of completed ballots from Bethpage, New York, to Pennsylvania.[224] On October 21, 2020, truck driver Jesse Morgan had twenty-four

---

224 Donald J Trump, "Jesse Morgan says he was suspicious of his cargo load of COMPLETED ballots from NY to PA," YouTube video, 5:03, December 19, 2020, https://www.youtube.com/watch?v=FAB2NVJtVVg.

large cardboard boxes containing tens of thousands of *completed* ballots loaded onto his trailer. These ballots were destined for postal facilities in Harrisburg, PA, and then Lancaster, PA. In Harrisburg, rather than unloading right away as usual, he was made to wait for six hours, from 9:15 a.m. to 3 p.m. for the transportation supervisor—a completely different experience from what usually happened. He was finally told by the transportation supervisor at the postal facility to drive, without being unloaded, from Harrisburg to Lancaster. Morgan asked for a ticket that detailed the time spent in Harrisburg, verifying that (oddly) nothing was offloaded, but the transportation supervisor refused and just told him to go to Lancaster. He then drove to Lancaster, unhooked, and parked his trailer. The next day he went back to the Lancaster postal facility to hook up to his trailer, but his trailer was gone.

Why would completed mail-in and absentee ballots be shipped from one state to another, since voting and counting always occur *within* each respective state? Why would so many ballots be on a single truck—wouldn't legitimate mail-in ballots and absentee ballots be mixed in with actual mail if they were legitimate?

Then there's the testimony (under oath) of Gregory Stenstrom that calls into question over one hundred thousand votes.[225] Stenstrom was a commanding officer in the Navy, a CEO of his own company, a data scientist, a forensic computer expert in security and fraud—and a Republican poll watcher for the 2020 election. On November 3, he began as a poll watcher in the PA city of Chester.

One irregularity he witnessed was that people who had sent in mail-in ballots wanted to vote in person as well (because their vote hadn't yet been uploaded yet, they were worried that it wouldn't be counted). Normally, they would be given provisional ballots, but

---

225 Freedom Thumper, "Witness #3 Gregory Stenstrom," YouTube video, 14:15, November 27, 2020, https://www.youtube.com/watch?v=C_TJ7Q1_yzg.

those in charge handed them regular ballots to vote, meaning that they would have voted twice. When Stenstrom brought that violation to the attention of the poll workers, who undoubtedly knew it was a violation, they stopped. That raises an important question: How often did this double-voting happen elsewhere?

But that was just the beginning of the problems in PA. The presence of fraud convinced Stenstrom and others that they should go down to the vote counting center, a remote building. Stenstrom had been told by election workers that there were ten to twenty Republican observers there. There were not. He arrived with four other Republican poll watchers at about 6 p.m. on election day, but they weren't allowed in the building until 11 p.m., and that was only after securing legal help. When he finally got in and observed what was happening, he concluded "that it would be impossible to verify the validity of 100,000 to 120,000 votes," out of Delaware County's 425,000 registered voters.

The problems? First, mail-in ballots were separated from their envelopes, thereby creating so-called "naked ballots," which lacked essential certification provided on the envelopes in a recount. In fact, Stenstrom found that they didn't follow any of the demanded chain of custody procedures for ballots.

It gets worse. He personally witnessed USB cards being uploaded to voting machines by the warehouse supervisor at least twenty-four times. No one official was watching over the supervisor. He wasn't an official part of the voting process. He simply walked in with baggies of USBs that he uploaded in the voting machines. Making matters worse, at the time of his testimony, forty-seven USB cards were mysteriously missing, making it impossible for Stenstrom to obtain the cards he saw uploaded.

The frustrated Stenstrom demanded that those in charge show him the updated voting tallies, so that he could see if there was indeed a vote jump at the time he saw the USB uploads. There were fifty thousand votes added—all for Biden.

And there's more. It took three days to get a court order to gain admission to the locked back office. There, Stenstrom and two other observers, one of them a Democrat, found seventy-thousand unopened mail-in ballots in boxes of five hundred (filled out, just like the kinds shipped in from New York). No answers were given as to why the mail-in vote, that was already completed (with 120,000 votes), did not have these votes added. My own guess was that these were spare mail-in votes, to be used in accordance with the Goldilocks Principle of adding not too many votes, not too few, but just enough to win.

Finally, Stenstrom was notified that virtually all chain-of-custody logs, i.e., all forensic evidence mandated by law to ensure the integrity of the vote, had disappeared. And keep in mind: that's only one county in Pennsylvania, but the votes called into question would have been far more than Trump needed to win PA.

Elsewhere, in Philadelphia, Republican poll watchers were forced to leave ballot counting areas or made to stand so far away from them that observation was impossible,[226] and a Democrat sheriff refused to enforce a court order restoring proper polling observation procedures.[227]

I think all of that is more than enough to legitimately call into question the integrity of the election in Pennsylvania, and that means calling into question Biden's presidential win.

---

226 Dorothy Cummings McLean and Raymond Wolfe, "GOP poll watchers are denied access in Philadelphia," LifeSiteNews, November 3, 2020. https://www.lifesitenews.com/news/gop-poll-watchers-are-denied-access-in-philadelphia/.

227 "Philadelphia sheriff defies court order, refuses poll watchers access to counting," *Metro Voice*, November 6, 2020. https://metrovoicenews.com/philadelphia-sheriff-defies-court-order-refuses-poll-watchers-access-to-counting/.

WHAT HAPPENED IN MICHIGAN

Again, Biden won Michigan by 154,188 votes in 2020, but did it even though he got 68,539 fewer votes than Obama did in 2008 (dropping from Obama's getting 57.4 percent of the vote, down to 50.62 percent of the vote). In fact he lost votes in sixty-five of Michigan's eighty-three counties. How could Biden have beaten Obama's record for popular votes and won Michigan as well?

By throwing a lot of effort—or, more exactly, a lot of absentee and mail-in votes—into a small number of counties: Oakland (increased by 16 percent over Obama), Ottawa (increased by 25 percent), Kent (25 percent), and Washtenaw (20 percent). That's where Biden picked up the most votes, an additional 138,883 more than Obama had in these counties. Even that barely won him Michigan. If there were going to be mail-in and absentee vote fraud, a good bet for places to look for it would be in these four counties.

But as with Pennsylvania, the really disturbing aspect for me was the violations of the Constitution. The Michigan secretary of state directly violated the Constitution by issuing "guidance" on October 6, 2020, that clearly violated state laws by loosening voting restrictions in regard to signature verification on absentee ballots.

After the election, the violations were made evident in court. On March 9, 2021, Chief Court of Claims Judge Christopher M. Murray ruled that Democratic Secretary of State Jocelyn Benson had indeed violated state laws by issuing "Absent Voter Ballot Processing: Signature Verification and Voter Notification Standards" to local clerks charged with inspecting signatures on absent voter ballot applications and ballots.[228] Judge Murray pro-

---

228 Genetski v Benson, March 9, 2021, Case No. 20-000216-MM, p. 2. https://www.scribd.com/document/498855479/Genetski-v-Benson-No-20-216-MM-in-the-Court-of-Claims-for-the-State-of-Michigan.

vides the following description that shows how loose Benson's standards were:

> Under a heading entitled "Procedures for Signature Verification," the document stated that signature review "begins with the presumption that" the signature on an absent voter ballot application or envelope is valid. Further, the form instructs clerks to, if there are "any redeeming qualities in the [absent voter] application or return envelope signature as compared to the signature on file, treat the signature as valid." "Redeeming qualities" are described as including, but not being limited to, "similar distinctive flourishes," and "more matching features than nonmatching features." Signatures "should be considered questionable" the guidance explained, only if they differ "in multiple, significant and obvious respects from the signature on file."[229]

As Judge Murray rightly observed, "Nowhere in this state's election law has the Legislature indicated that signatures are to be presumed valid, nor did the Legislature require that signatures are to be accepted so long as there are any redeeming qualities in the application or return envelope signature as compared with the signature on file."[230] The reason the state legislature didn't do this should be obvious: the point of the law was to protect *against* voter fraud, not invite it. Judge Murray rejected Benson's excuse that the COVID emergency situation demanded such loosening, because any emergency actions still have to be in conformity with the law.[231]

---

229 Genetski v Benson, March 9, 2021, Case No. 20-000216-MM, p. 3.
230 Genetski v Benson, March 9, 2021, Case No. 20-000216-MM, p. 10.
231 Genetski v Benson, March 9, 2021, Case No. 20-000216-MM, pp. 12-13.

Let's state the obvious here: Democratic Secretary of State Jocelyn Benson's "guidance" was unconstitutional on the day it was issued, October 6, 2020. It was unconstitutional on Election Day, November 3, 2020. It was unconstitutional on January 6, 2021, the day that Trump supporters by the tens of thousands were in Washington, DC, peacefully protesting exactly the kinds of actions taken by Michigan's Democrat secretary of state to skew the election in favor of Joe Biden.

How many fraudulent or invalid ballots were there? That's a good question, given the record number of absentee ballots. According to Michigan's secretary of state herself, "Despite the pandemic, 2020 shattered state records for voter turnout, with more than 5.5 million total ballots cast (the previous record was 5 million, set in 2008). Approximately 3.3 million of ballots cast were absentee ballots, also a new state record; by comparison, the 2016 election, with an overall turnout of 4.8 million, saw 1.3 million voters cast absentee ballots."[232] Remember, Biden won Michigan by only 154,188 votes in 2020.

One very interesting clue that something suspect was happening was a couple of very sudden, very large spikes in the number of votes for Biden that came in the (you guessed it) wee hours of the morning. The first one came at 3:50 a.m. (EST) on November 4th, 2020, which shows 54,497 votes for Joe Biden and 4,718 votes for Donald Trump, that is, 92 percent for Biden. It was even more out of whack at 6:31 a.m. (EST) when a ballot dump showed 141,258 votes for Joe Biden and 5,968 votes for Donald Trump, that is, over 95.9 percent for Biden.[233]

---

232 Jocelyn Benson, Secretary of State, "Audits of the November 3, 2020 General Election," April 21, 2021, pp. 1-2. https://www.michigan.gov/documents/sos/BOE_2020_Post_Election_ Audit_Report_04_21_21_723005_7.pdf.

233 Vote Integrity, "Anomalies in Vote Counts and Their Effects on Election 2020," November 24, 2020. https://votepatternanalysis.substack.com/p/voting-anomalies-2020.

Percentages like that are sure signs of election fraud. The explanation from the mainstream media was that this was the result of big batches of absentee and mail-in votes were counted, which favor Democrats, and anyway they added, Trump got votes too.[234]

But that's not really an explanation because the problem is that the *ratio* of Biden to Trump votes is way, way out of whack, as if nearly all the mail-in and absentee ballots were Democrat votes. Or, more simply, as if a large batch of prepared mail-in votes were ready for dumping when needed. The first batch wasn't enough to put Biden over Trump; the second batch was, and that's why it was even more out of whack.

One of the oldest tricks in the book: the early-morning ballot dump that manufactures just enough votes to win over the opponent's seeming late-night vote-count victory.

Where did they come from? One of the big counting houses was the TCF Center in Detroit. About 3:30 a.m. a Detroit Election Bureau truck pulled up, and about fifty boxes of ballots were unloaded seven and a half hours after the 8 p.m. deadline for ballot arrivals. One of the witnesses of this literal ballot dump was former Michigan state senator, Pat Colbeck. Another load of ballots was delivered over an hour later.[235] Just what was needed to boost Biden to victory.

WHAT HAPPENED IN WISCONSIN

Again, Biden won Wisconsin by a mere 20,467 votes over Trump, even though he did it with 46,345 *fewer* votes than Obama had

234 Reuters Staff, "Fact check: Vote spikes in Wisconsin, Michigan and Pennsylvania do not prove election fraud," Reuters, November 10, 2020. https://www.reuters.com/article/uk-factcheck-wi-pa-mi-vote-spikes-idUSKBN27Q307.

235 Jim Hoft, "EXCLUSIVE: Suspicious Vehicle Seen Escorting Late Night Biden Ballot Van at TCF Center on Election Night (VIDEO)," The Gateway Pundit, February 8, 2021. https://www.thegatewaypundit.com/2021/02/exclusive-suspicious-vehicle-seen-escorting-late-night-biden-ballot-van-tcf-center-election-night-video/.

in 2008 and lost votes in sixty-seven of Wisconsin's seventy-two counties. As you already suspect, in conformity with what would happen if the Democrat strategy was to flood a small number of key counties with mail-in and absentee ballots, and let everything else go, a very few counties made Biden's victory possible, and they are easy to spot: they're the two counties that increased from Obama's 2008 record-breaking victory: Dane (28 percent) and Waukesha (22 percent). That's a total of 75,967 votes in these counties over Obama's in 2008.

As with Michigan, we've got a telltale sign of voter fraud, an early morning ballot dump that produced a sudden spike in votes that put Biden over the top. The update in Wisconsin occurred at 3:42 a.m. (CT) on November 4th, the wee hours of the morning after election night: 143,379 votes for Joe Biden and 25,163 votes for Donald Trump, slightly over 85 percent for Biden.[236] Again, just enough votes, in the wee hours, to put Biden over Trump. Of course, Trump got votes in the ballot dump, but the number of Biden's votes are way out of line with the usual ratio of Democrat to Republican votes of mail-in and absentee ballots, just enough out of whack to bring Biden the victory.

Where did all those extra votes come from? Let's take a closer look at the situation in Wisconsin and see what we find, beginning with the most important fact for assessing the legitimacy of the 2020 vote.

As with Pennsylvania and Michigan, there was a clear violation of the Constitution in Wisconsin, as the Wisconsin Supreme Court ruled on December 14, 2020,[237] one that loosened voting restrictions designed to keep voter fraud from occurring. As the judgment notes, it was done under cover of COVID.

---

236 Vote Integrity, "Anomalies in Vote Counts and Their Effects on Election 2020," November 24, 2020. https://votepatternanalysis.substack.com/p/voting-anomalies-2020.
237 Mark Jefferson v Dane County, Wisconsin, December 14, 2020, 2020AP557-OA. https://law.justia.com/cases/wisconsin/supreme-court/2020/2020ap000557-oa.html.

Here's the story, according to the ruling. Democrat Governor Tony Evers issued his Safer at Home, Emergency Order # 12 on March 24, 2020. The next day Dane County, WI, clerk Democrat Scott McDonell stated on his personal Facebook page that he informed all "Dane County Municipal Clerks that during this emergency and based on the Governors Stay at Home order I am declaring all Dane County voters may indicate as needed that they are indefinitely confined due to illness…. I urge all voters who request a ballot and have trouble presenting a valid ID to indicate that they are indefinitely confined." He then provided easy instructions: go to "myvote.wi.gov to request a ballot," and then click on the box that says, "I certify that I am indefinitely confined due to age, illness, infirmity or disability…." And that means that "the voter is then able to skip the step of uploading an ID in order to receive a ballot…."[238]

In other words, voters can skip all voting identification requirements, thereby opening up the widest possible door for absentee voter fraud. Dane County is the second most populous county in Wisconsin and the seat of the state government in Madison. Of the 220,404 who declared that they were indefinitely confined, 77.1 percent claimed that status for the first time in 2020.[239]

The Milwaukee County Clerk George Christenson did the exact same thing on his Facebook page later that day, urging "all voters who request a ballot and do not have the ability or equipment to upload a valid ID to indicate that they are indefinitely confined."[240] Milwaukee County is the most populous county in Wisconsin, and the city of Milwaukee the most populous city.

Win Dane and Milwaukee counties, and you pretty much win the state of Wisconsin and its ten electoral votes. It's interesting,

238   Mark Jefferson v Dane County, Wisconsin, December 14, 2020, 2020AP557-OA, pp. 2-3.
239   State of Wisconsin, Legislative Audit Bureau, Elections Administration, October 2021, p. 50. https://legis.wisconsin.gov/lab/media/3288/21-19full.pdf.
240   Mark Jefferson v Dane County, Wisconsin, December 14, 2020, 2020AP557-OA, pp. 3-4.

to say the least, that the percentage of ballots cast as absentee were extraordinarily high in these two counties, 74.4 percent in Dane County and 70.6 percent in Milwaukee County, the two highest of all Wisconsin counties.[241] Both are far above the national percentage of 46 percent voting by absentee or mail-in. That in itself should give us pause, given how much easier voter fraud is with absentee and mail-in, and how removing the safeguards in Wisconsin made it even more so.

The Wisconsin Supreme Court understood that very clearly, noting that in accordance with Wisconsin Statute 6.84 "voting by absentee ballot is a privilege exercised wholly outside the traditional safeguards of the polling place." For this reason, the law continues, "matters relating to the absentee ballot process...shall be...mandatory," and "its exercise requires strict compliance." Therefore, in accord with previous decisions, "[b]allots counted in contravention of the procedures...may not be included in the certified result of any election."[242]

Unsurprisingly, the court ruled that "a county clerk may not 'declare' that any elector is indefinitely confined due to a pandemic." First of all, it's the Wisconsin Elections Commission "that is responsible for guidance in the administration and enforcement of Wisconsin's election laws, not the county clerks."[243] Second, individual voters are the ones who make the determination about their status of being "indefinitely confined" in accordance with Wisconsin state law; "[N]either county clerks nor an order of the Governor may declare persons indefinitely confined" because of COVID or any other reason.[244]

---

241 State of Wisconsin, Legislative Audit Bureau, Elections Administration, October 2021, p. 39. https://legis.wisconsin.gov/lab/media/3288/21-19full.pdf.

242 Mark Jefferson v Dane County, Wisconsin, December 14, 2020, 2020AP557-OA, pp. 8-9.

243 Mark Jefferson v Dane County, Wisconsin, December 14, 2020, 2020AP557-OA, p. 12.

244 Mark Jefferson v Dane County, Wisconsin, December 14, 2020, 2020AP557-OA, p. 13.

So, declared the court, "The presence of a communicable disease such as COVID-19, in and of itself, does not entitle all electors in Wisconsin to obtain an absentee ballot...." Furthermore, "an emergency order that required all Wisconsinites to remain in their homes except for limited circumstances, standing alone, was not a condition based on age, a physical illness, or an infirmity" in accordance with the allowable conditions under Wisconsin law. "Finally, having trouble uploading or providing proof of a photo identification does not permit electors to avoid both the absentee voting laws and the voter identification laws."[245] And so the court concluded that the Democrat's "interpretation of Wisconsin's election laws is erroneous," and "Emergency Order #12 did not render all Wisconsin electors 'indefinitely confined,' thereby obviating the requirement of a valid photo identification to obtain an absentee ballot."[246]

In short, the whole thing was a sham, or better a scam to allow massive absentee ballot voting without having to present valid voter identification. It was unconstitutional on March 25, 2020, when the county clerks of the two largest counties posted it on Facebook. It was unconstitutional on November 3, 2020. It was unconstitutional on January 6, 2021.

We should also mention that Wisconsin had 1,304,554 absentee ballots returned, and only 2,981 rejected—a rejection rate of 2/10 of 1 percent, one of the lowest rejection rates in the nation for 2020.[247] That's a pretty strong indication that the unconstitutional measures had their intended effects for the Democrats: a low rejection rate signals loose oversight.

Remember Biden won Wisconsin by only 20,467 votes in 2020. The mysterious ballot dump in the wee hours of the morning

---

245 Mark Jefferson v Dane County, Wisconsin, December 14, 2020, 2020AP557-OA, p. 15.
246 Mark Jefferson v Dane County, Wisconsin, December 14, 2020, 2020AP557-OA, p. 18.
247 See Ballotpedia, "Election results, 2020: Analysis of rejected ballots." https://ballotpedia.org/Election_results,_2020:_Analysis_of_rejected_ballots.

brought him that victory, and now we know where all those extra ballots came from. It's not enough to point out that Democrats tend to vote by mail-in or absentee more than Republicans, because the percentage of the one-time dump is all out of proportion with the normal ratio of Democrat to Republican rates in regard to that kind of voting, *and* to state the obvious, if the mail-in and absentee votes were being counted all night, the regular ratio would have been maintained, not violated.

But that's not all the problems that undermined the integrity of the 2020 presidential election in Wisconsin. Remember from Chapter 3 how Democrats "mined" votes at nursing homes? Well, that happened in Wisconsin in 2020, as discovered by investigators at the Racine County Sheriff's Office. Wisconsin law mandates the use of Special Voting Deputies who, for the sake of voting integrity, deliver the absentee ballots to any residents who requested them, and they oversee the voting process to ensure its integrity. But the Wisconsin Elections Commission (WEC) issued an illegal directive not to use the official deputies and instead allowed for sending the ballots by mail (with no oversight). The WEC then informed "care facility administrator[s] and staff member[s]" that they could "assist residents in filling out their ballots or certification envelops," an open invitation to fraud that directly violates Wisconsin law.

Sgt. Michael Luell, who led the investigation for the Racine County Sheriff's Office, was alerted to problems by a woman who complained that her mother at the Ridgewood Care Center, who had significantly diminished mental capacities and had died on October 9, 2020, had somehow cast an absentee ballot. Sgt. Luell then discovered that a total of forty-three residents at that nursing home had voted in the November 3 election, over four times the usual number that voted in presidential elections, and six of the families of these residents declared their family member was not mentally capable of voting.

This was not an isolated problem. As Sheriff Christopher Schmaling noted, "Ridgewood is one of 11 facilities within our county," and Racine County only "one of 72 counties" in the state. "There are literally hundreds and hundreds of these facilities throughout the entire state of Wisconsin," and so "we would be foolish to think for a moment that this integrity issue, this violation of the statute, occurred to just this small group of people at one care facility in one county in the entire state."[248]

That's not all. Wisconsin law demands that an absentee ballot must be signed by a witness, who is also required to list his or her address in order to validate the identity of the voter. But the WEC issued a memo, "Spoiling Absentee Ballot Guidance" on October 19, 2020, that asserted, "Please note that the clerk should attempt to resolve any missing witness address information prior to Election Day if possible, and this can be done through reliable information (personal knowledge, voter registration information, through a phone call with the voter or witness),"[249] rather than returning them to voters to correct, as the law demands. That's a lot of illegal leeway to give a clerk in verifying the witness of an absentee ballot. Personal knowledge?

There were other potential problems pointed out by the non-partisan Legislative Audit Bureau of Wisconsin in its Elections Administration Report of October 2021.[250] Wisconsin law demands that the WEC verify personal information of those registered to vote with the Department of Transportation. There were 45,665 registrants to vote whose information didn't match the DOT's. While a significant number of these could have been

248 Margot Cleveland, "Wisconsin Investigation Uncovers Potential Tip of a Voting Fraud Iceberg," The Federalist, November 1, 2021. https://thefederalist.com/2021/11/01/wisconsin-investigation-uncovers-potential-tip-of-a-voting-fraud-iceberg/.

249 WEC, "Spoiling Absentee Ballot Guidance," October 19, 2020. https://elections.wi.gov/node/7190.

250 State of Wisconsin, Legislative Audit Bureau, Elections Administration, October 2021. https://legis.wisconsin.gov/lab/media/3288/21-19full.pdf.

easily reconciled (e.g., a man registers his name as Bob but DOT had him as Robert), the report noted that "one county clerk was unaware of the need to review non-matches, and one municipal clerk indicated not having time to review non-matches."[251] How many clerks didn't know or didn't check, and didn't admit it? We can't tell. In any case, there were far too many registrants not matching the DOT database to be explained away so easily.

And then there's the issue of drop boxes. According to the Legislative Audit Bureau report, Wisconsin "statutes do not permit or prohibit ballot drop boxes," and so drop boxes were used by about 30 percent of the clerks.[252] Since there was no legislative direction, the WEC took it upon itself to issue guidance in July of 2020, part of which was that even book return slots at municipal libraries were a permissible ballot drop box![253]

Taking all of this into account, it's pretty easy to conclude that Biden didn't win Wisconsin because—to state the obvious—he wouldn't have just enough extra votes if all of these things were subtracted.

WHAT HAPPENED IN GEORGIA

Even though Obama won the all-time record for the popular vote in 2008, he didn't win Georgia, and Hillary only did worse. Although she got 33,826 more votes than Obama, she dropped in the percentage of the Georgia vote from Obama's 47 percent to her 45.9 percent.

Trump had a big lead on election night in Georgia, and as I said above, there was every reason to believe that he'd win big again, just as he did in 2016.

---

251 State of Wisconsin, Legislative Audit Bureau, Elections Administration, October 2021, pp. 22-23.
252 State of Wisconsin, Legislative Audit Bureau, Elections Administration, October 2021, p. 46.
253 State of Wisconsin, Legislative Audit Bureau, Elections Administration, October 2021, p. 46.

It took fifty-eight hours *after* the polls closed for Biden to "pull ahead" by 12,636 votes.[254]

That's beyond suspicious, fitting perfectly into the Mayor Daley pattern of "finding" just enough extra votes to win in the wee hours of the morning—although the wee hours stretched into fifty-eight hours.

It's not difficult to see where the suspicious rise in the number of Democrat votes occurred when we do a county-by-county analysis. Again, let's compare Biden's performance with Obama's 2008 record-breaking vote. There was a suspicious rise in the number of votes in the following counties: Cobb (57 percent), DeKalb (21 percent), Douglas (54 percent), Fayette (63 percent), Forsyth (174 percent), Fulton (40 percent), Gwinnett (88 percent), and Henry (81 percent). The extra votes gained over Obama in any single one of these counties was more than enough to account for 12,636 votes Biden won by. But the real angle to understand how "amazing" Biden's victory was is that, if we add all of the votes together from these counties that Biden got over Obama (442,836), it was just barely enough, as it turns out, for Biden to squeak by Trump.

Much has been made—and rightly so—of the shenanigans at the State Farm Arena in Atlanta, where the Fulton County was counting the mail-in and absentee ballots. That's understandable, given that Biden got a total of 380,212 votes there (108,212 more than Obama in 2008). But as evident from the jump in votes in the other counties I've listed, it would be foolish just to focus on Fulton. Gwinnett County rose by 88 percent (as compared to Fulton's 40 percent) and accounted for an additional 112,969 votes more than Obama's total. Cobb's 57 percent increase accounted for an additional 80,631 votes more than Obama racked up. And certainly something is very strange about Forsyth County jetting up by 174 percent.

---

254 Laura Bronner, Anna Wiederkehr, and Nathaniel Rakich, "What Blue and Red Shifts Looked Like in Every State."

Perhaps you're not surprised to find that there was another mysterious vote dumping spike in the wee hours of the morning in Georgia. At 1:34 a.m. (EST) on November 4th, 2020, there was a big vote spike: 136,155 votes for Joe Biden and 29,115 votes for Donald Trump, over 82 percent for Biden.[255] That's way out of proportion, a typical sign of fraud. As usual in this old trick, that was enough votes to push Biden over Trump, or at least bring him close enough so that the needed number of mail-in and absentee ballot votes could be "found" over the next fifty hours.

It won't do, I repeat, to say that this was due to a big load of absentee and mail-in ballots being uploaded at once, and these favor the Democrats. They don't favor the Democrats *that* much unless something fishy occurred that allowed that many more Democrat votes in that particular vote dump and *not* during the rest of the night.

While I'd like to see broader investigations, I admit that there was something especially unsettling about the Fulton County fiasco. Stopping the vote for a water main break that turned out to have been, at most, an overflowed urinal. Keeping Republican poll watchers from effectively watching the recount. Shooing the Republican poll watchers out at 10:30 p.m., pretending that the counting had stopped, and then four election workers pulling boxes of ballots out from under a table and continuing the count after everyone had left. Running the same ballots through multiple times. This was clearly a fraudulent situation that was famously caught on security cameras. And guess what—that huge spike in Biden votes occurred during that very time when this was all happening with no oversight.[256]

---

255   Vote Integrity, "Anomalies in Vote Counts and Their Effects on Election 2020," November 24, 2020. https://votepatternanalysis.substack.com/p/voting-anomalies-2020.

256   See the extensive footage at the Georgia Senate Judiciary subcommittee hearing: https://www.bing.com/videos/search?q=running+ballots+through+multiple+times&&view=detail&mid=6710E09273369E5F813B6710E09273369E5F813B&rvsmid=9B9219D9F867C10E54789B9219D9F867C10E5478&FORM=VDQVAP.

We might get the idea from the press coverage that the only problem was at one location. But we should also hear the sworn affidavits of Robin Hall and Judy Aube, both of whom were certified audit monitors at the World Congress Center in Atlanta overseeing the absentee and mail-in ballot counts on November 14, 2020. Hall and Aube observed many "boxes of absentee or mail in boxes" that were "perfectly filled out as if they were preprinted" which were "100% for Biden and 0% for Trump." Hall and other observers wrote down the "batch headers and box number ranges [that] were suspicious."[257]

Then there's the sworn affidavit of Susan Voyles, a poll manager, also working at the World Congress Center that day, in her case, counting the actual votes. She began counting absentee ballots at 9 a.m., but was "not given any information or standards on how to interpret spoiled ballots or other discrepancies." Most of the ballots were obviously handled and worn, but "one batch [of 100 ballots] stood out. It was pristine," and there was an obvious "difference in the feel" of the ballots. "There were no markings on the ballots to show where they had come from, or where they had been processed." Further, "the markings for the candidates on the ballots were unusually uniform," as if done with a "ballot marking device." How were they marked: "98% constituted votes for Joseph Biden. I only observed two of these ballots as votes for President Donald J. Trump."[258] What surer sign of fraud does one need?

That matches the experience of Barbara Hartman, also tasked with counting votes that day at the World Congress Center. In her sworn affidavit, she states that she was given several stacks of absentee ballots to count. "I could not observe any creases in the ballots and [they] did not seem like they were ever folded and

257 L. Lin Wood v Brad Raffensperger, Exhibits C and D. https://law.justia.com/cases/federal/appellate-courts/ca11/20-14813/20-14813-2021-08-06.html.

258 L. Lin Wood v Brad Raffensperger, Exhibit E. https://law.justia.com/cases/federal/appellate-courts/ca11/20-14813/20-14813-2021-08-06.html.

put into envelopes and mailed out." The markings for candidates "were filled in with black ink perfectly in the circle. It looked like they had been stamped." And imagine this: "The majority of the mail-in ballots I received contained suspicious black perfectly bubbled markings for Biden."[259]

And there were more problems than that in Georgia, as revealed in Governor Brian Kemp's "Review of Inconsistencies in the Data Supporting The Risk Limiting Audit Report" (November 17, 2021).[260] Because the race was so close, an audit was ordered. But that recount itself was riddled with errors, or as seems obvious in some cases, outright fraudulent manipulation—the error rate of 60 percent being, to say the least, extraordinarily high. There were thirty-six instances of duplicate or misidentified batches, resulting in 4,255 votes being added. There were also seven falsified tally sheets. In the words of the election integrity organization VoterGA (founded in 2006), "A batch containing 60 ballot images voted for Joe Biden, and 40 voted for Donald Trump was reported as 100 for Biden and 0 for Trump. The 7 batches of ballot images with 554 votes for Joe Biden, 140 votes for Donald Trump and 11 votes for Jo Jorgenson [sic] had tally sheets in the audit falsified to show 850 votes for Biden, 0 votes for Trump and 0 votes for Jorgenson [sic]."[261] You can see the problem.

VoterGA also found that seventy-four Georgia counties can't produce 2020 ballot images, and fifty-six counties say such images aren't even available, although that violates retention laws both on

---

259 L. Lin Wood v Brad Raffensperger, Exhibit F. https://law.justia.com/cases/federal/appellate-courts/ca11/20-14813/20-14813-2021-08-06.html.

260 "Review of Inconsistencies in the Data Supporting the Risk Limiting Audit Report," State of Georgia, November 17, 2021. https://voterga.org/wp-content/uploads/2021/11/Brian-Kemp-Audit-Inconsistencies-Report-Joe-Rossi-11.18.2021.pdf.

261 "Georgia Governor Brian Kemp's Election Audit Report Admits Massive Fulton Errors First Revealed by VoterGA," VoterGA Press Release, November 27, 2021. https://voterga.org/wp-content/uploads/2021/11/Press-Release-GA-Gov-Brian-Kemp-Admits-Fulton-Audit-Errors-Revealed-by-VoterGA.pdf.

the federal and state level.[262] Such laws are there to ensure that a proper audit of the vote can take place, but that would seem to be extremely difficult, to say the least, with so many "missing" ballot images. What do they have to hide?

In addition, VoterGA reports a "chain of custody study that revealed nearly 107,000 drop box ballots in the November 2020 election results have improper chain of custody forms that call into question the authenticity of those ballots."[263]

That brings us back to Dinesh D'Souza's movie (with True the Vote) that contains damning video evidence of Democratic "mules" stuffing ballots in drop boxes. On January 4, 2022, Georgia Secretary of State Brad Raffensperger revealed that, as a result of True the Vote's work, his office is investigating allegations that large-scale ballot harvesting took place in the 2020 election. Ballot harvesting, where third-party groups volunteer to pick up and deliver ballots for other people, is illegal in Georgia for the obvious door it opens to voter fraud. According to one report, True the Vote "informed the secretary its evidence included video footage from surveillance cameras placed by counties outside the drop boxes as well as geolocation data for the cell phones of more than 200 activists seen on the tapes purportedly showing the dates and times of ballot drop-offs…." How many? Thousands.[264]

True the Vote reports that over 40 percent of the drop box ballot stuffing occurred—as you might have guessed—between midnight and five in the morning. The Georgia investigation is an especially important development because Raffensperger, a

---

262 "74 Georgia Counties Can't Produce Original 2020 Election Ballot Images," VoterGA Press Release, November 9, 2021. https://voterga.org/wp-content/uploads/2021/11/Press-Release-VoterGA-2020-Election-Ballot-Images-Destroyed-11-09-21-1.pdf.

263 "Custody Chain Analysis Finds 106,000+ Suspect Ballots, Uselessness of Drop Box Videos," VoterGA Press Release, January 20, 2022. https://voterga.org/wp-content/uploads/2022/01/Press-Release-VoterGA-Drop-Box-Custody-Chain-Analysis.pdf.

264 John Solomon, "Georgia opens investigation into possible illegal ballot harvesting in 2020 election," Just the News, January 4, 2022. https://justthenews.com/politics-policy/elections/georgia-opens-investigation-possible-illegal-ballot-harvesting-2020

Republican, originally denied that President Trump's allegations of voter fraud in Georgia had merit.

WHAT HAPPENED IN ARIZONA

Biden's win in Arizona was also deeply suspicious. Again, other than Bill Clinton's win in Arizona in 1996, Republicans had won Arizona in *every* election since 1952. Trump won it in 2016 by over ninety thousand votes. But Biden snatched it from Trump by a mere 10,457 votes, and it took him 637,436 more votes than Obama got in Arizona in 2008 and 510,976 more votes than Hillary got in 2016 to do it. That's a whole lot of extra votes. It's certainly hard to believe that Biden got a larger percentage of the state vote than Obama had in 2008 (49.36 percent, as compared to Obama's 45.1 percent).

Where did all those votes come from? Arizona has only fifteen counties, and Biden managed to increase the number of votes over what Obama achieved in every one of those counties. On the face of it, that doesn't indicate fraud because Republicans increased their vote count substantially in all Arizona's counties as well. A simple explanation might be that Arizona's population increased by about 12 percent from 2008 to 2020.

But when we dig into the county-by-county details, things become quite suspicious when we compare Biden's lackluster performance over Obama's benchmark numbers in 2008, especially in the following counties: Coconino (65 percent increase over Obama), Maricopa (92 percent), Pima (59 percent), Pinal (75 percent), and Yuma (82 percent). Those are enormous increases and add a total of 676,450 votes, and even that was barely enough for Biden to beat Trump because the Republican vote was increasing as well. Maricopa is the obvious place where a disproportionately large number of Democrat votes were "found," and by the Democrats' own admission, they were found among the mail-in and absentee votes. Even when we account for the rise of the Republican vote in Maricopa, the Democrat vote rose by almost twice as much.

Just based on those numbers alone, if you were a detective, you'd look in those counties for evidence of fraud, especially Maricopa. If you were following the news, you recall that state Republicans had a group call Cyber Ninjas to perform a forensic analysis, which showed all kinds of integrity failures and voter fraud red flags.[265] Then, Maricopa County put out a point-by-point refutation.[266]

Rather than try to settle that debate, I think it's best to trust my fellow Republicans in Arizona whose judgment was that the election integrity of the 2020 election in their state was fatally compromised. I'm going to quote from HCR2033, introduced on February 9, 2022.[267] In it, they set forth the evidence that, for them, demands Arizona's 2020 electors should be decertified. Let's look at some of the most serious charges.

First, as with the other states I've mentioned, there was a direct violation of the Constitution, with the judiciary usurping the rightful power of the state legislature to define election law: "Voter registration was extended by the federal judiciary to October 23 in direct conflict" with Arizona state law.[268]

In addition, "Maricopa County reported 1,455 ballot envelopes having no signatures, yet they were counted contrary" to state law. The number of chain of custody breaches were also numerous,

265 "Maricopa County Forensic Audit," September 24, 2021. https://www.documentcloud.org/documents/21068477-20210919-maricopa-county-forensic-audit-volume-i-executive-summary.

266 Maricopa County Elections Department, "Correcting the Record," January 2022. https://recorder.maricopa.gov/justthefacts/pdf/Correcting%20The%20Record%20-%20January%202022%20Report.pdf.

267 Arizona HCR2033, "Decertifying Arizona's 2020 electors," TrackBill, 2020. https://trackbill.com/bill/arizona-house-concurrent-resolution-2033-decertifying-arizonas-2020-electors/2223128/.

268 For this and all of the following, please read Arizona HCR2033, pp. 1-6. https://www.azleg.gov/legtext/55leg/2R/bills/HCR2033P.pdf.

calling into question the legitimacy of ballots—gaps in chain of custody are where voter fraud takes place.

And here's a sure sign that something was wrong with the ballot counting: "Poll watchers and observers were not allowed to be on site or close enough to observe whether poll workers were following proper identification processes,…poll workers were made to stay seated or in a particular area far away from where voting activity was occurring,…poll workers were reprimanded for asking questions and…poll workers observed bias in voting.…"

Or how about this: "Batches and trays of ballots by the thousands in one 4-5 hour shift were carried to rooms and offsite where they were not overseen.…" If that weren't bad enough, "signatures on absentee ballots did not match and thousands more in a 4-5 hour period were not verified before being counted or 'run through' electronic signature adjudication, which alone could comprise hundreds of thousands of ballots in Maricopa County, in which 1.875 million out of 2 million were cast by mail.…" Slow down and think of that, almost 94 percent of the ballots in one county were cast by mail. How much room for fraud does that cause?

Then there were "some ballots…changed from candidate Trump to candidate Biden but observers were never provided answers regarding how or when they were to be rectified.…" Given that observers were often kept from watching the counting, you have to wonder how many times that happened when there were no Republican observers.

Shouldn't we be suspicious if we found "30 of the same signature on 30 different ballots?" For some reason, though, "The Attorney General's Election Fraud Unit was not notified.…"

On November 30, 2020, "Members of the Legislature of the State of Arizona sitting as an ad hoc public fact-finding hearing on election integrity…heard testimony and received evidence that through extraordinary means the vote count in some counties was electronically altered to award enough votes to a candidate that did not actually receive said number of votes in such a volume so as to alter the outcome of the election…."

That's only a partial account of the evidence of fraud in the election. But there's also a cover-up afterward. So, "There is clear evidence of intentional remote overwriting of the security logs by the Elections Management System Administrator…." For example, "On February 11, 2021, 462 log entries were overwritten, on March 3, 2021, 37,686 log entries were overwritten and on April 12, 2021, 330 log entries were overwritten…."

What didn't they want seen? If that weren't bad enough, "Maricopa County Supervisors admitted on the Congressional Record that general election results were purged from the Election Management System (EMS) as evidenced by a February 1, 2021 SQL Log entry."

Remember what I said about Dinesh D'Souza's movie and the problem with ballot stuffing in drop boxes? Well, "Maricopa County reported that 923,000 early voter ballots were accepted at vote centers or drop box locations and that the county lacks chain of custody documents for at least 740,000 of those early voter ballots…." In fact, "The Maricopa County Recorder, who is responsible for enforcing the chain of custody of all ballots, failed to enforce the counting of ballots and record the number of ballots retrieved from each ballot drop box location."

That's only one county. As the authors of the bill add, there is significant evidence of the same kind of problems in Pima County as well.

WHAT HAPPENED IN TEXAS

I'd like to end looking at my own home state. Trump won Texas by only 631,221 votes in 2020. That's not much and puts the Democrats within striking distance for turning the state blue in 2024. Is there any sign of cheating in Texas? Certain numbers make one suspicious, and pointing them out might help Republicans in the 2022 and 2024 elections know where to watch.

Remember, prior to the 2020 election, Obama held the all-time popular vote record. That's, again, why I'm using him as a benchmark. One notable thing that happened in 2020 is that the lackluster Biden increased the number of his votes in Texas by 49 percent over Obama's 2008 win. That's significant. Not enough to win the state, but a lot.

In certain counties Biden beat Obama by a far greater increase: Collin (113 percent), Denton (108 percent), my own Fort Bend County (99 percent), Hays (109 percent), Montgomery (104 percent), and Williamson (114 percent). That accounts for a total of 463,421 more votes than Obama had in 2008 in these counties.

There were other suspiciously large Democratic gains in other counties, smaller by percentage of the gain over Obama, but larger by the number of total votes because of the density of the population: Bexar (63 percent), Dallas (41 percent), Harris (56 percent), Tarrant (50 percent), and Travis (72 percent). The total votes added by Biden in these increases: 997,167.

Granted, the population of Texas grew by almost 16 percent during this period, and that's certainly part of the rise in Biden's vote tallies (and explains the rise in Republican voting numbers as well). But what we're looking for are exceptional spikes that might indicate voter fraud had occurred, especially through absentee and mail-in voting (and so where it's likely to occur in 2022 and 2024).

So, taking into account that voter totals in Texas rose for both Democrats and Republicans from 2008 to 2020 because of an increase in population, an additional clue that might allow us to detect potential fraud would be those counties where the difference in the percentage rise in the Democrat vote was far higher than the percentage rise in the Republican vote during the same period.

For example, in my own Fort Bend County, the Democrat vote rose by 99 percent from 2008 to 2020, while the Republican vote rose by only 53 percent. That's a pretty big difference between the rise of the two: a 46 percent greater rise by the Democrats. Other counties that had a notable rise in the Democrat as compared to the Republican vote were Bexar (38 percent), Collin (76 percent), Denton (59 percent), Dallas (42 percent), Montgomery (42 percent), Travis (53 percent), and Williamson (55 percent).

How much of this suspicious rise in the Democrat vote in 2020 might be due to voter fraud? I can't tell, but if there are going to be any more investigations of the 2020 elections, we'd know what were the most likely places to look in Texas—and, as I said, where to be on guard in 2022 and 2024.

AND SO...TRUMP WON THE ELECTION IN 2020

Given everything we've gone over, I don't think there's any doubt that Trump won the 2020 election. The great shadow conspiracy's effort to boost the absentee and mail-in ballot vote was probably enough to rig the election, especially since part of the effort was to loosen the restrictions that protected against fraud—and there's too much evidence of fraud, regardless of what the mainstream media says. Given that big tech has methodically done everything it can to silence evidence by declaring any such evidence as "disinformation" to be censored, we must conclude that most of the fraud has either been undetected or smothered before it could see the light and enter into our assessment of the 2020 election.

The mainstream media and big tech have colluded to cover the fraud so they could beat Trump by any and every means possible, just as they colluded in regard to the Steele Dossier, the Russian hoax, and COVID. The Democrat Party was clearly in on it as well.

We cannot let our investigations of the 2020 elections stop just because they aren't the hot news item of the day. The more we know about what was done behind the scenes to rig the election against Trump, the more prepared we'll be in 2022 and 2024 to have a free and fair election.

And make no mistake: the other side will be doing everything it can to win by who-knows-what methods—a mix of the old and some new tricks as well. Just because Biden's presidency has been an unmitigated disaster so far doesn't mean it will translate into a Republican victory in 2022 unless we are intensely vigilant at every turn (rather than merely reacting when it's too late).

That brings us back to January 6, 2021, and the Capitol Hill riot, because if Trump actually won, then as I've said, all those peaceful protestors were rightfully in Washington, DC, that day. They knew if the Democrats got away with it, then they would never have a voice again. A sign that they were right in that assessment was the Democrat attempt to pass HR 1, the so-called Voting Rights bill that would have cemented in place all the unconstitutional changes they pushed through in 2020 under cover of COVID. Big tech is still on their side. The mainstream media is still on their side. And you can be sure that the great shadow conspiracy has been working overtime and will continue to do so.

If the peaceful protestors were right, then how did a constitutionally protected demonstration turn into a riot? That's the subject of the next chapter.

CHAPTER 9

JANUARY 6TH, A CLOSER ANALYSIS

It's time to take a deeper look at January 6th itself and do so in light of all that we've covered. In the first chapter, I gave an account of how January 6th looked to me in the moment; now, I'd like to give an account after much consideration, taking into account what we've covered in this book. I imagine that what I have to say will make some folks uncomfortable, to say the least.

I'm going to split things into two parts. First, we're going to look at the "innocent" failures, institutional and individual negligence, incompetence, and misjudgment. I put "innocent" in quotes because it's now clear to me that if these failures hadn't occurred, then there would have been no breach of the Capitol. Second, we're going to ask harder questions about the possibility that there was a purposeful strategy to turn a peaceful demonstration into a riot *for political purposes*.

THE DISMAL ASSESSMENT OF THE CAPITOL POLICE

As someone involved in law enforcement for so many years, I'm used to setting aside my political and personal opinions and aims, and looking at the straightforward facts. In regard to what happened on January 6th, the Inspector General Report of the United States Capitol Police (March 2021) and the Senate Report (June 2021) are essential reading.[269] Admittedly, both reports are difficult to get through, partly because of the number of agencies and their endless acronyms, and partly because of the complexity of the interactions with these agencies. I'm going to do my best to boil it down.

If you look back over the videos of what happened at the Capitol that day—especially with the eyes of a trained law enforcement officer—one thing is startlingly clear: the Capitol Police seem to be fairly quickly overwhelmed, as if they were taken by surprise, ill-equipped, poorly trained, and badly led. Both reports confirm these problems.

Let's begin with the curious failure in intelligence informing them of what to expect. The group tasked with providing that intelligence was the USCP's Intelligence and Interagency Coordination Division (IICD). The IICD provided three separate "Special Event Assessments," one on December 15, 2020, a second on December 30, 2020, and a third on January 3, 2021.

In the first Special Event Assessment of December 15, 2020, the IICD asserted that there was a "LOW level of concern at this time," because "there is no information to indicate any type of violence or civil unrest will be associated with the Joint Session of Congress—Electoral College Certification." Yet, in its Overall Analysis, it stated that "due to the tense political environment following the 2020 election, the threat of disruptive actions or violence cannot be ruled out."[270]

---

269 United States Capitol Police, Office of Inspector General, "Review of the Events Surrounding the January 6, 2021, Takeover of the U.S. Capitol," Investigative Number 2021-I-0003-B, March 2021 (hereafter, OIG Report); United States Senate, "Examining the U.S. Capitol Attack: A Review of the Security, Planning, and Response Failures on January 6" (hereafter, Senate Report).

270 IICD Special Event Assessment, December 15, 2020, 21-A-0468.

In the December 30, 2020, Special Event Assessment, things have heated up, the IICD reporting that "some protestors have indicated they plan to be armed." Along with the tens of thousands of peaceful supporters of Donald Trump, "It is also expected that members of the Proud Boys, Antifa, and other extremist groups will rally on January 6, 2021," the Antifa groups being Refuse Fascism and Shutdown DC. If things go as they had in the past, there will be "clashes between pro-Trump and opposing groups." There were, in fact, multiple arrests made in previous clashes at rallies in November and December of 2020, with charges ranging from "assault with a dangerous weapon, assault on police, simple assault, weapons violations, riotous acts, destruction of property, disorderly conduct, resisting arrest, and crossing a police line."[271]

Oddly, in the Overall Analysis, the IICD simply repeats what it said in December 15, rather than express a heightened sense of potential disorder. Even more odd—as the Office of Inspector General (OIG) Report notes[272]—the IICD didn't reference an Investigative Research and Analysis Report of December 2, 2020. That report included a number of red-flag social media posts about the upcoming January 6th events, for example, posts showing maps of the tunnels used by members of Congress, with a response saying, "Forget the tunnels. Get into the Capitol Building, stand outside congress. Be in the room next to them. They wont [sic] have time to run if they play dumb." Another chimes in that "we should just go to there [sic] houses," and someone else adds, "I vote to just straight up burn down Pelosi's & McConnell's DC homes." One post suggest that the Supreme Court should be burned down as well and another that "anyone going armed needs to be mentally prepared to draw down on LEOs [Law Enforcement Officers]." "Bring shovels," is followed by "And guns."[273]

---

271   IICD Special Event Assessment, December 30, 2020, 21-A-0468 v. 2.
272   OIG Report, p. 24.
273   OIG Report, Appendix E, pp. 90-93.

The third IICD Special Event Assessment of January 3, 2021, repeats the warning about possible armed protestors and adds that "white supremacist groups may be attending the protests." The same concern about clashes between pro-Trump supporters and groups like Antifa is expressed, and the number of known protest groups has grown to twenty. Its Overall Analysis shows even more concern. In addition to noting the "tense political environment" as it had before, the IICD adds that,

> *Supporters of the current president see January 6, 2021, as the last opportunity to overturn the results of the presidential election. This sense of desperation and disappointment may lead to more of an incentive to become violent. Unlike previous post-election protests, the targets of the pro-Trump supporters are not necessarily the counter-protesters as they were previously, but rather Congress itself is the target of the 6th. As outlined above, there has been a worrisome call for protesters to come to these events armed and there is the possibility that protesters may be inclined to become violent.*

The IICD notes its concern about the pro-Trump group Stop the Steal in particular, which it says "does not have a permit" and has a "propensity to attract white supremacists, militia members, and others who actively promote violence," which "may lead to a significantly dangerous situation for law enforcement and the general public alike."[274]

If this intelligence were in fact accurate, these were (recalling what I said in Chapter 4) the "individuals or small groups" who would "infiltrate the larger protest" and try to turn it into a riot.

---

274 IICD Special Event Assessment, January 3, 2021, 21-A-0468 v. 3.

If that was the assessment of the intelligence division connected to the Capitol Police and the Civil Disturbance Unit (CDU) *three days before January 6th*, any reasonable person would think that the Capitol Police would have been ready to meet the heightened sense of danger, especially since it had been previously warned on December 21st and 30th.

But as the Senate Report makes clear, while the IICD "was aware of the potential for violence in the days and weeks ahead of January 6th," it "failed to fully incorporate this information into all of its internal assessments about January 6th and the Joint Session. As a result, critical information regarding threats of violence was not shared with USCP's own officers and other law enforcement partners."[275] The Capitol Police on the ground didn't understand what they might be up against.

Setting aside these failures in intelligence, how ready were Capitol Police? As it turns out, they were not only unprepared for what might occur on January 6th, they were unprepared *period* because they didn't have sufficient training and equipment to deploy Less-than-Lethal Force (Level Four on the Use of Force Continuum).

In regard to the equipment, people may not realize that, like food and medicine, it has a limited shelf life. As the OIG makes clear, much of the equipment had "expired," which resulted in (for example) "riot shields shattering upon impact" on January 6th, an effect of "either improper storage or the age of the shield."[276]

Moreover, Less-than-Lethal projectile weapons used for riot control were also expired by over a year and in some cases by four years. This included 40mm CS Smoke Projectiles, 40mm Sting-Ball Smokeless .60CAL Rubber Pellets, 40mm Riot OC Powder Muzzle Blasts, Riot CS Smoke Grenades, Riot CS Red Smoke

---

275 Senate Report, p. 2.
276 OIG Report, p. 10.

Grenades, Riot CS Smoke Grenade Triple Phasers, 40mm Outdoor White Smoke Long Range Projectiles, 40mm Sting-Ball Smokeless .31CAL Rubber Pellets, CS Baffled Riot CS Smoke Grenades, White Smoke Canister Grenades, OC Vapor Grenades, and CS Jet-Lite Rubber Ball Grenades.[277]

And then there were the personnel and leadership issues. Within the Capitol Police Department, the Civil Disturbance Unit (CDU) was the main Capitol Police unit dealing with the crowds on January 6th. The CDU's mission is to "ensure the legislative functions of Congress are not disrupted by civil unrest or protest activity, while respecting the Civil Rights of all citizens."[278]

But the CDU is an *ad hoc* unit, meaning that it's "without dedicated full-time staffing," and so the "administration of the CDU is an ancillary responsibility." In fact, the Capitol Police Department "did not have an accurate listing of which employees were in CDU."[279] As the OIG report further notes, "The lack of policies and procedures for CDU creates ambiguity and lack of accountability and coordination among the various offices and bureaus involved in the deployment of CDU...."[280]

And so, in facing the crowds at the Capitol on January 6th, the Capitol Police Department "did not have established policies identifying areas such as the process for activating CDU, responsibilities of CDU officers, issuance of gear to CDU officers, tactics used when CDU is activated, and the command structure within CDU."[281] One result of this, as the Senate Report points out, was that although the Capitol Police "activated seven specialty Civil Disturbance Unit ('CDU') platoons in advance of the Joint Session, only four of those platoons were outfitted with special pro-

---

277 OIG Report, pp.11-12.
278 OIG Report, p. 4.
279 OIG Report, p. 14.
280 OIG Report, pp. 7-8.
281 OIG Report, p. 7.

tective equipment, including helmets, hardened plastic armor, and shields. The many other USCP officers who fought to defend the Capitol were left to do so in their daily uniforms."

That's poor leadership and inexcusably inadequate given the nature of the potential danger and the size of the crowds. Small wonder. The OIG report gives us the reason: "No leadership development training exists for CDU officers."[282]

Another bad result was that "heavier less-lethal weapons and corresponding munitions that included the 40mm grenade launcher, 37mm grenade launcher, and Sting Ball grenades were not used that day because of orders from leadership," the very things that would have helped them "push back the rioters...."[283]

An additional problem was that the CDU had only a very limited number of personnel (called grenadiers) trained to use this riot control equipment. How limited? Well, "approximately 10." Given the small number of grenadiers and the lack of leadership, one officer in the midst of the chaos that day reported that "he was unable to summon grenadiers for support while fighting off the crowd."[284]

Would they have been effective if summoned? One wonders: "Of those 10 grenadiers, zero received the required semiannual training."[285] Furthermore, the "grenadier teams did not [initially] deploy with 40mm weapons and munitions" when the chaos first erupted. It was only after the crowd dispersed, and they were preparing for "a second wave of violence," that "40mm weapons and munitions were deployed, but not used."[286] Too late.

Lack of training was a problem with all the officers of the CDU using "hard protective gear," who are "required to complete annual refresher training that ranges from 16 to 24 hours." This is

282 OIG Report, p. 8.
283 OIG Report, p. 12.
284 OIG Report, p. 13.
285 OIG Report, p. 14.
286 OIG Report, p. 11.

extremely important because the officers in the "hard" CDU are the ones designated to "control violent crowds." But as the report makes clear, "The majority of officers…have not completed the training during the past few years." Perhaps part of the problem was that the Capitol Police Department "did not have formal training standards and lesson plans for its CDU refresher training."[287]

Other issues arose that day, some almost comical, if the result of such incompetence hadn't been so tragic. One CDU platoon was deployed *without* riot shields, which for some reason were being kept in a nearby bus. "When the crowd became unruly, that CDU platoon attempted to access the bus to distribute the shields, but were unable because the door was locked," and so they were forced "to respond to the crowd without protection of their riot shields."[288]

It's an understatement to say that the Capitol Police were not ready for what they had to face. But why didn't they call in help once things were obviously out of control? They did, but for some reason, help was *purposely* withheld.

THE CAPITOL POLICE CHIEFS WATCH AND DO NOTHING

With that question, we take up the second part of our inquiry where it seems to be that there was some kind of conspiracy. Let's begin with words from the Senate Report.

> *As the attack unfolded, USCP [US Capitol Police] and the Metropolitan Police Department of the District of Columbia ("MPD") both pleaded with DOD [Department of Defense] officials for immedi-*

---

287 OIG Report, pp. 8, 14.
288 OIG Report, p. 13.

ate assistance.... Miscommunication and confusion during response preparations, demonstrated by conflicting records about who authorized deployment and at what time, contributed to the delayed deployment. DCNG [DC National Guard] began arriving at the Capitol Complex at 5:20 p.m.—nearly three hours after DOD received USCP's request for assistance and more than four hours after the barriers at the Capitol were first breached.[289]

On this account, it took over four hours for the National Guard to arrive after the trouble started, just in time to be (conveniently?) too late to help the overwhelmed Capitol Police. This is *not* how any police and military should respond to a riot emergency.

It's all the more suspicious because, given the intelligence and the size of the crowds, *the National Guard should have been ready for immediate deployment, with plans in place*. It's as if they had been purposely told to stand down and drag their feet. As it turns out, the Senate Report states, once informed of the need for immediate assistance, the Department of Defense spent hours "mission planning."[290] The report continues, the "DOD and DCNG have conflicting records of when orders and authorizations were given, and no one could explain why DCNG did not deploy until after 5:00 p.m."[291]

Since these two reports came out, other revelations only add to our suspicions. Deputy Chief Jeffrey J. Pickett (now retired) was deployed on January 6th and has written an inside look at what was really going on. He did so in an official "whistleblower" document I obtained that was filed with Nancy Pelosi, Chuck Schumer, Kevin McCarthy, and Mitch McConnell (dated September 28, 2021).

---

289 Senate Report, pp. 3-4.
290 Senate Report, p. 8.
291 Senate Report, p. 8.

Officer Pickett focuses on the leadership failures of Capitol Police Chiefs Yogananda Pittman and Sean Gallagher, and the "failed honesty" of the leadership of Congress itself. According to Officer Pickett, "The truth of the leadership/intelligence failures of the 6th is purposely not being delivered to the officers and public."

To begin with, Pittman and Gallagher had the intelligence beforehand that alerted them to the real possibility of a riot, "but never shared it with the rest of the Department, particularly those commanders with real operational experience. If provided, this information would have changed the paradigm of that day." As a result, the "incident commanders" actually on the ground in the midst of the chaos, "were doomed from the start." Even worse, Pittman testified to the Senate that she had shared the appropriate intelligence with the assistant and deputy chiefs of the Capitol Police, which is "unconditionally false. It was never sent or shared."

But even more suspicious, as things heated up, Pittman and Gallagher "simply watched mostly with their hands in their laps" in the "control center.... They did not try to help or assist as officers and officials were literally fighting for each other, their lives, and Congress." Instead, they sat "like two bumps on a log."

"What I observed," reports Officer Pickett, was Pittman and Gallagher "mostly sitting there, blankly looking at the TV screens showing real time footage of officers and officials fight for Congress and their lives," and "their inaction [was] reported and collaborated by other officials and non-USCP entities." Then afterward, they had the gall to blame incident commanders for their own failures.

Their inexplicable inaction was so astounding that Pickett alleges "that these two with intent and malice opted to not try and assist the officers and officials," and indeed, "chose to try and use this even for their own personal promotions," which did, in fact, occur soon afterwards.

Officer Pickett blames the failures of Pittman and Gallagher on incompetence. Through "political favors" they got "unmerited promotions" and rose to a level of command that they were simply unfit to exercise. That would mean that Congress was responsible, and it would be "immensely embarrassing to the congressional leadership and those key staffers for championing the promotions of inexperienced and incapable leaders that directly led to the events of the 6th."

Another possibility beyond incompetence exists, and I state that this is only conjecture, and therefore it may turn out not to be true. Perhaps Pittman and Gallagher were told to sit on their hands *so that* Capitol Police on the ground would be overwhelmed. That possibility fits with the strange delay by the DC National Guard. It's as if somebody wanted things to get out of the control and for the rioters to enter the Capitol Building that day so they could finally destroy Donald Trump.

THE ARMY HOLDS BACK THE NATIONAL GUARD UNTIL IT'S TOO LATE

Perhaps the DC National Guard was not to blame but someone else in the chain of command. That's the assertion of Major General William Walker, Commanding General of the District of Columbia National Guard at the time, along with his Staff Judge Advocate, Colonel Earl Matthews. Their "The Harder Right: An Analysis of a Recent DoD Inspector General Investigation and Other Matters"[292] is a scathing reply to a Department of Defense report[293] that Walker maintains attempted to shift the blame from

---

292   Colonel Earl G. Matthews, "The Harder Right: An Analysis of a Recent DoD Inspector General Investigation and Other Matters." https://www.scribd.com/document/545012748/Matthews.

293   "Review of the Department of Defense's Role, Responsibilities, and Actions to Prepare for and Respond to the Protest and its Aftermath at the U.S. Capitol Campus on January 6, 2021 (DODIG-2022-039)," Department of Defense Office of Inspector General, November 16, 2021. Available at https://www.dodig.mil/reports.html/Article/2844941/review-of-the-department-of-defenses-role-responsibilities-and-actions-to-prepa/.

itself for the hours-long delay of DC National Guard deployment on January 6th.

According to Walker, he received a "series of frantic telephone calls" from Chief of the US Capitol Police Steven Sund "beginning at 1:49 p.m. on 6 January 2021" informing him that "the security perimeter at the U.S. Capitol had been breached by hostile rioters." The breach had occurred about an hour earlier at the walkway into the Capitol Hill area by the Peace Monument,[294] the most direct path for crowds to flow from where Trump was speaking. During the intervening time, Sund had been desperately working his way through the bureaucratic chain of command to get approval for National Guard deployment, finally contacting Walker directly. "Chief Sund, his voice cracking with emotion, indicated that there was a dire emergency on Capitol Hill and requested the immediate assistance of as many D.C. National Guard personnel as MG Walker could muster...."[295] The delays weren't over. Assistance would finally come three and a half hours later.

In a meeting soon after of those responsible for making the decision how and when to respond, Chief Sund repeated the need for urgent help from the DC National Guard but the Department of Defense was interested only in obstruction. In the established chain of command, the Department of Defense was in charge of granting the request, but according to the National Guard's Walker and Matthews, its representative, "LTG Piatt stated that it would not be his best military advice to recommend to the Secretary of the Army that the D.C. National Guard be allowed to deploy to the Capitol at that time." Furthermore, Piatt "stated that the presence of uniformed military personnel could inflame the situation and that the police were best suited to handle the situation," and that

---

294 "Peace Monument," Architect of the Capitol, https://www.aoc.gov/explore-capitol-campus/art/peace-monument.

295 Colonel Earl G. Matthews, "The Harder Right: An Analysis of a Recent DoD Inspector General Investigation and Other Matters," p. 3.

"the optics of having uniformed military personnel deployed to the U.S. Capitol would not be good."[296] The Army's LTG Charles Flynn seconded Piatt. In short, the Army was the one dragging its feet, or more exactly, the feet of the National Guard.

In corroboration of this, President Trump said in an interview with Fox News's Steve Hilton that (to quote a Fox report) "his team alerted the Department of Defense days before the rally that crowds might be larger than anticipated and 10,000 national guardsmen should be ready to deploy. He said that—from what he understands—the warning was passed along to leaders at the Capitol, including House Speaker Nancy Pelosi—and he heard that the request was rejected because these leaders did not like the optics of 10,000 troops at the Capitol."[297]

Unlike the Capitol Police, the DC National Guard was a "seasoned forced when it came to civil disturbance response operations, having conducted these missions, or prepared to conduct such missions, extensively over the previous 6 months."[298] MG Walker directed the Guard's Quick Reaction Force (QRF) to move "from Joint Base Andrews to the Armory" at 2:12 p.m., a bit over twenty minutes after Sund called him directly.[299] As Walker reports, they were ready for action: "all D.C. National Guard personnel preparing to go to the Capitol were already fully kitted out with riot gear."[300]

Under normal circumstances, MG Walker would have full authority to deploy the DC National Guard immediately, *but for*

---

296 Colonel Earl G. Matthews, "The Harder Right: An Analysis of a Recent DoD Inspector General Investigation and Other Matters," p. 4.

297 Edmund DeMarche, "Trump says he requested 10K National Guard troops at Capitol on day of riot," Fox News, March 1, 2021. https://www.foxnews.com/politics/trump-says-he-requested-10k-national-guard-troops-at-capitol-on-day-of-riot.

298 Colonel Earl G. Matthews, "The Harder Right: An Analysis of a Recent DoD Inspector General Investigation and Other Matters," p. 6.

299 Colonel Earl G. Matthews, "The Harder Right: An Analysis of a Recent DoD Inspector General Investigation and Other Matters," p. 8.

300 Colonel Earl G. Matthews, "The Harder Right: An Analysis of a Recent DoD Inspector General Investigation and Other Matters," p. 8.

some strange reason, a "restriction withholding QRF employment authority from MG Walker...was inserted [in a letter] by Army Staff officers late on the evening of 4 January," even though it was not mentioned at a meeting Walker had with the Army that very day. "The restriction, or at least the more stringent language was added at the request of the Judge Advocate General of the Army."[301] The original correspondence from Ryan McCarthy, the Secretary of the Army, affirmed MG Walker's authority to employ the National Guard according to his judgment; the second version substitutes, "I withhold authority to approve employment of the DCNG Quick Reaction Force..." for the original, "You may employ the DCNG Quick Reaction Force...."[302]

If that restriction hadn't been mysteriously added, Walker would have sent in the Quick Reaction Force to the Capitol immediately. But the restriction meant that Walker finally received "the approval of civilian leadership to deploy to the Capitol at 5:08PM."[303]

Why, on the evening of January 4th, less than two days before the Capitol was breached, did the Army mysteriously withhold authority for the Guard's deployment from MG Walker? That restriction inexplicably kept the Guard waiting until after 5:00 p.m. to deploy. MG Walker's Staff Judge Advocate, Colonel Earl Matthews, expressed the Guard's frustration that day in an email sent to Acting Secretary of Defense, Christopher Miller, at 2:21 p.m.: "Sir: Army has DCNG [DC National Guard] on stand down despite request for support."[304]

---

301 Colonel Earl G. Matthews, "The Harder Right: An Analysis of a Recent DoD Inspector General Investigation and Other Matters," p. 14.

302 I myself have a copy of this correspondence. The change is covered in Colonel Earl G. Matthews, "The Harder Right: An Analysis of a Recent DoD Inspector General Investigation and Other Matters," pp. 28-29.

303 Colonel Earl G. Matthews, "The Harder Right: An Analysis of a Recent DoD Inspector General Investigation and Other Matters," p. 14.

304 Colonel Earl G. Matthews, "The Harder Right: An Analysis of a Recent DoD Inspector General Investigation and Other Matters," p. 15.

The Army's excuse was that it had to formulate a plan, but the DC Guard did not need help from the Army. As Matthews makes clear, "The DCNG had a great deal of experience handling civil unrest in Washington in support of local and federal law enforcement. It had a 40-member Quick Reaction Force and MG Walker could pull troops off of the traffic control points or could direct other trained and experienced personnel present at the Armory to immediately don riot gear and respond to support USCP [the U.S. Capitol Police] and MPD [Metropolitan Police Department] at once."[305]

The entire command of the Guard "wanted to respond immediately," reported Matthews. "They could have directed their 40 person QRF to move immediately from Joint Base Andrews to link up with USCP near the Capitol. DCNG could also have diverted personnel supporting the traffic control mission to the Capitol. These soldiers and airmen possessed the requisite riot gear in their vehicles. DCNG estimates 131 riot gear-equipped troops could have been mustered immediately and an additional 200 Guardsmen within the following 2 hours."[306]

"To a person, every leader in the DCNG wanted to get to Capitol Hill with deliberate speed when the Capitol security perimeter was breached. Their attitude was 'This is What We Do.' 'Send Me.' In fact, responding to civil unrest within the confines of the District of Columbia was a foundational mission, a statutory mission of the D.C. National Guard, given it by the Congress."[307]

That guardsmen were not immediately deployed had only one cause: "Inaction and inertia at the Pentagon."[308] Later, Walker and

---

305 Colonel Earl G. Matthews, "The Harder Right: An Analysis of a Recent DoD Inspector General Investigation and Other Matters," p. 18.

306 Colonel Earl G. Matthews, "The Harder Right: An Analysis of a Recent DoD Inspector General Investigation and Other Matters," p. 24.

307 Colonel Earl G. Matthews, "The Harder Right: An Analysis of a Recent DoD Inspector General Investigation and Other Matters," p. 27.

308 Colonel Earl G. Matthews, "The Harder Right: An Analysis of a Recent DoD Inspector General Investigation and Other Matters," p. 25.

Matthews leveled a most serious charge: Army officials lied both in their sworn testimony and in their accounts of what actually occurred on January 6th, pinning the blame for inaction on the DC National Guard.

But clearly it wasn't the National Guard that caused the delay. "Every leader in the D.C. Guard wanted to respond and knew they could respond to the riot at the seat of government. They sat stunned watching in the Armory while for the first time in its 219 year history, the D.C. National Guard was not allowed to respond to a riot in the city."[309]

Let's add up what we do have so far. The Capitol Police were woefully underprepared and left to face the Capitol rioters for several hours (while the Capitol Police chiefs sat idly by), even though the DC National Guard, who was fully prepared to respond immediately, was inexplicably held back by the Army until after 5:00 p.m. In the time provided by this delay, the breach of the Capitol Building itself was allowed to transpire.

It certainly seems as if Capitol Police Chiefs Yogananda Pittman and Sean Gallagher, and the Secretary of the Army Ryan McCarthy were all following the same orders...from somewhere. That order certainly seems to have come from, or been affirmed by, Nancy Pelosi.

On January 13, 2022, I attended a meeting organized by the Republican Conference, the purpose of which was to allow Republican members to ask questions of Capitol Police Chief Thomas Manger and General William Walker (now House Sergeant-at-Arms). In the meeting, I commented that Assistant Chief Pittman continues to oversee the intelligence section in the Capital Police, which I find problematic.

I also noted that Paul Irving, who as the previous House Sergeant-at-Arms was partly responsible for issuing the order to

---

309 Colonel Earl G. Matthews, "The Harder Right: An Analysis of a Recent DoD Inspector General Investigation and Other Matters," p. 33.

bring in help from the National Guard on January 6th, hesitated to declare an emergency because he had to "run it up the chain of command," a chain that runs up to House Speaker Nancy Pelosi. I told General Walker I believe Speaker Pelosi herself played a role in the delayed response of the DC National Guard.

I then asked General Walker, "Now that you serve as House Sergeant-at-Arms, do you feel you need Speaker Pelosi's approval, as Mister Irving apparently did, to deploy troops to the Capitol should something like this take place again?"

He replied "No."

I expected that answer. It seems like there were some special behind-the-scenes orders governing Irving's response that day.

I then asked General Walker, "If the DC National Guard would have been deployed to the Capitol Building on January 4th, as intelligence suggested, do you feel our Capitol would *not* have been breached?"

He replied, "Yes."

I agree.

The inexplicable delay was suspicious, as if it were planned in advance. Things grow even more so as we look at what happened while the National Guard was made to wait.

TURNING A PROTEST INTO A RIOT: PROVOCATEURS IN THE JANUARY 6TH CROWD

That a small number of people with a distinct agenda—provocateurs—can strategically turn a peaceful protest into a destructive riot is not some kind of wild, baseless speculation. We've already seen, in significant detail, that's what Antifa adherents regularly do.

To repeat Andy Ngo's words, "Antifa know the effect that smashed windows, breached businesses, and fires have on crowd mentality." They know, given the psychology of crowds, that such acts "can turn protesters into rioters." That's why Antifa cells teach adherents how to provoke a riot through acts of initial destruction—such as tearing down barricades and breaking windows at the Capitol. As we know from endless footage of 2020 riots, such acts are not out of character for Antifa activists (although they are out of character for Trump supporters, who are almost invariably peaceful and law-abiding).

If we look, as we have, at the larger, longer history of Antifa, we also are made aware of another tactic. In the 1950s, Antifa activists in Britain dressed up like the characteristic Blackshirts of British fascist groups so they could infiltrate their headquarters undetected, and then, once in, would steal records and trash the offices.[310]

Dressing up in its signature black bloc is the usual modus operandi of Antifa today; its members also carry alternative clothes in backpacks so they can appear and disappear into the crowd at will. Since Antifa regards Trump and his supporters as modern-day fascists, Antifa dressing up as MAGA supporters in the January 6th rally is not inconceivable, nor is it beyond the pale to suggest that Antifa provocateurs would then follow the "breaking windows" strategy to whip the normally quiet, law-abiding Trump supporters into undertaking destructive activity at the Capitol. We also know, according to the Intelligence and Interagency Coordination Division's Special Events Assessment that Antifa was expected.

Does that *prove* that there were Antifa provocateurs? Of course not, but it shows that it is not impossible or even out of character for Antifa. We also know that on the eve of the Capitol Hill riot, Antifa and Black Lives Matter protestors clashed with Trump supporters, so both Antifa and BLM were still in Washington on January 6th. And, as I've noted, there certainly could have been a small percentage of Trump supporters that were intent on something other than peaceful protest, and they would have been easy targets for Antifa provocateurs to turn into rioters.

---

310   Mark Bray, *Antifa: The Anti-Fascist Handbook*, p. 45.

We also know that there were indeed provocateurs at the Capitol that day because we have extensive footage of them doing everything they can to push Trump supporters up to and into the Capitol Building.

The Revolver website has put together one of the most extensive accounts that tried to piece together footage from various sources, and I urge readers to watch all the videos contained in the two-part analysis and make their own judgment.[311] I will be referring to material in those two articles in my analysis below.

In order to figure out what turned a peaceful protest about election integrity into a riot at Capitol Hill we first need to have a grasp of the timeline on January 6th (although we'll add something important from January 5th). You'll need to refer to it as I try to sort out what happened.

JANUARY 5, 2021

10:30 p.m.-midnight A man later identified as Ray Epps, dressed in a red TRUMP cap, repeatedly urges Trump supporters to go *into* the Capitol the next day. Antifa and Black Lives Matter protestors clash with Trump supporters.

JANUARY 6, 2021

10:24 a.m. Long before President Trump speaks, Ray Epps (standing near the Washington Monument) urges Trump supporters on their way to the rally at the Ellipse to go to the Capitol after the speech.

---

311 "Meet Ray Epps: The Fed-Protected Provocateur Who Appears To Have Led The Very First 1/6 Attack On The U.S. Capitol," Revolver, October 25, 2021, https://www.revolver.news/2021/10/meet-ray-epps-the-fed-protected-provocateur-who-appears-to-have-led-the-very-first-1-6-attack-on-the-u-s-capitol/; and "Meet Ray Epps, Part 2: Damning New Details Emerge Exposing Massive Web Of Unindicted Operators At The Heart Of January 6," Revolver, December 18, 2021, https://www.revolver.news/2021/12/damning-new-details-massive-web-unindicted-operators-january-6/.

10:48 a.m. Capitol Police estimate the crowd at the Ellipse where President Trump will speak to be twenty-five thousand to thirty-thousand.

11:50 a.m. Donald Trump starts speaking at the Ellipse (about a twenty-five-minute walk from the Capitol Building).

12:44 p.m. Capitol Police investigate explosive device at Republican National Committee Headquarters, thereby drawing off Capitol Police resources.

12:48 p.m. Ray Epps is at the very front of the first breach site at the Peace Monument that was set up to block the walkway to the Capitol Building. For some strange reason, there are only a few Capitol Police protecting the barrier.

12:50 p.m. The first breach: Ray Epps and a handful of protestors push away the barrier and enter the restricted area.

12:58 p.m. Capitol Police Chief Sund asks for and receives help from the Metropolitan Police Department.

1:03 p.m. Capitol Police find vehicle with eleven Molotov cocktails and a firearm.

1:04 p.m. Capitol Police Chief Sund first asks for declaration of emergency authorization of National Guard support.

1:07 p.m. Capitol Police investigate explosive device at Democratic National Campaign Headquarters.

1:09 p.m. Chief Sund asks for declaration of emergency authorization from another agency in order to get National Guard support.

1:10 p.m. President Trump ends his speech nearly twenty minutes after first breach.

1:11 p.m. Capitol Police evacuate Cannon Building because of explosive devices at Republican and Democrat National Committee Headquarters.

1:21 p.m. Additional Metropolitan Police arrive to help.

1:22 p.m. Chief Sund asks again for emergency declaration authorization of National Guard support.

1:49 p.m. Chief Sund requests support directly from the DC National Guard's General Walker.

2:03 p.m. Chief Sund asks again for emergency declaration authorization of National Guard support.

2:11 p.m. Vice President Pence escorted from Senate Chamber.

2:19 p.m. Capitol Rotunda breached.

2:26 p.m. Chief Sund begs for National Guard support during teleconference meeting, but the Army won't authorize due to "optics."

2:35 p.m. At approximately this time, I have moved to the back door of the House Chamber to help deal with protestors who are trying to enter the Chamber.

2:43 p.m. Capitol Police Officer Lieutenant Michael Byrd shoots and kills Ashli Babbitt.

2:57 p.m. House members fully evacuated.

5:08 p.m. MG Walker of the National Guard finally receives authorization to deploy.

5:47 p.m. Seven National Guard buses head to north barricade at the Capitol.

Two things stand out immediately when we look at the timeline. To begin with, the first breach of the Capitol perimeter occurs at 12:50 p.m., *a full twenty minutes before* President Trump has finished speaking. That's odd because Trump supporters go to hear Trump; that's what they're there for. Why would a smaller group of them be at the Capitol Building area long before Trump finished?

Second, in confirmation of what we've just gone over, there is a huge gap between the first breach (12:50 p.m.) and Capitol Police chief's first call for help from the National Guard (1:04 p.m.), and the final authorization of the National Guard to deploy (5:08 p.m.) and its actual deployment.

What was going on during that long delay? Before Trump's speech was done, an advance group of protestors breached the restricted Capitol Building area, took down fencing, removed signs that would have warned soon-to-be-arriving Trump supporters that they were entering a restricted area, and then spent the next hours shepherding Trump's supporters into the restricted area and urging them to enter the Capitol Building.

At the center of this operation is the now-famous Ray Epps (see the video footage in the Revolver articles). We first see Epps on the late evening of January 5th (wearing a TRUMP hat) milling about the crowds strangely insistent on convincing Trump supporters the night before the rally that *the* most important thing that they need to do is breach the Capitol Building.

In the videos we hear Epps shouting, "Keep your focus! Stay focused on what we're here for…. Tomorrow, we need to go *into* the Capitol! *Into* the Capitol!" He is immediately booed by Trump supporters who drown him out by chanting, "Fed! Fed! Fed! Fed!" They smell a rat.

At one point that evening, while Epps is trying to convince Trump supporters to follow his instructions, standing next to him is none other than John Sullivan, alleged Antifa and Black Lives Matter supporter. We hear Sullivan remarking that, given Epps's strange behavior, he must be an undercover agent. The following day both Epps and Sullivan will (separately) urge Trump supporters into the Capitol.

The next day, January 6th at 10:24 a.m., Ray Epps is near the Washington Monument shouting to those who are going to hear President Trump speak at the Ellipse, "After the speech, we are going to the Capitol. Where our problems are. It's that direction. Please spread the word!"

Ray Epps is then at the first breach site at the northwest walkway leading into the Capitol at the Peace Monument at least forty-five minutes *before* it happens at 12:50 p.m. As noted, the first breach will occur here before Trump finished his speech, as if it were done in as a kind of planned preparation.

This walkway is the place where, after Trump is finished speaking, the thousands upon thousands of supporters will then be funneled as they walk from the Ellipse down either Constitution Avenue or Pennsylvania Avenue. (Constitution Avenue merges into Pennsylvania Avenue about two thousand feet from the Peace Monument.) Since Epps and others begin the breach before Trump finished, the plan seems to have been to accomplish it before Trump supporters would arrive.

Even though this is the main walkway where thousands and thousands of Trump's supporters will obviously converge, the videos taken before the breach show only about five Capitol Police officers standing at the barricades. Wouldn't this be the most important place the Capitol Police should have been deployed?

At 12:48 p.m., a video shows Epps shouting instructions into the ear of a man (later identified as Ryan Samsel but first known by the FBI as Most Wanted Suspect # 51), and two minutes later, at 12:50, Samsel and a handful of protestors push back the barricades, with Ray Epps and the protestors following right behind.

As the footage gathered by Revolver shows, almost immediately after the breach a male individual (wearing sunglasses, a maroon ski cap, but no Trump gear) calmly and methodically cuts down and rolls up fences and takes down signs that would indicate to the soon-to-be-arriving Trump supporters that this was a restricted area, and consequently, that they could be arrested for entering the Capitol area. (Oddly, even though there's plenty of footage, he did not make it onto the FBI Most Wanted List.) As footage attests, this fence cutting man was waiting at the site of the breach at 12:31 p.m. (twenty-one minutes *before* it happened). Does that look like an accident?

There was also another small group about thirty feet south of the breach site also removing fencing at the very moment the breach occurred (led by a man in a black ski mask, who then runs up with the crowd with Epps in it as it advances on the Capitol). He is on the FBI's wanted list as Suspect #148. Although there is a very clear picture of his face, he has yet to be arrested. This is extremely odd since on January 5th he was taken out of a bus full of Trump supporters by police who believed the bus had weapons within.

This methodical fence and sign removal is important. Normally, this area is open to the public but had been declared restricted, both on multiple signs and by the fencing. With all that so quickly removed, the arriving Trump supporters would have no idea they were entering a restricted area.

Now you can understand the importance of the first breach of the Capitol area being about twenty minutes *before* Trump finished speaking at the Ellipse. That gave the Epps and the "first breach team" time to remove the barricades, fences, and warning signs so that the wave of Trump supporters would unknowingly (and illegally) enter the restricted area around the Capitol, thereby making them subject to arrest.

Also waiting at the breach site at least twenty minutes before it happened was another man (a middle-aged white male wearing glasses, a hoody, and a blue hat), who came to be known to internet sleuths as Scaffold Commander. We first see him waiting outside the breach area, then once the breach occurs, he helps fence-cutting man take down the fences. He then climbs the media tower next to the inauguration platform, and from about 1:00 to 2:30 issues endless, urgent commands through a megaphone to Trump supporters as they wander into restricted area: "Don't just stand there! Move Forward! Move Forward! Help somebody over the wall!" Once the Capitol Building itself was breached, Scaffold Commander begins yelling, "Okay we're in! We're in! Come on! We gotta fill up the Capitol! Come on! Come now! We need help! We gotta fill up the Capitol! They got in!"

Interestingly, adding to suspicions of a conspiracy, from about 1:00 onward, Epps can be seen under the media tower, in concert with Scaffold Commander, directing Trump supporters forward.

Even though Scaffold Commander was probably the most visible of any of the protestors, and consequently there are multiple pictures of him, he did not make the FBI Most Wanted List.

Ray Epps did make the FBI's Most Wanted List on January 8th as Suspect #16. Given the number of pictures of Epps at the Capitol and already on the internet prior to January 6th, internet sleuths were able to identify him within three days. As more and more information surfaced, Epps began to look more and more like an FBI informant/provocateur whose goal (along with the others mentioned) was to shepherd Trump supporters up and into the Capitol where they could then be arrested as insurrectionists (which the FBI soon did, with great zeal, hunting down Trump supporters and hauling them in).

But even though Epps was fully identified, he was not arrested. Mysteriously, Ray Epps disappeared as Suspect #16 without a trace from the FBI's Most Wanted List on July 1, 2021, with no explanation by the FBI. He was not arrested; he was simply erased as a suspect.

Very, very suspicious.

What to make of this? Clearly, Ray Epps and the others working with him were not Antifa infiltrators (although Antifa agitators would seem to have the same goal). The most likely people one would suspect of being Antifa on January 6th would be those who were attacking police and smashing windows and doors. That kind of behavior is uncharacteristic of Trump supporters whose protests and rallies are always peaceful and deeply respectful of law enforcement. Until clearer evidence arises, I can't say much more than that about possible Antifa infiltration.

The most likely explanation seems to be that Ray Epps and the others were FBI directed informants whose task was to ensure that during the time the Department of Defense stalled in authorizing the arrival of the National Guard, Trump supporters would be tricked into entering into the restricted Capitol grounds and then into the Capitol Building.

Why implicate the FBI? It isn't just that the FBI wouldn't arrest Epps and the others engaged in the same activities. That's suspicious enough. But the FBI had already shown quite recently in the plot to kidnap Gretchen Whitmer, the Governor of Michigan, that it's quite capable of manipulating people into committing serious crimes. The alleged right-wing plot to kidnap Governor Whitmer was very publicly foiled by the FBI in October of 2020—less than a month before the presidential election and less than three months before the presidential inauguration in January of 2021. It was revealed that they wanted to storm the Michigan State Capitol, seal legislators inside, and set fire to the building, then execute hostages publicly. Immediately, Trump was blamed by Whitmer, major Democrats, and the media for the outrage as the most vocal supporter of White Supremacist revolution by his loyal deplorables. When January 6th rolled around, Whitmer, the Democrats, and the media could then claim that storming the Capitol was exactly the kind of thing we know Trump supporters do.

The problem is that the whole Michigan kidnapping plot has since been unraveling. Not only were there FBI informants and infiltrators among the conspirators, but there were very good reasons to believe that they were actually leading them forward. This possibility is put forth, not by some conservative news agency, but by investigative reporters at the very liberal BuzzFeed. "An examination of the case by BuzzFeed News…reveals that some of those informants, acting under the direction of the FBI, played a far larger role than has previously been reported. Working in secret, they did more than just passively observe and report on the actions of the suspects. Instead, they had a hand in nearly every aspect of the alleged plot, starting with its inception. The extent of their involvement raises questions as to whether there would have even been a conspiracy without them."[312] On top of that, the moral and legal caliber of the FBI agents and informants has been seriously undermined.[313]

If further investigation completely undermines the credibility of the Whitmer kidnapping plot and shows that it was something that the FBI was involved in a kind of entrapment, then similar FBI involvement on January 6th would be all the more believable.

But there are other very telling "ifs."

If the Capitol Police hadn't been responding to bogus bomb threats at the RNC and DNC headquarters, they would have had more officers available.

---

312   Ken Bensinger and Jessica Garrison, "Watching the Watchmen," BuzzFeed News, July 20, 2021, https://www.buzzfeednews.com/article/kenbensinger/michigan-kidnapping-gretchen-whitmer-fbi-informant. See also Glenn Greenwald, "FBI Using the Same Fear Tactic From the First War on Terror: Orchestrating its Own Terrorism Plots," July 24, 2021, https://greenwald.substack.com/p/fbi-using-the-same-fear-tactic-from?token=eyJ1c2VyX 2lkIjoxMzQ4OTgsInBvc3RfaWQiOjM5MDIxODgzLCJfIjoiQVRBc1MiLCJpYXQiO-jE2MjcxNDQzNDcsImV4cCI6MTYyNzE0Nzk0NywiaXNzIjoicHViLTEyODY2MiIsIn-N1YiI6InBvc3QtcmVhY3Rpb24ifQ.e9ku1dufQw_QtSv9lcdjdh2nftQtKlfrrpvgLjKu--o.

313   Ken Bensinger and Jessica Garrison "The FBI Investigation Into The Alleged Plot To Kidnap Michigan Gov. Gretchen Whitmer Has Gotten Very Complicated," Buzzfeed News, December 16, 2021. https://www.buzzfeednews.com/article/kenbensinger/fbi-michigan-kidnap-whitmer.

If someone at the top of the Capitol Police—presumably Capitol Police Chiefs Yogananda Pittman and Sean Gallagher—hadn't stationed a literal handful of officers at the most obvious and vulnerable site where Trump supporters would soon be streaming in by the thousands, the nearly effortless breach that began the whole thing might have been stopped before it got anywhere.

And there's another really big "if," one that seems to implicate the top Democrats themselves in this plot. As we've seen, video footage is essential to help sort out what really happened on Capitol Hill that day. Nancy Pelosi refuses to allow the release of over fourteen thousand hours of video footage taken at the Capitol that day.

Like almost every other building these days, there are security cameras everywhere at the Capitol Building. One of the things that Trump supporters reported, and some videoed, was Capitol Police *opening up doors* for them to stream into the Capitol Building thereby inviting them to be prosecuted.

If Speaker Pelosi would release all this footage—as she should—what else might those fourteen thousand hours reveal?

As we all know, Nancy Pelosi set up the January 6th Committee to investigate what happened that day. I myself was originally going to be assigned to that committee, along with my fellow Republicans Jim Jordan, Jim Banks, Kelly Armstrong, and Rodney Davis. But Pelosi wouldn't allow it—she wants the January 6th Committee to be defined by and for the Democrat Party agenda, and to serve the Democrat narrative for that day.

If we would have been part of the committee, it really would have gotten to the bottom of things.

And what is the Democrat agenda in regard to January 6th?

Putting everything together so far, it's not difficult to figure out. For the sake of permanently destroying President Trump politically, the January 6th rally had to be turned into an insurrection. Doing so allowed the FBI to treat all Trump supporters (and not just the ones at the Capitol that day) as being not only White Supremacists but political revolutionaries bent on destroying our democracy.

There's more. As I said in the very first chapter, the breach of the Capitol area and building stopped short the Republican attempt on January 6th to call for an investigation into the myriad voter integrity issues. If there hadn't been a riot, that's what we would have done. I believe the riot was meant to happen to ensure that no investigation would take place. Given the amount of fraud uncovered, no wonder such a diversionary tactic seemed necessary (dare I say it) to the shadow conspirators.

I have one last aspect of January 6th that I must address, a very sad aspect that, like the riot itself, didn't have to happen.

THE MURDER OF ASHLI BABBITT

I mentioned activist John Sullivan above, the one caught on video commenting that Ray Epps must be an FBI plant. Sullivan hated Trump and was clearly a provocateur who did everything he could to draw Trump supporters into breaching the Capitol, but he also took about ninety minutes of quality footage during the riot. One of the things he caught on camera was the shooting of Ashli Babbitt, a shooting which, speaking as a police officer with years of experience, I regard as murder.

Sullivan was right there outside the Speaker's Lobby in the Capitol Building when Babbitt was shot. In an interview with *Rolling Stone* he describes what he saw:

> By no means did I see her bash in a window or even break the windows. Somebody else did that, for sure. But then all of a sudden, I see her start trying to climb through the window, and I'm like, "Don't go in there,

*don't go in there," but I know she could not hear me.
So my thought was to get that moment on camera. I
wanted to show the gun firing, and the bullet hitting
her, and how she dropped to the ground. All of this
is going through my mind at that moment, because I
knew that this was going to be the only record of how
she would have died. Because I knew she was going
to die. The guy who was pointing a gun at her was
leaning with an intent to shoot; he was not playing.
There's a difference between holding a gun up and
warning somebody versus, like, really leaning into it.
I was like, all right, I'm going to show the world why
she died. And I'm not going to let her death go in vain.
Because I didn't think that she deserved to die. She
didn't have a weapon. She didn't have anything. This
is what I'm thinking about in this moment, in this
small sliver of time.* [314]

I agree with Sullivan: Ashli Babbitt did not deserve to die, and
Capitol Police Officer Lt. Michael Byrd should have been tried
for murder, rather than cleared by the Capitol Police. I listened to
Lt. Byrd's personal testimony, giving his account of the shooting
of the unarmed Trump supporter Babbitt on January 6th. [315] His
claim that he "saved countless lives" by killing Babbitt is, frankly,
despicable.

I'm in no way condoning Ashli's behavior. As I said in the first
chapter, she and everyone else who broke into the Capitol should
never have entered the building. Nor do I condone any threats

---

314 Tim Dickinson, "'I Don't Think She Deserved to Die': Black Activist Who Filmed Ashli Babbitt
Shooting Speaks Out," *Rolling Stone*, January 14, 2021. https://www.rollingstone.com/culture/
culture-features/ashli-babbitt-shooting-video-jayden-x-maga-riot-interview-1112949/.

315 Rich Schapiro, Anna Schecter, and Chelsea Damberg, "Officer who shot Ashli Babbitt
during Capitol riot breaks silence: 'I saved countless lives,'" NBC News, April 6, 2021.
https://www.nbcnews.com/news/us-news/officer-who-shot-ashli-babbitt-during-capitol-riot-
breaks-silence-n1277736.

made against Lt. Byrd since the shooting. But despite the constant rhetoric describing those who broke into the Capitol as terrorists, Lt. Byrd was the only person who pulled a trigger that day. As a law enforcement officer for nearly thirty years, I have serious questions about Lt. Byrd's decision and his exoneration.

I've reviewed multiple tapes of her shooting. As I've noted previously, police officers are all trained to respond to difficult situations in accordance with a five-level Use of Force Continuum, which runs from mere Police Presence all the way up to Lethal Force—the last resort. Police officers don't just "clear leather," i.e., whip guns out, at the slightest provocation.

According to his own admission in the interview, Lt. Byrd moved from Verbal Commands (level 2) to Lethal Force (level 5), without going through the proper de-escalation levels in between (level 3, Physical Control by Hand; level 4, Less-than-Lethal Force such as using pepper spray, a baton, or a taser).

Why leap to Lethal Force? By his own admission, Lt. Byrd reported that he could not see her hands and therefore didn't know whether she was armed or unarmed. She was unarmed. That's why you don't shoot if you don't know.

At no point was Ashli violent towards any law enforcement officer. While she was trying to climb through a broken window, she never swung at or hit any of the officers nearby. Had Ashli gotten through the window, there were numerous Less-than-Lethal options at Lt. Byrd's disposal to defuse and control the situation.

It is never appropriate for an officer to fire on a suspect who is unarmed and no clear threat to that officer's safety. As a former county sheriff watching over 850,000 residents in Texas, I feel more than confident that if a similar situation played out in Texas, the shooting officer *would be charged with manslaughter at least, if not murder.*

I therefore question Lt. Byrd's training and his competence (and, bringing us back to the beginning of this chapter, I consider it one more sign of the defects of Capitol Police training and discipline that we've already noted in detail above).

Believe me, having spent so many years in law enforcement, I know that we must keep in mind that officers face life and death split-second decisions daily. But that's exactly why they must be well-trained and competent. The pressure, the bias, emotions, experience, and training all come into play in those moments. That having been said, the way Lt. Byrd handled his firearm and his decision to use lethal force against Ashli Babbitt make me question his training, decision-making, and experience.

Credit: Stefani Reynolds/Bloomberg via Getty Images

Lt. Byrd was previously reprimanded for leaving his firearm, loaded and unattended, in the Capitol Hill Visitor Center bathroom. Additionally, there are pictures of Lt. Byrd on the House floor on January 6th with his finger on the well of his gun, despite being completely surrounded by fellow law enforcement officers and facing no threat whatsoever. Any competent law enforcement officer—indeed, any competent gun owner—knows that you don't put your finger in the trigger area unless you are ready to shoot.

Lt. Byrd was *too ready* to shoot. Even more damning, if you look at several of the videos taken by others, there were several Capitol Police officers on the other side of the door, standing very near Babbitt, and officers in riot gear on the steps. The unarmed Babbitt was literally surrounded by armed Capitol Police, yet Lt. Byrd pulled the trigger at nearly point-blank range.

Lt. Byrd was cleared of any wrongdoing by what some Capitol Police officers (whose identities I can't reveal) have described to me as the "quickest investigation they've ever seen into a shooting, even as compared to situations where the Capitol Police officer shot an armed suspect."

I'm appalled. Anyone with two eyes and law enforcement experience can see his decision to shoot was highly questionable. I don't make those comments lightly. I know *exactly* what Lt. Byrd was facing that day. As I recounted in the first chapter, I myself stood at the back doors in the House Chamber helping Capitol Police barricade it as rioters tried to break through. When the shattered glass started flying, I ducked, as did the Capitol Police officers nearby. One of the officers got on the radio and said, "Shots fired! Shots fired!" Although the police had their guns drawn, they did *not* shoot.

That was the right decision—not Byrd's. Byrd should have done exactly what I did: I helped fellow officers work on de-escalating the situation. That was the proper response. It was my duty to defuse the situation knowing, with Capitol Police guns drawn, just how dangerous it was for those on the other side of the door.

I am not a hero. I did my best to preserve life that day and would do the same tomorrow. I never felt my life was in real danger, so I don't believe I would have been justified in using deadly force on those protestors without exhausting all other options available. My experience being deployed into combat zones has taught me to manage stress and fear, and work above them. Lt. Byrd was clearly not well-trained.

But that's not all that bothers me about the murder of Ashli Babbitt. Again, there were riots all during the previous summer, far worse than what occurred at Capitol Hill that day. Imagine if the same scenario played out in one of those riots, and Lt. Byrd was a white police officer and Ashli Babbitt was a black woman protesting racial injustice, climbing through a broken window. What would the media narrative be surrounding Lt. Byrd?

And that reminds me of another point. I've seen video myself of Lt. Byrd kneeling, on duty and in uniform, which is against protocol, in solidarity with Black Lives Matter protestors. As a law enforcement officer, the video astounded me. The same organization that has called for violence against law enforcement officers, has burnt police precincts to the ground, and has called for defunding police, is supported by Lt. Byrd.

Did this play into Lt. Byrd's response on January 6th—the fact that rioters inside the Capitol were predominantly white Trump supporters? As I said, the pressure, bias, emotions, experience, and training all come into play in those moments when a police officer has to make split-second decisions.

We may not be able to settle that. But we can ask a much simpler question: Why didn't Lt. Byrd attempt to de-escalate the situation with Ashli Babbitt before resorting to lethal means? I have yet to find a law enforcement officer who believes the shooting was clearly justifiable, and after listening to Lt. Byrd's interview, I find myself even more confident that it wasn't.

There are so many "ifs" that make clear that the Capitol riot didn't have to happen, and if it hadn't happened then Ashli Babbitt would be alive today. I close with the words of John Sullivan who, whatever his faults were, captured the sad moment with the deepest clarity and sympathy.

> *I remember she dropped to the ground, and I don't think that's the part I was ready for. That was emotional for me. I remember just like looking into her eyes, like she was staring at me. She's just staring straight at me, and I just see her soul leave her body… the light just leave her eyes. I felt a lot of anger, I felt a lot of sadness and sorrow, frustration. I don't think I could ever have prepared myself for it. This was the first time I saw somebody die. I'm still trying to deal with it.*[316]

---

316 Tim Dickinson, "'I Don't Think She Deserved to Die': Black Activist Who Filmed Ashli Babbitt Shooting Speaks Out," *Rolling Stone*, January 14, 2021. https://www.rollingstone.com/culture/culture-features/ashli-babbitt-shooting-video-jayden-x-maga-riot-interview-1112949/.

CHAPTER 10 CONCLUSION

On Saturday, November 20, 2022, while members of Congress were away for Thanksgiving, a Capitol Police officer entered my office (as it was reported to me later, because he saw that the door to my office suite was "wide open"). That officer took a picture of my white board. What else he may have done, I don't know.

Allegedly, this officer took the picture of my whiteboard because he believed that there was something suspicious on it—the words "body armor" and a crude diagram of the Rayburn Building with an X marked on it. I had been discussing with my staff the fact that we are buying our body armor from China, and that shouldn't be. The X on the diagram was there to direct an intern to an ice machine.

The Capitol Police officer, believing this was some kind of threat, contacted the Command Center, which in turn, contacted a supervisor of the Protective Services Bureau's Threat Assessment Section. The matter was then referred to IOS agents, who came and talked to my staff on November 22nd to clarify things. They asked in particular about the words "body armor" and the X, and were given the reasons.

This all seemed very suspicious to me and became even more so when an article from *Politico* came out revealing that "after the Jan. 6 insurrection, the Capitol Police's intelligence unit quietly started scrutinizing the backgrounds of people who meet with lawmakers," which certainly seems as if Capitol intelligence is using January 6th as an excuse to spy on members of Congress, their staff, and their constituents.[317] This was the result of changes that began in the fall of 2020 when the Capitol Police hired former Department of Homeland Security official Julie Farnam to run its intelligence unit. According to the article, Farnam directed the intelligence unit's analysts "to look closely at the people meeting privately and publicly with members" of Congress, and search through the social media of members of Congress and attendees at their events, as well as make background checks. Not only that, but analysts were directed to learn everything about the buildings members of Congress used in their events, and were even "tasked with sifting through tax and real estate records to find out who owned the properties that lawmakers visited." All of this was done, allegedly, to protect members of Congress.

Given the way that the Democrats have politicized our other intelligence agencies, I don't think it's out of bounds to suspect this is one more potential example of the partisan "capture" of the Capitol Police's intelligence unit.

This is not some kind of paranoia on my part. Since January 6, 2021, I have been doing my own investigations into what really happened on that day, including asking a lot of questions about the Capitol Police (especially its leadership), calling into question the caliber and intentions of its leadership, and finally declaring publicly that the shooting of Ashli Babbitt should be considered a murder. All of this and more I've included in this book you're now reading, a book that obviously isn't something that Democrats and their shadow co-conspirators want published. I think you can see why I believe that the incident at my office was a sign that I was being spied on.

---

317 Betsy Swan and Daniel Lippman, "Capitol Police examines backgrounds, social media feeds of some who meet with lawmakers," Politico, January 24, 2022. https://www.politico.com/news/2022/01/24/capitol-police-social-media-00000948.

Using the Capitol Police for unconstitutional surveillance of members of Congress is, to state the obvious, illegal. Those in charge I contacted assured me that this was all quite routine, but I remain suspicious. They claimed that they were only trying to protect me, but there are too many red flags. First, there is no reason whatsoever that my office door would have been left ajar over the Thanksgiving recess. Second, something is a bit fishy about the given reasons why the officer thought the words "body armor" and a crude diagram with an X on it signaled a possible danger *to me*. Did the officer and intelligence agents really think that a terrorist would break into my office on Thanksgiving recess and write "body armor" on my white board, and under it write three points having to do with National Institute of Justice (NIJ) certification of body armor, the fact that body armor bought from the Chinese falsely claims certification, and that this false claim is a felony? What exact kind of a threat would that be?

That doesn't make any sense. Did Capitol Police think that I was planning to put on body armor and attack the Rayburn Building from the X? That makes even less sense. That's why I remain convinced that Capitol Police intelligence had been tasked with investigating me, and that's why someone was in my office. Perhaps the intelligence agents thought that "body armor" tied me to some alleged White Supremacist paramilitary organization. Perhaps they were just looking for anything to undermine my integrity. I don't know. But given what you've read in all the previous chapters, I hope you're suspicious as well.

I do know that Democrats don't want you to know what's in this book, and I've made no secret of the fact that I've been working on it for the last year. The Capitol Police take orders from Nancy Pelosi, and she made sure that I wasn't on the January 6th Committee. She has had no qualms about misusing the intelligence agencies in her attacks on Donald Trump during his presidency, so why wouldn't she use the Capitol Police to try to undermine my political future as well?

But let's return to the big picture. I hope you can see the truth about January 6, 2021, the truth that Democrats don't want you to know, the truth that I hope can protect us from future stolen elections. That day represents a critical point in our nation's history. The Democrats and their shadow conspirators wanted to capture political power permanently on that day, and to do it, they knew they had to completely undermine any opposition. That plan to capture political power—using the combined efforts of big tech, the mainstream media, and immensely powerful behind-the-scenes co-conspirators—would fail if evidence that the 2020 election had been stolen came to light. As I've said, turning the peaceful protest into a riot, and the riot into the political weapon of the completely partisan January 6th Committee, was part of the grand strategy to destroy the future prospects of Donald Trump and his supporters and to turn democracy into an oligarchical dictatorship of the Left.

If that sounds like nonsense, then you need to understand how deep the connections are between China—the world's most powerful oligarchical dictatorship of the Left—and the Democrat Party, big tech, the mainstream media, the intellectual elite in our universities, and all too many establishment Republicans. I urge those who are skeptical to read Peter Schweizer's *Red-Handed: How American Elites Get Rich Helping China Win*. Remember that Donald Trump rightly pegged China as *the* most powerful and insidious enemy of the US, and he did everything he could to undermine China's influence over America. I don't doubt for a minute that China— whom Trump also rightly blamed for the outbreak of COVID— did everything it could to ensure that Biden would win in 2020.

It's not the purpose of this book to dig deeply into that connection. My goal has been to make clear that, given the Democrat history of voter fraud, manipulation, and intimidation, it was almost predicable that they would try to steal the election in 2020—and all the evidence points that way.

We cannot let this happen again in 2022. It looks like the absolutely miserable job Joe Biden has done as president would be enough to ensure that the Republicans will take both the House and the Senate in 2022, and that Donald Trump will win the presidency again in 2024. However, given all that I've set forth in this book, we know that an even more powerful shadow conspiracy has already formed to do everything it can to retain political power. We must be prepared, and I hope that this book has helped that effort.

A SPECIAL THANKS

A special thanks to Kevin Countie, Trey Zanutto, and Daniel Gribble for their hard work in researching and compiling the evidence around the 2020 election and January 6th.

ABOUT THE AUTHOR

 Congressman Troy E. Nehls is a pro-Trump, America-first conservative who served our nation for twenty-one years in the US Army Reserve, retiring with the rank of major and two Bronze Stars. He also served nearly thirty years in law enforcement, with eight of those years as a county sheriff in Texas. He's a freshman congressman from Texas who garnered national attention for defending the House Chamber from rioters on January 6 and subsequently being chosen by Republican Leader Kevin McCarthy as the only freshman congressman to serve on the January 6 committee.